RED SOX

vs.

YANKEES

HOMETOWN EXPERTS
ANALYZE, DEBATE, AND ILLUMINATE
BASEBALL'S ULTIMATE RIVALRY

BILL NOWLIN AND DAVID FISCHER

SPORTS
PUBLISHING

DF: For Mike Torrez—for obvious reasons.

BN: To the entire 2004 Red Sox team—for similarly obvious reasons.

Sports Publishing books may be purchased in bulk at special discounts for sales promotion, corporate gifts, fund-raising, or educational purposes. Special editions can also be created to specifications. For details, contact the Special Sales Department, Sports Publishing, 307 West 36th Street, 11th Floor, New York, NY 10018 or sportspubbooks@skyhorsepublishing.com.

Sports Publishing® is a registered trademark of Skyhorse Publishing, Inc.®, a Delaware corporation.

Visit our website at www.sportspubbooks.com.

10 9 8 7 6 5 4 3 2 1

Library of Congress Cataloging-in-Publication Data is available on file.

Cover design by Qualcom and Brian Peterson
Cover photos: AP Images and Getty Images (Ted Williams)

All simulations were supplied by

Print ISBN: 978-1-68358-304-2
Ebook ISBN: 978-1-68358-305-9

Printed in the United States of America

TABLE OF CONTENTS

Introduction   vi

I. THE ALL-TIME TEAMS

II. THE BEST TEAMS

EDITOR'S NOTE

Being a born-and-bred New Yorker, I know full well the rivalry between the Yankees and Red Sox—and their fans. Thankfully, as a Mets fan, I've been able to watch and observe from a distance.

While many rivalries have their ebbs and flows, this one has stayed strong for over a century. Whether we're talking about the Curse of the Bambino, Bucky *^&%* Dent, Aaron *^&%* Boone, Pedro and Zimmer, or the epic 2004 comeback, the bad blood shows no signs of slowing down.

So when the idea came up of having a book where a Yankee and a Red Sox writer would have to sit down and *work* together ... well, to say I had a bit of trepidation would be an understatement.

Luckily, I had the privilege of previously working with both Bill Nowlin and David Fischer, and knew their love of the sport trumped all else. While they're both die-hards in their own right, I hoped that they would be able to have fun with this project and see the bigger picture.

The role taken as this book's editor was not only to handle my standard duties while also keeping an eye on statistical insight and accuracy, but to make sure everything stayed civil. Thankfully I did not have to do much policing, as both Bill and David were on their best behavior (for the most part).

At the end of the day, our love of sports is what brings us together. So whether it's Red Sox vs. Yankees, Celtics vs. Lakers, Bears vs. Packers, Flyers vs. Penguins, Auburn vs. Alabama, or UNC vs. Duke, being able to have a friendly discussion about our teams (with obviously a bit of chiding here and there) is the reason we love sports so much: they are a part of us.

So whether you support the Bronx Bombers or the BoSox, we hope you can enjoy this book for what it is, and maybe strike up a discussion with friends and family about who *you* think should win.

—J. K.

INTRODUCTION

The idea for this book came from our editor at Sports Publishing, Jason Katzman. He approached the two of us as authors he knew and felt us out to see what we thought about the idea of a book that would look at what has often been dubbed "Baseball's Greatest Rivalry"—Red Sox vs. Yankees—by pitting partisans of each team against each other.

It wouldn't be much of an argument to ask which team won the most world championships. That's a math question, and the Yankees easily hold a 3–1 edge there, 27 to 9. But pretend you're two guys who met each other in a bar and started talking about which team had the best player, position by position, and then looking at which actual team was the best for each franchise.

We may each have been a little wary heading into the project. Collaborating with the enemy? Would we ever be able to come to agreement … on anything? Medical teams were standing by in each corner. "I planned to mention frequently names like Babe, Bucky, and Boone," said Fischer, a Yankees fan, "to dredge up painful memories and assert my team's dominance." In response, Red Sox stalwart Nowlin replied, "I see you're still mostly living in the last century, back when the Yankees dominated. It's a new day now." As it happened, our mutual love of baseball carried the day. And mutual respect for each other, and each other's teams. It turned out to be a very enjoyable experience, with no bruises at all.

We'd never met each other, but early in the 2018 season we met at the Skyhorse offices in Manhattan, and then we dug in, planning to finish the day after the World Series, so the book could be ready by the start of the 2019 season. Naturally, we could have no way of knowing how either team would fare.

We each had our favorite players—Derek Jeter and Ted Williams. But we had to pick one for each position, with the idea of then running simulations for our all-time dream teams against each other. We dug in and did our research. We each found surprising things we hadn't realized about the players we selected, and came up with a better appreciation of some of the opposition, too.

* * *

The Yankees-Red Sox rivalry is the most storied in all of baseball, and arguably in all of sports. Maybe it began in 1904, when the pennant was decided on the final day of the season. Boston pretty much dominated the first couple of decades of the twentieth century. The rivalry took on an entirely different dimension when Red Sox owner Harry Frazee (a New Yorker at that) sold off baseball's biggest star, Babe Ruth, to the Yankees. It was only one of many sales that moved good players from Boston to New York, and the Yankees never looked back. They started winning … and kept on winning. And winning.

The Yankees became the most successful franchise in baseball. By the year 2000, they'd won 26 World Series titles and produced countless Hall of Fame players, including legends such as Mickey Mantle and Joe DiMaggio. Playing in the same league, and then the same division, the teams faced each other often. Geographic proximity helped stoke the rivalry. Allegiance to the teams divided neighbors, friends, and families. Red Sox fans blamed the Yankees for all their problems, and Yankees fans gloated in return.

And the Red Sox did have a lot of problems. One could say that the Red Sox became a star-crossed band of lovable losers. They reached the World Series only four more times that century, losing Game Seven each time in dramatic fashion, to the endless frustration of their fans. They also lost two single-game playoffs—in 1948 to the Indians and 1978 to the Yankees. Red Sox fans were bitter, and often surly. But they just expected to lose, one way or another, and this kept on into the early twenty-first century, through 2003—when they lost Game Seven of the American League Championship Series … to the Yankees.

Things have changed dramatically in the past fifteen years. Today, when the two teams face each other, it is no longer a battle between cocky uber-victors and pessimistic perpetual losers. Any demons were exorcised thanks to Boston's playoff win (over the Yankees, arising from the depths of despair) in 2004 to sweep the final four games of the ALCS and then the World Series. And then win three more World Series in the next fourteen years.

That has helped temper the narrative, and in the twenty-first century the Red Sox are leading in the World Series sweepstakes, four championships to one, and in 2018 there even arose (in part due to multiple Patriots, Bruins, and Celtics championships) the question of "parade fatigue." Any attempt to label the Red Sox as an "underdog" has become utterly laughable. The Yankees don't even have the highest payroll in baseball anymore (by 2018). That prize went to the Red Sox.

From a New York state of mind, the Yankees have those 27 titles, so long-term history remains on their side. But curses, the Red Sox have won four World Series in the past fifteen seasons. The modern relationship is getting awfully one-sided. It includes Boston capturing the past three American League East division titles and knocking out the Yankees in the 2018 Division Series (after a 100-win season), en route to a world championship. If there is a "curse" anymore, it is spewing from the mouths of Yankees fans as they witness what their greatest rival has become.

There are two sorts of Red Sox fans in 2018. Younger fans—say those who are under the age of thirty—don't really remember the years when the Yankees seemed to routinely win, year after year, even though they closed out the twentieth century with three consecutive championships. Older Red Sox fans still find it a little hard to comprehend the new reality. It's like it's *not* real. But either Sox fan might well tweak a Yankees fan by asking, "Oh, the Yankees? Right! They were sure a great team … back in the last century."

This book offers a unique way of looking at this 100-year-old rivalry—position by position, regardless of the years in which the players played. With certain concessions for balance and flow, we have chosen who, in our judgment, is the most deserving player at each position for their respective team, along with "honorable mentions" of the four or five next most significant players, in ranking order. We then compared the best from each team directly against the other's best to determine a winner. We repeated this selection process in choosing the best team in the history of each franchise, too.

A word about our procedure. Certain players—Ted Williams, Derek Jeter, Carl Yastrzemski, and Mariano Rivera—played their entire careers with the Red Sox or Yankees, and dominated their respective positions. They are the no-brainers, if you will. Other players—Tris Speaker and Dave Winfield, to name just two—spent part of their Hall of Fame careers playing with other teams in addition to the Red Sox and Yankees. For our purposes here, their seasons spent playing for the Red Sox and Yankees are primary.

Nevertheless, we've attempted to be definitive in choosing the greatest single-season teams for each franchise, as well as the top players at the eight positions, plus a designated hitter, a right-handed and left-handed starting pitcher, a reliever, and a closer. We accepted three premises: That some players and teams may become more—or less—compelling when viewed with the hindsight of time. That individual and team statistics cannot be interpreted apart from the era in which they played. And that the stigma of the steroid era could shadow our thought process but should not disqualify accused or admitted players from consideration. Hours of debate went into the broth, and so difficult were some selections that on two occasions we chose a tie between players and teams.

This book isn't a product of looking at dry statistics. It is a book of informed opinions. Ours, to be sure, but also the informed opinions of dozens of experts who are closely identified with the game, and the super-fans we know who sit in the grandstands at Fenway Park and Yankee Stadium on a regular basis. Opinions formed by firsthand eyewitness accounts are certainly important. Yet no special emphasis has been given to players we saw in person or on television to the exclusion of those long retired who we never watched in action on the field.

This book would not have been possible without the creativity, sound judgment, and tireless work of our collaborators, including all those at Sports Publishing, including Kirsten Dalley, as well as the astute eye of our fact checker/proofreader Ken Samelson. The scope and appearance of the book was greatly enhanced by the wise counsel of Jason Katzman. We also appreciate the time of Dave Koch and Action! PC Baseball for handling all the simulations that appear in this book. And the project in a real sense would have been next to impossible to accomplish without the understanding and support of our family, friends, and colleagues for contributing ideas, time, advice, and encouragement. To all of them, and to numerous other friends and associates who shared our vision, our deep and abiding thanks.

DAVID FISCHER
River Vale, New Jersey
Yankees fan since attending my first game at the old Stadium in 1970

BILL NOWLIN
Cambridge, Massachusetts
Sox fan through thick and thin, from Ted Williams to Mookie Betts

RED SOX

vs.

YANKEES

CATCHER

RED SOX CATCHER: JASON VARITEK

Career	H	HR	RBI	BA	Awards
1997–2011 (15-year career)	664	193	757	.256	3x All-Star 2005 Gold Glove 2005 Silver Slugger 2x World Series Champ

Red Sox All-Time Rankings:
Games Played: 1546 (10th All-Time)

Doubles: 306 (10th All-Time)

Extra-Base Hits: 513 (10th All-Time)

Runs Batted In: 757 (10th All-Time)

Reason for Decision

Jason Varitek came to Boston in one of the most lopsided trades in baseball history, arriving with fellow Red Sox Hall of Famer Derek Lowe in a trade with the Seattle Mariners for reliever Heathcliff Slocumb.

Varitek caught almost 500 more games than any other Red Sox catcher. He was never an MVP or a ROY, but was a three-time All-Star, with a Gold Glove and Silver Slugger Award. He also helped lead the team to six postseason appearances and two World Series titles, in 2004 and 2007.

He played his full career with the Red Sox, parts of 15 seasons.

Rarely did a pitcher shake off Tek's signs, and it is perhaps no coincidence that he has caught four "official" no-hitters: Hideo Nomo (in 2001), Derek Lowe (2002), Clay Buchholz (2007), and Jon Lester (2008). And he caught Devern Hansack's no-hitter on October 1, 2006—in the record books as a complete-game shutout and a win, with no hits (but not "official" because an "act of God"—rain—prevented the game from being nine innings long). The only other major-league catcher to catch four official no-hitters is Carlos Ruiz.

In December 2004, Varitek was designated team captain—the first captain the Red Sox had had since Jim Rice in 1990, and he wore a "C" on his jersey to reflect the honor. The switch-hitting Varitek had driven in a career-high 85 runs to take the Sox deep into the postseason in 2003. Just after the All-Star break in 2004, he cemented his image with Sox fans and may have given the team as a whole some extra resolve during the nationally televised game on July 24 when he pushed his glove into the face of the Yankees' Alex Rodriguez, igniting a bench-clearing brawl and creating a photographic image that embodied the rivalry in the back-to-back years when the Red Sox and Yankees traded Game Seven ALCS wins.

As a bit of a footnote, it's of interest that Varitek is one of only three players who has played in the Little League World Series, College World Series, and Major League Baseball World Series. He also played for Team USA in the Olympic Games and in the World Baseball Classic. He continues to work for the Red Sox as a special assistant.

Honorable Mention

Carlton Fisk was an 11-time All-Star and the American League Rookie of the Year in 1972. He hit one of the most iconic home runs in Red Sox—and World Series—history, in Game Six of the 1975 Series. Yes, he went on to play more years for the "other Sox" (the ones in Chicago) and hit more homers and drove in more runs for them than he did for Boston, but he wears a "B" cap in the Hall of Fame.

There are others who could be listed: **Bill Carrigan** (three world championships to his credit: 1912, 1915, and 1916), **Lou Criger** (Cy Young's personal catcher), **Rick Ferrell** (enshrined in Cooperstown), **Rich Gedman**, **Birdie Tebbetts**, and **Sammy White** among them—but truly it came down to a look at Tek vs. Fisk.

David Fischer's Response

Upon learning of Bill's choice of **Jason Varitek** as the greatest catcher in Red Sox history over **Carlton Fisk**, my knee-jerk reaction was befuddlement. But please don't think me a jerk. Anyone who followed baseball in the 1970s knows Fisk and respects his place in the pantheon. He was Rookie of the Year and won a Gold Glove in 1972, and he just kept getting better from there. A New Hampshire product, Pudge kept the Sox's hopes alive in Game Six of the 1975 World Series with a 12th inning home run that he willed fair—an image that is framed atop many a New Englander's mantel.

If that iconic moment is not enough to give Fisk the upper hand over Varitek, well, he's also a Hall of Famer. And before we go on, let's dispel any ideas you may have as to Varitek's Hall of Fame worthiness. While Jason Varitek was an All-Star, a two-time World Series champion, a Gold Glover, and a Silver Slugger recipient, he doesn't sniff the Hall without a ticket. But this debate is not based on career accolades and accomplishments; it's centered on a player's performance while playing for the Red Sox.

With Boston, Fisk slashed .284/.356/.481 with 162 home runs and 568 RBIs. Varitek slashed .256/.341/.435 with 193 homers and drove in 757 runs. Varitek also played in Boston much longer than Fisk, appearing in the tenth most games of anyone in Red Sox history, 468 more games than Fisk played for Boston. Varitek hit the 11th most homers, scored the 16th most runs, had the 15th most hits, and has the 12th most total bases of anyone to wear a Red Sox uniform. Fisk does get the nod by a long shot over Varitek in All-Star selections, however, at seven to three. Fisk also finished in the top 10 in MVP balloting three times with the Sox; Varitek never once broke into the top 20.

While Fisk was known as a good-hitting catcher, Varitek was a pitcher's catcher. He prepared harder for every game than anyone, according to his teammates. He knew what pitch should be thrown and when. (Ask Curt Schilling, who lost a no-hitter with two outs in the ninth inning because he shook off Varitek.)

'Tek was a good defensive catcher, though he was poor at throwing out runners. But his knowledge of opposing batters, the comfort he gave to his pitchers, and his gritty play more than made up for his weak arm.

As for the all-important intangibles, both men were strong clubhouse leaders and rock-steady influences on their respective teams. Both men were tough as nails. Pudge enjoyed brawling with the Yankees, especially Lou Piniella, in seemingly every series. And at Varitek's retirement press conference, video of 'Tek giving A-Rod a face full of glove played on an endless loop.

The main factor Varitek has over Fisk is durability. Fisk became the starting catcher in 1972 and, over his subsequent nine seasons in Boston, he played in fewer than 100 games three times due to injuries. Varitek, by comparison, played in fewer than 130 games only twice from 1999 through 2008, seasons when he reliably served as Boston's top backstop.

Varitek over Fisk is one of the tougher calls in filling out the all-time Red Sox roster, and I don't begrudge your decision. But after much thought, I give the nod to Fisk, since it wasn't his fault that he didn't spend his entire career in Boston. When his contract expired after the 1980 season, the Red Sox front office mailed him a new contract one day after the deadline and, as a result, Fisk became a free agent. When the Pale Hose made him an offer he couldn't refuse, he didn't.

Judging from the remaining six honorable mentions, the catching position has been, well, um, under-represented throughout the franchise's storied history, though Babe Ruth called Carrigan the best manager he ever played for. The list focuses on defensive catchers, evidenced by Ferrell's brother, Wes, a pitcher who slugged more career home runs (38) than his catching brother, who hit 28. Speaking of defense, didn't Gedman fail to handle a pitch thrown by Bob Stanley in Game Six of the 1986 World Series? It was scored as a wild pitch, but many thought Gedman botched it. The tying run came in to score, and then Mookie Wilson hit a ball that went through first baseman Bill Buckner's legs to win the game for the Mets, forcing a deciding seventh game, also won by the Metropolitans. (Sorry, I couldn't resist.)

YANKEES CATCHER: YOGI BERRA

Career	H	HR	RBI	BA	Awards			
1946–1963, 1965 (19-year career)	2150	358	1430	.285	15x All-Star 3x MVP 10x World Series Champ Hall of Fame Inductee (1972)			

Yankees Career	H	HR	RBI	BA
1946–1963	2148	358	1430	.285

Yankees All-Time Rankings:
Games Played: 2116 (4th All-Time)
Plate Appearances: 8350 (6th All-Time)
Hits: 2148 (8th All-Time)
At-Bats: 7546 (5th All-Time)
Singles: 1420 (6th All-Time)
Home Runs: 358 (5th All-Time)
Extra-Base Hits: 728 (7th All-Time)
Total Bases: 3641 (7th All-Time)
Runs Scored: 1174 (8th All-Time)
Runs Batted In: 1430 (5th All-Time)

Reason for Decision

For pure staying power, no dynasty compares to the New York Yankees' version from 1949 to 1964. Those Yankees won nine World Series in 14 tries over 16 seasons, including a record five straight from 1949 to 1953. The constant of that era was their catcher, Yogi Berra. So integral was Berra to the Yankees' fortunes that he was voted the American League's Most Valuable Player award three times (1951, 1954, and 1955) over a five-year span—in a league that boasted such future Hall of Famers as Mickey Mantle, Ted Williams, and Al Kaline. Even more impressive: from 1950 to 1957, Berra never finished lower than fourth in the MVP voting.

Bridging the team's transition from Joe DiMaggio to Mantle, Berra played on all 14 pennant winners during that prodigious stretch. In fact, he is the only player in history to play on 10 World Series championship teams. He also holds World Series records for at-bats (259), games (75), hits (71), and doubles (10). He played 19 years in the majors and in 15 straight All-Star Games. Upon retiring, his 313 career home runs as a catcher (358 overall) stood as the record until Johnny Bench, Carlton Fisk, and then Mike Piazza broke it. He was elected to the National Baseball Hall of Fame in 1972, and was chosen to baseball's All-Century Team.

Berra was squat and clumsy when he joined the Yankees in 1946, but manager Casey Stengel believed in him from the start. Berra knew how to call a game, and Stengel dubbed him "my assistant manager." Yankees catcher Bill Dickey had just finished his Hall of Fame career, and he took the young Berra on as a student. Dickey was a great teacher, showing Berra the basics of catching, and he proved to be an excellent pupil. "Bill is teaching me all his experience," said Yogi.

In 1949, Berra became the Yankees' full-time starting catcher, a job he would hold for a decade. Behind the plate he was one of the top defensive catchers in the game and a great handler of pitchers. The jug-eared catcher, who was built like a fireplug, had cat-like reflexes. "He springs on a bunt like it was another dollar," said Stengel. Berra led the league in games caught eight times, led in double plays six times, and went the entire 1958 season without an error. He called two no-hitters thrown by Allie Reynolds in 1951 and caught Don Larsen's perfect game in the 1956 World Series—the only one in Series history. "It never happened before, and it still hasn't happened since," said Berra.

He was one of the great clutch hitters of his day, "the toughest man in baseball in the last three innings," said Paul Richards, who managed the Orioles and White Sox during the 1950s. In addition to his glove, Berra was an amazing bad-ball hitter—skilled at reaching for balls out of the strike zone and hitting them out of the park. Yet for all his aggressiveness at the plate, he rarely struck out—only 414 times in 7,555 at-bats. In 1950, he fanned only 12 times in 597 at-bats. During that 1950 season, though not one in which he won the MVP, he hit a career-best .322 with 28 homers and 124 runs batted in. A dependable run producer, Berra drove in at least 90 runs nine times during his career.

Honorable Mention

The switch-hitting **Jorge Posada** played on five World Series winners and was also a five-time All-Star and five-time Silver Slugger winner. One of the "Core Four" along with Derek Jeter, Andy Pettitte, and Mariano

Rivera, Posada emerged as one of the game's best-hitting backstops. He finished his career with 275 homers, 1,664 hits, and 936 walks. More than just an exceptional hitter with a keen eye (as well as considerable pop), Posada was a respected handler of pitchers and an emotional leader on a team that made the playoffs in every year of his career (except for 2008, when a right shoulder injury required season-ending surgery). A fan favorite, his at-bats were accompanied by a rousing cheer of "Hip Hip Jorge!"

Thurman Munson is still a revered figure in Yankees history. He won both the Rookie of the Year (1970) and Most Valuable Player (1976) awards while leading the team to consecutive World Series titles in 1977 and 1978. A seven-time All-Star and recipient of three Gold Glove awards, Munson hit for a .292 average over 11 seasons and was at his best in the clutch, batting .357 in 30 postseason games between 1976 and 1978. Munson had a tough outer shell, but his teammates knew him as a leader. He was named the first Yankees team captain since Lou Gehrig four decades before. Like Gehrig, Munson is also remembered as a tragic figure. He died in a plane crash on August 2, 1979, at the age of thirty-two.

Hailed as one of the greatest catchers of all time—yet incredibly rates only as an honorable mention—**Bill Dickey** was an 11-time All-Star and seven-time World Series champion. Dickey reached double digits in home runs nine times, the 100 RBI mark four times, and batted better than .300 11 times during his 17-year career (all with the Yankees).

Bill Nowlin's Response

How could anyone disagree with the choice of Yogi Berra? As a Red Sox fan, I would rather have Dale Berra behind the plate—particularly since he was an infielder.

Yogi had to be doing something right—playing in 14 World Series (and winning 10 of them—a ring for each finger on both hands, including his thumbs). He hit .274 in World Series competition, close to his regular-season career batting average of .285, as well as 12 home runs and 39 RBIs in World Series play.

And—Yogi-isms aside—he had to have been communicating very

effectively with all those Yankees pitchers all those years, 1947 to 1963 in the World Series alone. (He played seven Yankees games in 1964, and in four games with the Mets in 1965, under manager Casey Stengel, but that 1947 through 1963 span pretty much embraced his career.)

The one day I played hooky in junior high school was October 8, 1956. The Dodgers had won the first two games of the World Series, and then the Yankees evened it up with wins in Game Three and Game Four. I was rooting for the Dodgers, but in the seventh inning—for the first time and last time in the twentieth century, I started rooting for the Yankees. Well, not for the Yankees, but for Don Larsen to complete the perfect game he had going.

(There was one other game, in the aftermath of 9/11/2001, when I found myself rooting for the Yankees. I'd been in Yankee Stadium with my friend Jim Prime for the Red Sox games on 9/8 and 9/9, and I was rooting for the Red Sox then, but the first game the Yankees played at the Stadium after 9/11, I found myself pulling for New York to win.)

But I digress. One thing about Yogi that always impressed me was him wearing another uniform, as Seaman Second Class Lawrence P. Berra, assigned to an LCS(S) Rocket Boat aboard the attack transport APA-33 *USS Bayfield*. It was the flagship command vessel for the Utah Beach landing during D-Day, and shortly afterward headed through the Strait of Gibraltar to take part in the invasion of southern France on August 15. So Yogi Berra truly was involved in the D-Day invasion, with his life at stake.

Anyone has to be impressed with what I noted, following Dave Fischer's observation—that in the days when All-Star selection was not a popularity contest with the fans but voted on by peers in the league, Berra was named an All-Star every year he played, save a couple of bookend seasons.

Now, as to your honorable mentions, maybe it's partly because he's further back in history, but I think I might have rated **Bill Dickey** higher. I thought he might have been an All-Star in the seasons 1929 through 1932 (before there was an All-Star Game), but then I realized the Tigers' Mickey Cochrane probably would have locked that down all four years. When it comes to the postseason, though, a catcher's handling of a pitching staff is an important key to success, and the seven world championships rank higher in my mind than the five under **Jorge Posada** and the two under **Thurman Munson**; Dickey's teams were 7-for-8 in World Series competition, only losing once (to the Cardinals in 1942). A close call. I'll defer to the Yankees expert in the house.

HEAD-TO-HEAD

Bill Nowlin: Naturally, it would be nice to see a seven-game American League Championship Series in which the two teams faced off—the Red Sox with Varitek catching and the Yankees with Berra catching—and it would be nice (if nerve-wracking) to see it go the full seven games.

David Fischer: The last two ALCS meetings between the teams went seven games, in 2003 the Yankees won, and in 2004 the Red Sox won, so odds are this dream match-up wouldn't be any different. Varitek was behind the plate for both of those ALCS face-offs. This time, though a fantasy, the difference-maker would be Yogi; he was the ultimate winner.

BN: Having them match up face-to-face is something we can never see, but I'd be glad to take my chances with Jason Varitek. In any given series, one never knows which team might prevail and who would be the stand-out players on that team.

DF: Yogi was a clutch hitter, and he came through more times than not in big spots. Varitek was a solid backstop and a consummate leader, but Berra is the pick here, if for no other reason than he was hands-down the much better offensive player.

BN: I have to say that on paper, based on their respective histories, Yogi has a sizable edge over Tek. I'll concede that. But I'll continue to admire Varitek's work ethic, his diligence in preparation, and his spirit and determination on the field of play. The Red Sox would have a good fighting chance with him behind the plate.

DF: Intangibles get you only so far. At some point, you've got to swing the bat. You've got to produce. You've got to drive in runs. Yogi would hold his own against Tek handling the pitching staff. But when it comes to intimidating the opposing pitcher, Tek doesn't hold a candle to Yogi in the batters' box, especially with runners in scoring position.

BN: The catcher who scares me most these days is Gary Sanchez, but it's too early in his career to do more than mention him here.

DF: Sanchez has unlimited upside potential. The Yankees always have an advantage at the catcher position due to his powerful bat. He'll surely be included in the discussion in a few years when we update this book!

Winner: Yogi Berra

FIRST BASE

RED SOX FIRST BASEMAN: CARL YASTRZEMSKI

Career	H	HR	RBI	BA	Awards
1961–1983 (23-year career)	3149	452	1844	.285	18x All-Star 7x Gold Glove 3x Batting Champ MVP (1967) Triple Crown (1967) Hall of Fame Inductee (1989)

Red Sox All-Time Rankings:
Games Played: 3308 (1st All-Time)
Plate Appearances: 13,992 (1st All-Time)
At-Bats: 11,988 (1st All-Time)
Hits: 3419 (1st All-Time)
Singles: 2262 (1st All-Time)
Doubles: 646 (1st All-Time)
Home Runs: 452 (3rd All-Time)
Extra-Base Hits: 1157 (1st All-Time)
Walks: 1845 (2nd All-Time)
Stolen Bases: 168 (4th All-Time)
Total Bases: 5539 (1st All-Time)
Runs Scored: 1816 (1st All-Time)
Runs Batted In: 1844 (1st All-Time)

Reason for Decision

Why Yaz? I started looking at the universe of Red Sox first basemen and quickly narrowed down the field to five: alphabetically, they were Jimmie Foxx, George Scott, Mo Vaughn, Carl Yastrzemski, and Kevin Youkilis. (Sorry, Phil Todt. You might have made the top six, but I only dug into the top five.) Yaz only played about a quarter of his games as the Sox first baseman and twice as many games in left field than he did at first base.

But when you've got Ted Williams in left field, well, there wasn't even a hesitation as to who'd get the left-field assignment.

In the eight years where he played 40 or more games at first base, he was an All-Star each year. His MVP year was 1967, when he played left field and the three batting titles he won were when playing left field. The very fact of his versatility and his ability to excel wherever he was positioned is a reason I've chosen him.

Yaz also DH'd in 412 games, but he played 765 games at first base—and was the team's first baseman during the pennant-winning year of 1975, playing significant time there in both 1972 (42 games) and 1978 (50 games), two years the Sox took the pennant race to the very last game of the season.

Only four first basemen played more games at first base for Boston: Scott, Vaughn, Todt, and Foxx. Only three had a better career fielding percentage: Youk, Stuffy McInnis, and Pete Runnels. Only four recorded more putouts, more assists, took part in more double plays. That might seem to rank Yaz a little further down on defense, but it was on offense (and in the imprecise category of leadership) where Captain Carl stood out.

The first year he played first base was 1970—and he led the league in runs scored, on-base percentage, total bases, and slugging percentage; and was just .0004 from the lead for the batting title.

Studying his splits, he performed marginally better on offense during the years he played left field as opposed to first base. For instance, dividing RBIs into at-bats, he produced an RBI 15 percent of the time (.150) in the games he played first base and was .155 in the games he played left. When he DH'd, the figure was .152.

Yaz was named team captain in 1966—the first one in 20 years—and the moniker "Captain Carl" was his again once manager Dick Williams left town. Years later, in 2009, Jim Rice told John Powers of the *Boston Globe*, "I don't know if he was the captain in 1975 or not, but I called him Captain and I call him Captain now."

Honorable Mention

If I were told I couldn't have Yaz as my first baseman, I'd go with **Jimmie Foxx**. Though many of his better years were with the Philadelphia

Athletics (he won the Triple Crown in 1933), Foxx—"The Beast"—played seven seasons for the Red Sox and still holds the team record for RBIs in one season (175 in 1938, leading the league. That was the year he was voted Most Valuable Player for the third time). He hit 50 homers (but came in second to Hank Greenberg's 58) and hit for a league-leading .349 batting average. His lifetime batting average for Boston was .320, and he homered 222 times while driving in 788 runs. Twice he led all of baseball in OPS: 1938 and 1939. A member of the National Baseball Hall of Fame, he was also an excellent fielder, with a career .992 fielding percentage at first base.

Mo Vaughn, the "Hit Dog," hit 230 homers in his eight years with the Sox, leading the league with 126 RBIs in 1995. He was the league MVP that same year, and finished in the top five in 1996 and 1998. The three-time All-Star drove in 752 runs over those years, batting .304. Four times, he drove in more than 100 runs; his 143 RBIs in 1996 was his career high. As Dave Fischer helpfully reminded me, he went 4-for-4 with three home runs against the Yankees in Boston's 10–4 win on May 30, 1997. He was hit by pitches 71 times in those eight seasons with the Sox, perhaps not all by accident. One of Vaughn's most memorable hits came on Opening Day in 1998 when he hit a walk-off grand slam in the bottom of the ninth inning to beat the Seattle Mariners.

George "Boomer" Scott played nine years for Boston, with 154 homers and 562 RBIs, and a .257 average. He was an excellent fielder as well, with eight Gold Gloves to his credit (three with the Red Sox). He broke in with the Red Sox in 1966, hitting 27 homers and driving in 90 runs. He was named to the All-Star team and placed third in Rookie of the Year voting. He was traded to Milwaukee after the 1971 season and traded back to Boston five years later. In his second stint for the Red Sox, he was again named an All-Star in 1977.

David Fischer's Response

Jimmie Foxx was one of the great sluggers of all-time; perhaps the most feared right-handed hitter of the twentieth century. Speaking of Foxx, left-handed Yankees pitcher Lefty Gomez said, "He has muscles in his hair." Despite Foxx's prodigious power, I agree with your selection of Carl Yastrzemski. Not only was Yaz a terrific player and a worthy Hall of Famer, he was, and remains, a quintessential Boston legend, on par with Larry Bird, Bobby Orr, and Tom Brady.

It's ironic that Carl Yastrzemski, born in Southampton, New York, grew up a Yankees fan. Several times each season, he and his father made the 200-mile round trip to the Bronx to watch Joe DiMaggio or Mickey Mantle patrol center field. Yastrzemski's childhood dream was to play for the Yankees. During his senior year of high school a Yankees scout offered him a $60,000 contract. The young Carl desperately wanted to accept the offer, but his father insisted on holding out for $100,000. When the Yankees refused to increase their offer, Carl decided to attend Notre Dame on a baseball scholarship. After one year the Red Sox signed him for $108,000. That worked out well for Boston and for Yastrzemski.

My first-ever baseball glove was a Carl Yastrzemski model. I cherished that mitt, and it enabled me to impress my friends with the ability to correctly spell his last name at an early age. It also forced me to focus on the player himself. My memories of Yaz against the Yankees include one of the greatest games ever played. The 1978 Yankees-Red Sox playoff to settle the AL East title carries a special place in this rivalry's lore. New York overcame a 14-game deficit to end the season in a first-place tie with Boston. One game would decide which team made the trip to the AL Championship Series.

The Red Sox struck first, as Yastrzemski, hungry for a World Series triumph, homered off Ron Guidry to lead off the bottom of the second inning. I was not amused. Boston's 2–0 lead was wiped out in the seventh when light-hitting shortstop Bucky Dent hit a lazy fly ball to left field that Yastrzemski was sure he would catch … but the ball drifted and drifted and landed in the netting of the Green Monster for a home run—and a 3–2 Yankees lead. In my mind's eye, I can still see Yaz slumping his shoulders in disgust. Another run and a homer by Reggie Jackson gave the Yankees a 5–2 lead, and I was giddy. But the Red Sox mounted a comeback, and another RBI by Yaz helped trim the Yankees lead to 5–4. The old man was still clutch. So I was extremely nervous in the bottom of the ninth, with the tying run on third base, and Yankees reliever Goose Gossage facing Yaz, Boston's last hope. To my great relief, Gossage got

Yaz to pop out to third for the final out of the game, sending the Yankees to the playoffs. New York would go on to defeat the Los Angeles Dodgers in the World Series in six games in a rematch of the 1977 Series for their 22nd championship in franchise history. The curse of the Bambino lived on!

The next year, on September 12, 1979, with both the Yankees and Red Sox having awful seasons, I couldn't begrudge Captain Carl for achieving a career milestone against the Yanks. Yaz stroked a single off Jim Beattie in the eighth inning to highlight a 9–2 Boston win, becoming the fifteenth player to reach 3,000 hits and the first American Leaguer to reach 3,000 hits and 400 homers. This same game also marked the final appearance at Fenway Park for Hall of Fame pitcher Catfish Hunter, who received a standing ovation from the Fenway faithful after being knocked out in the fifth inning.

YANKEES FIRST BASEMAN: LOU GEHRIG

Career	H	HR	RBI	BA	Awards
1923–1939 (17-year career)	2721	493	1995	.340	7x All-Star 1934 Batting Champ 2x MVP Triple Crown (1934) 6x World Series Champ Hall of Fame Inductee (1939)

Yankees All-Time Rankings:
Games Played: 2164 (3rd All-Time)
Plate Appearances: 9665 (3rd All-Time)
At-Bats: 8001 (3rd All-Time)
Hits: 2721 (2nd All-Time)
Singles: 1531 (3rd All-Time)
Doubles: 534 (2nd All-Time)
Triples: 163 (1st All-Time)
Home Runs: 493 (3rd All-Time)
Extra-Base Hits: 1190 (1st All-Time)
Walks: 1508 (3rd All-Time)
Total Bases: 5060 (2nd All-Time)
Runs Scored: 1888 (3rd All-Time)
Runs Batted In: 1995 (1st All-Time)
Batting Average: .340 (2nd All-Time)
On-Base Percentage: .447 (2nd All-Time)
Slugging Percenage: .632 (2nd All-Time)
On-Base Plus Slugging: 1.080 (2nd All-Time)

Reason for Decision

Baseball history regards Lou Gehrig as the greatest first baseman ever, so an easy choice as the Yankees' best at the position. In his career, Gehrig hit 493 home runs and had a .340 batting average. He was a member of six World Series–winning teams.

Lou Gehrig was born in New York City in 1903, and never strayed too far from his roots. He attended Columbia University and signed with the Yankees in 1923. Gehrig became the Yankees' starting first baseman in 1925, and from then until 1932 he and Babe Ruth were the two greatest hitters ever to play together. Ruth and Gehrig finished first and second, respectively, in the home-run race each season from 1927 to 1931. They scared opposing pitchers in a way two batters had never done before.

Gehrig had good seasons in 1925 and 1926, but it was in 1927 as part of the famous "Murderers' Row" lineup that he exploded as a superstar, batting .373 with 47 homers and 175 runs batted in. In spite of the Babe's record 60 home runs in 1927, Gehrig was picked as the American League's Most Valuable Player. The 1927 Yankees—considered by many to be the greatest offensive team of all time—swept the Pittsburgh Pirates in the World Series. In 1928, Gehrig blasted four home runs in the Yankees' World Series sweep over the St. Louis Cardinals.

For the entirety of his career, Gehrig was the picture of consistency and offensive production. He drove in at least 100 runs for 13 consecutive seasons, topping 150 RBIs seven times and setting the American League record with 184 RBIs in 1931. He had at least 100 RBIs and 100 runs scored in every full season of his career. On June 3, 1932, Gehrig became the first AL player to hit four home runs in a game. In 1934, he achieved the batting Triple Crown by leading the league in home runs (49), RBIs (165), and batting average (.363).

Gehrig was known as "The Iron Horse" for playing in 2,130 consecutive games from 1925 to 1939, a remarkable record surpassed by Cal Ripken Jr. in 1995. Feeling fatigued, Gehrig removed himself from the lineup on May 2, 1939. He was soon diagnosed with amyotrophic lateral sclerosis, forever after known as Lou Gehrig's disease. It was incurable and fatal. To express their admiration, the Yankees held "Lou Gehrig Appreciation Day" on July 4, 1939, to honor the man they called "the Pride of the Yankees." That day, Gehrig referred to himself as the "luckiest man on the face of the earth," a scene forever immortalized by screen actor Gary Cooper's stoic portrayal in the 1942 film, *The Pride of the Yankees*.

At season's end the club retired Gehrig's No. 4, making his the first retired number in sports. Then the Hall of Fame waived its five-year eligibility requirement and voted Gehrig into the Hall of Fame immediately. He died two years later at the age of thirty-seven.

Honorable Mention

During his 14 seasons in the Bronx, **Don Mattingly** grew to be one of the most popular and well-respected Yankees in team history. He showed promise from the start, winning the batting title with a .343 average in his first full season of 1984. He was the American League MVP in 1985 when he hit .324 with 35 home runs and 145 runs batted in. The Indiana native with the flowing long hair and rock-star mustache kept getting better. In 1986, he set team records for doubles (53) and hits (238), becoming the first Yankee since Lou Gehrig to collect at least 200 hits for three seasons in a row. In 1987, Mattingly put his name in the record books by belting a home run in eight consecutive games. That season he also hit six grand slams to set a new single-season mark. The record-setting sixth grand slam was hit off Boston's Bruce Hurst on September 29, 1987.

Mattingly matched his hitting with outstanding defense, and won seven Gold Gloves for his fielding excellence at first base. "Donnie Baseball" put up Hall of Fame–caliber numbers at the plate when healthy. He had a lifetime batting average of .307 with 222 home runs and 1,099 RBIs in a career hampered by a painful back. In 1991, the Yankees appointed Mattingly as the tenth captain in team history. When the aching back was more than he could bear, Mattingly retired after the 1995 playoff series loss to Seattle, a rare Yankees legend to have never reached the World Series. In 1997, his uniform No. 23 was retired and a bronze plaque unveiled, the last line reading: "A Yankee forever."

Here's where the choices gets a little murky. **Tino Martinez**, **Mark Teixeira**, **Jason Giambi**, and **Chris Chambliss** each played the position in the Bronx for seven years, and **Moose Skowron** played it for nine. Skowron has the most All-Star selections for the Yankees (five), Giambi the most homers (209), Teixeira the most Gold Gloves (three), and Chambliss hit the walk-off homer that made the Yanks AL champs in 1976 after a 12-year postseason absence. But I select Martinez, who led the group with 739 Yankee RBIs and stacks up well with the rest in most other hitting numbers. Only Teixeira, with league-leading totals of 39 homers and 122 RBIs in 2009, almost matched Martinez's best season of 44 homers and 141 RBIs in 1997—seasons in which both finished second in MVP voting. While only Skowron could match Tino's four world championships with the club, there's a reason Martinez got his very own plaque in Monument Park back in 2014: he had his share of dramatic moments in pinstripes. October highlights include the go-ahead grand slam in Game One of the 1998 World Series against Padres lefty Mark Langston, and the dramatic game-tying two-run homer against D-backs closer Byung-Hyun Kim in the ninth inning of Game Four of the 2001 World Series.

Bill Nowlin's Reponse

Was there anyone else? Despite having his career cut short by ALS, only Derek Jeter (2,747) and Mickey Mantle (2,401) ever played in more games as a Yankee. Once he edged aside poor Wally Pipp (lest we forget, Pipp led the league in home runs in 1916 and 1917), Gehrig played in 2,164 games, all but 34 of them encompassed by his nearly incomparable consecutive-games streak. The eras were different but in 1925, his first full year in pinstripes, Gehrig homered 20 times, one more than Pipp's two HR crown totals put together. And he had an Ivy League education to boot!

I'm not wading into trying to think through the Tino/Teixeira/Giambi/Chambliss/Moose competition, but will readily agree that Don Mattingly is a fine choice for tops among the honorable mention crew.

Leave it up to me to choose the Yankee I might most prefer at first base, and I might choose Tony Clark (.221, with a .297 on-base percentage in 2004, a year I'm particularly fond of for a number of reasons). Then again, Clark did a much better job playing for the Yankees than he did for the Red Sox in 2002.

HEAD-TO-HEAD

Bill Nowlin: I guess if it's true that "baseball history regards Lou Gehrig as the greatest first baseman ever," he must have been better than Carl Yastrzemski. I can't really mount a lengthy counter-argument.

David Fischer: As great a player as he was—and Yastrzemski was a great player—Captain Carl falls short when his numbers are put up against the outstanding Yankees captain. But anyone else would place second behind the quiet hero. Gehrig is an immortal, a player for the ages. How can you compare mere greatness to an immortal?

BN: Gehrig had 10 seasons of 30 or more home runs and Yaz had three. Gehrig had 13 seasons driving in 100 or more runs—and, as you point out, Dave, he did that a nearly unbelievable 13 years in a row. They both led the league five times in on-base percentage, so are comparable there.

DF: Gehrig's production is made even more remarkable when you consider he was able to drive in all those runs while hitting *after* Babe Ruth. Gehrig batted fourth in the powerful Yankees batting order (hence, he wore No. 4), protecting Ruth in the lineup (who batted third, hence, the Babe wore No. 3). Taking into account Ruth's career homers, Gehrig came to the plate about 700 extra times with no runners on base! Yastrzemski and Gehrig both drew a ton of walks and neither struck out very much. While both led the league in on-base percentage five times, as you say, Gehrig's career on-base percentage is .447 compared to Yaz's .379.

BN: Yaz had a marginally better (.994 to .991) fielding percentage in the games he played at first base, but Gehrig played almost three times as many games at the position. Yaz was never on a team that won a World Series. Gehrig was—six times.

DF: Yaz may rate the better defender statistically, but he had the advantage of playing with a modern first baseman's glove. As for the World Series appearances, it's a matter of being on the right team at the right time.

BN: Maybe all I can fall back on are two things: if we're going not just head-to-head overall, but looking at a hypothetical series between the two "best" teams, Yaz had a versatility that saw him play more than 2,000 games in the outfield, 412 as a DH, and 33 at third base. That versatility might count for a lot, given injuries or the need to shuffle around players in a playoff series. Yaz also had, particularly in 1967, demonstrated the ability to carry a team for a week or more when the chips were really down. In the final 12 games of the '67 season, with the pennant only decided on the final day, Carl Yastrzemski had 23 hits in 44 at-bats, driving in 16 runs and scoring 14. That included 10 hits in his last 13 at-bats. And when it came to the last two games, Yaz was 7-for-8, driving in six runs.

DF: Gehrig played nine games in the outfield and one game at shortstop (a left-handed shortstop? I'd like to know what happened on that day in 1934!), but with the dominant teams the Yankees were fielding in the 1920s and 1930s, versatility was not an important tool in a manager's bag of tricks. Still, what Yastrzemski accomplished during the Impossible Dream season of 1967 will never be forgotten. His achievement of winning the batting Triple Crown—during a season when pitching was so dominant that major league baseball would soon lower the height of the mound—is a truly remarkable feat. I feel a twinge of sympathy for Yastrzemski. Even the most die-hard Yankees fan, the kind who are fans of two teams—the Yankees and anyone who plays the Red Sox—can't help but have a soft spot for Yaz. He was a superb ballplayer and, like Gehrig, a consummate professional. If you're a baseball fan, you have to appreciate what Yaz brought to the ballpark—both on the field and in the clubhouse. But Gehrig was the GOAT, the greatest of all time at the position. End of story.

Winner: Lou Gehrig

SECOND BASE

YANKEES SECOND BASEMAN: TONY LAZZERI

Career	H	HR	RBI	BA	Awards
1926–1939 (14-year career)	1840	178	1194	.292	1933 All-Star 5x World Series Champ Hall of Fame Inductee (1991)

Yankees Career	H	HR	RBI	BA
1926–1937	1784	169	1157	.293

Yankees All-Time Rankings:
Triples: 115 (5th All-Time)
Runs Batted In: 1157 (9th All-Time)
Walks: 830 (9th All-Time)

Reason for Decision

A trio of worthy options was considered at second base for the Yankees. Two are Hall of Famers—Tony Lazzeri and Joe Gordon—and Robinson Cano was on his way until a PED suspension put his candidacy into question. I decided to go with Lazzeri, even though (full disclosure) Cano is one of my all-time favorite players to watch. Reliable keystoners Willie Randolph and Bobby Richardson also deserve praise, while Horace Clarke (the personification of the 1970s doldrums) does not.

Over his 12 years with New York, from 1926 to 1937, Tony Lazzeri batted .293 with an OBP of .379 and a slugging percentage of .467 for an OPS of .847. He also finished in the top 15 for MVP voting five times, including a third-place finish in 1928. He hit .300 or better five times, including a career-high .354 in 1929. Lazzeri hit for respectable power for the era: 169 homers and 1,157 RBIs. He won five World Series rings with the Yankees and probably would have won at least one MVP Award if it weren't for Babe Ruth and Lou Gehrig deservedly garnering all the accolades.

Despite following legendary teammates in the batting order, Lazzeri produced when called upon. He drove in 100 runs or more seven times. In the greatest run-producing day in American League history, Lazzeri drove in a league-record 11 runs in a victory over the Philadelphia Athletics at Shibe Park on May 24, 1936. The Yankees' second baseman became the first player to club two grand slams in one game. Lazzeri also hit a third homer and a triple. A day earlier, Lazzeri had three homers and four runs batted in during a doubleheader sweep, giving him an incredible six home runs and 15 RBIs in a three-game span.

A quiet leader for the "Murderers' Row" attack, Lazzeri's reputation for driving in clutch runs earned him the nickname "Poosh 'Em Up" Tony. In the 1928 World Series sweep of the St. Louis Cardinals, he doubled and scored the eventual winning run in the clinching game, and in the 1932 World Series he finished off the Chicago Cubs with two home runs in the clinching Game Four victory. In the 1936 Series against the Giants, also won by the Yankees, Lazzeri hit a grand slam in Game Two off Giants pitcher Dick Coffman; it was only the second grand slam ever hit in Series competition.

Although he earned a reputation for timely hitting, Lazzeri is often remembered for failing to deliver when the chips were down in the deciding seventh game of the 1926 World Series against the Cardinals. He was struck out in the seventh inning with the bases full by Grover Cleveland Alexander in one of baseball's most dramatic moments. One pitch earlier, Lazzeri had launched a ball out of Yankee Stadium—but just foul. Despite coming up short in this one instance, he was at his best on the big stage, producing 19 RBIs in 32 World Series games.

You really can't go wrong with any of the three. Lazzeri was a terrific hitter and fielder who played longer than anyone except Randolph, who was not nearly as talented a hitter as the rest of the bunch. Gordon's career was shortened due to World War II, but his high caliber of play on offense and defense from 1939–1943 comes surprisingly close to 2010–2013 Cano. Lazzeri didn't have Gordon or Cano's home run power, but no one even approaches Lazzeri's 115 triples, either. He was simply a strong all-around player who did just about everything right—and the right way.

The popular Lazzeri was a hero in the Italian American communities around the United States (especially in New York). He helped draw thousands of newly arrived immigrants to ballparks and helped foster an interest in baseball in many of America's newest citizens. Manager Miller Huggins called him the type of player that comes along "once in a generation." That endorsement is good enough for me.

Honorable Mention

Forgoing the selection of **Robinson Cano** was my most difficult decision. He can do it all: He hits for both average and power; and is smooth and effortless in the field with a strong arm. He spent nine seasons with the Yankees, from 2005 to 2013, during which he topped 100 RBIs three times, scored 100 runs four times, and hit over 200 homers.

Cano came up in 2005 and hit .297 with 34 doubles and 14 homers, good for a runner-up finish to Oakland's closer Huston Street in AL Rookie of the Year voting. In '06, Cano made his first All-Star team—he went to six All-Star Games in pinstripes—and his batting average of .342 ranked third in the AL behind teammate Derek Jeter and Twins catcher Joe Mauer. Cano also rapped 40 doubles that season for the first time, a milestone he would reach seven times with the Yankees—a franchise record he shares with that other extra-base machine, Lou Gehrig.

Cano's performance from 2008 to 2013 was positively electric. He hit .314, averaging 196 hits, 45 doubles, and 28 homers per season, an incredible peak for a second baseman. He started four All-Star Games in a row, won four Silver Sluggers in a row, took home a pair of Gold Gloves, and finished in the top six for MVP voting each year from 2010 to '13. He won a World Series with the Yanks in 2009 but came up two games shy of the Fall Classic in 2010 despite a four-homer ALCS against the Texas Rangers.

In his Yankee career, Cano hit .309 with 204 home runs, 822 RBIs, and an .860 OPS. He was unbelievably dependable throughout his tenure. From 2008 to 2013, he suited up for 1,120 out of the Yankees' 1,134 games, a remarkable 98.7 percent of total games played.

When he left New York in late 2013, signing a $240 million deal with the Seattle Mariners, it broke my heart. Cano has a good chance to top 3,000 hits and pass Jeff Kent for most home runs by a second baseman. (Cano has 296 through 2018, while Kent had 351 during his career.) That would qualify him as a surefire Hall of Famer—and likely he would wear a Yankee cap into Cooperstown—until a suspension for PEDs in 2018 put all those accomplishments—and his legacy—into question. That sound you hear is my heart breaking for a second time.

Joe Gordon spent seven seasons in pinstripes, from 1938 to 1946. He was an All-Star for five straight seasons beginning in 1939, and after his career was interrupted by World War II, again in '46. Though not a high-average hitter, Gordon hit for power and often ranked second to the great Joe DiMaggio as the team leader in home runs and runs batted in. As a rookie in 1938, "Flash" hit 25 home runs, setting the AL single-season record for second basemen that stood for 64 years until Bret Boone hit 36 in 2001. Gordon was a member of four World Series–winning teams with the Yankees. In the 1938 World Series, he hit .400 with six RBIs in their four-game sweep over the Cubs. Gordon hit .500 in the 1941 World Series and frustrated the Dodgers repeatedly with his glove, turning five double plays to set a record for a five-game series. Afterward, Yankees manager Joe McCarthy said, "The greatest all-around ballplayer I ever saw, and I don't bar any of them, is Joe Gordon." And Marse Joe saw a lot of ballplayers in his day. The 1942 season was Gordon's best, as he batted .322 and drove in 103 runs, edging Triple Crown–winner Ted Williams for the AL's MVP Award. He also teamed with shortstop Phil Rizzuto to complete more double plays than any other fielding combination in the league. When the Yankees traded Gordon to Cleveland for pitcher Allie Reynolds prior to the 1947 season, Gordon had exactly 1,000 hits in 1,000 games played for the Yankees. He could have gone even further had he not missed two of his prime seasons due to the war.

Bobby Richardson was a sure-handed fielder for the Yankees from 1955 to 1966. He was also a pesky batter who was nearly impossible to strike out. (He fanned only 22 times in 630 plate appearances during the 1963 regular season.) Richardson was at his best in World Series play. In 1960, he drove in 12 runs and made history as the only World Series MVP to be chosen from the losing team. Two years later, he caught a screaming line drive off the bat of Willie McCovey for the final out of Game Seven to win the World Series over the San Francisco Giants. In 1964, he collected 13 hits in a seven-game defeat against the St. Louis Cardinals.

Willie Randolph was a calm and constant presence amid the turbulent "Bronx Zoo" Yankees teams of the late 1970s. In his first six years with New York, the club won five division titles, four pennants, and two World Series. In all, Randolph played 13 seasons in pinstripes and teamed with 32 different shortstops.

Bill Nowlin's Response

I have to confess that, despite all the time I have spent looking at baseball history, I never had as full an appreciation of Tony Lazzeri as I should have. Maybe it's because Gehrig and Ruth so overshadowed everyone else on those teams. Heck, when I look at it now, I can anticipate Bob Meusel showing up here, too, when we get to the outfield—he drove in over 100 runs five separate times. But let's stick to second base for now.

Lazzeri's got the rings. One unfortunate at-bat in the 1926 World Series? It happens. He helped get them there in the first place.

I needn't recite all the stats Dave supplied. Suffice it to say that I fully agree: Lazzeri was very impressive. I was impressed by one line in Fred Glueckstein's SABR bio of Lazzeri. Making the point that Lazzeri was a born leader, ready to take charge when necessary, Glueckstein wrote: "Even Miller Huggins acknowledged him to be the brains of the Yankee infield."

There's an odd parallel in that he, like Bobby Doerr, entered the Hall of Fame via the Veteran's Committee route.

Maybe *anyone* who played on the "Murderers' Row" Yankees would benefit simply from being in the same lineup surrounded by all these other guys getting on base. But Lazzeri didn't just score runs, as you've pointed out; he drove in runs. I see he even hit 60 homers in one year (for Salt Lake City in the 1925 Pacific Coast League), two years before Ruth did.

It also turns out that Lazzeri battled epilepsy, something which fortunately never struck while he was on the field. That's impressive, too.

I note that, late in his career, Lazzeri played *against* the Yankees in the 1938 World Series. As a member of the Cubs, he was 0-for-2.

Before we get into the head-to-head discussion, I have to say something about both Joe Gordon and Robinson Cano, as I've got completely different opinions about the two of them. I'll get Cano out of the way first, because it's a complicated subject to which there is no ready answer. You alluded to it already, and we agreed between us (with the encouragement of our trusty editor, Jason Katzman) that we wouldn't get too wrapped up in the PEDs question. I won't say anything more than that he certainly was a steady performer, one who as a Red Sox fan I didn't like to see come to the plate—but look at his reliability: he averaged more than 152 games a year over nine seasons with New York. And yet the Yankees let him go through free agency.

Now, Joe Gordon. He was another Veteran's Committee inductee—I do have to say that I've never been one to be overly impressed by someone making the Hall. What rankles me—as I've always been a Ted Williams guy since my youngest days—is that MVP award in 1942. Joe Gordon won it. And there's something to be said for your team winning the pennant. But was Gordon even the best player on the Yankees? Joe DiMaggio hit more homers, drove in 11 more runs, and scored a staggering 35 more runs than Gordon.

Ted Williams won the Triple Crown that year—in fact, he won the major-league Triple Crown, leading all players in both leagues in batting average, home runs, and RBIs. He hit .356 to Gordon's .322, twice as many home runs (36 to 18), and drove in 137 runs to Gordon's 103. In part because Williams got on almost precisely half the time he came to bat (.499 on-base percentage) to Gordon's .409, Williams scored 141 runs, 53 more than Gordon's 88. Williams led in many categories. Gordon led the league in strikeouts, grounding into double plays, and errors committed at second base.

How's that for a rant?

RED SOX SECOND BASEMAN: BOBBY DOERR

Career	H	HR	RBI	BA	Awards
1937–1944, 1946–1951 (14-year career)	1094	223	1247	.288	9x All-Star Hall of Fame Inductee (1986)

All-Time Red Sox Rankings:

Games Played: 1865 (6th All-Time)

Plate Appearances: 8026 (6th All-Time)

At-Bats: 7093 (6th All-Time)

Hits: 2042 (7th All-Time)

Singles: 1349 (6th All-Time)

Doubles: 381 (7th All-Time)

Triples: 89 (4th All-Time)

Home Runs: 223 (8th All-Time)

Extra-Base Hits: 693 (6th All-Time)

Walks: 809 (7th All-Time)

Total Bases: 3270 (6th All-Time)

Runs Scored: 1094 (6th All-Time)

Runs Batted In: 1247 (6th All-Time)

Reason for Decision

This was not an easy decision. It came down to a choice between Bobby Doerr, who played for the Red Sox from 1937 through 1951 (excepting one year during World War II), and Dustin Pedroia, who debuted for the Red Sox in late 2006 and is still playing through 2018. Listing them alphabetically, Mike Andrews, Marty Barrett, Hobe Ferris, and Jerry Remy all received consideration, as did Billy Goodman and Doug Griffin.

Pedroia's career is still in progress, but through the 2018 season has put up some very impressive figures (see the summary in the Honorable Mention below). Before his career is done, he may edge Doerr out of the top spot. For now, though, we're going to go with "The Silent Captain"— as none other than Ted Williams dubbed him.

Doerr played in more games than any other second baseman in Red Sox history, some 1,852 games. Through 2018, Pedroia stands at 1,488. No one else reached 1,000. Doerr was a nine-time All-Star, accorded the honor seven seasons in a row (1941–1948), if one excepts the 1945 season when he was otherwise employed as Staff Sgt. Robert Doerr in the US Army. His three-run homer in the 1943 All-Star Game helped the American League win, 5–3.

Eight times he finished in the Top 20 in MVP voting, voting that was done by his peers and not by the fans. In 1946, he finished third.

In six seasons, Doerr drove in over 100 runs and there is a good chance he might have in 1944 (he was having his best year at the plate—batting .325 with 81 RBIs—when he had to report for Army induction at the beginning of September). The Sox had been in the thick of the pennant race, but the simultaneous loss of Doerr and pitcher Tex Hughson (18–5, 2.26 ERA at the time) cost them the opportunity. Doerr was nonetheless declared that year's American League Player of the Year by *The Sporting News*.

The Red Sox didn't have the success in reaching the World Series that the Yankees had, but they won the pennant in 1946 and lost it in the final games of the season in both 1948 and 1949. From 1946 through 1950, in fact, Doerr averaged 110 RBIs per year. His career high was the 120 runs batted in during 1950; the Red Sox finished four games out of first.

The only time Doerr was on a team that reached the World Series, 1946, the Red Sox lost to the St. Cardinals in a dramatic Game Seven. He led all the team's regulars in batting average, hitting .409 (9-for-22) with a homer and three runs driven in.

Over the course of his career, Doerr hit for a .288 average with a .362 on-base percentage, homered 223 times and drove in 1,237 runs. His career (spent entirely in Boston) fielding percentage was .980. He ranks first among all Red Sox second basemen with 4,928 putouts (Pedroia is second with 2,565 through 2018), 5,710 assists (Pedroia 3,997), and participating in double plays, 1,507 to Pedroia's 937. For 13 seasons he was the Red Sox second baseman on Opening Day.

In early August 1951, at just the age of thirty-three, Doerr's career was brought to a close by a serious back injury. He was elected to the National Baseball Hall of Fame by the Veterans Committee in 1986.

Honorable Mention

Dustin Pedroia stands above all other contenders. We have seen how he matched up with Doerr in a number of instances. Pedroia hit for a higher batting average (an even .300, with a .366 on-base percentage through the 2018 season).

After getting his feet wet in 31 late-season games in 2006, he put together back-to-back seasons that could hardly have been better. In 2007, he helped lead the Red Sox—even as a rookie—to a world championship with a .317 average and an even 50 RBIs. And in his very first at-bat in the 2007 World Series against the Colorado Rockies, leading off in Game One, he hit a home run over Fenway Park's Green Monster. He had hit .345 in the ALCS, driving in five runs in the Game Seven win over the Indians.

Rookie of the Year voting concluded before the 2007 playoffs began; Pedroia won the American League award with 24 first-place votes. Placing second, with three votes, was Tampa Bay's Delmon Young.

In 2008, Pedroia was voted Most Valuable Player in the American League. Again, it was not close. He received 16 first-place votes, while second-place finisher Justin Morneau received seven. Pedroia had hit .326 (.376 OBP), and his 213 base hits and 54 doubles both led the league. He has been a four-time All-Star. His career high in RBIs came in 2011, with 91. In 2013, he drove in 84 and won another ring, helping lead the Red Sox to ultimate victory over the Cardinals. Batting high in the order, he scored more runs than he drove in, four times scoring more than 100.

In terms of fielding percentage, Pedroia—known for his spectacular sliding stops of ground balls that might have otherwise gone through for singles to right field—ranks first among all Red Sox second basemen at .991. In 2016 and 2017 he put together a team-best streak of 114 consecutive errorless games. In 2009 and 2010 he once handled a team-tops 436 consecutive errorless chances.

In three of the last four seasons, however, he has struggled to stay on the field. The 2015, 2017, and 2018 seasons all saw him lose significant playing time to injury; he only appeared in three games in 2018. Pedroia hit .318 in 154 games in 2016, but we may never see another year like that.

Jerry Remy came to the Red Sox from the California Angels in time for the 1978 season, returning to his roots in Eastern New England. He was an All-Star that year, one in which the team took the drive for the pennant until the day after the scheduled 162 games were played, losing to a team from somewhere further south in a one-game tiebreaker (Remy was 2-for-4 in that game). He played seven seasons for the Red Sox with a .286 batting average, and he ranks fourth in games played at second base, fifth in fielding percentage. He was selected as president of Red Sox Nation when that group was first formed. Since 2001, he has been a fixture on Red Sox television broadcasts on NESN. He was inducted into the Red Sox Hall of Fame in 2006.

Mike Andrews was a member of the 1967 "Impossible Dream" Red Sox. Though he only played five seasons in Boston, he was an All-Star in 1969 but became most widely known in New England through his service for more than 30 years as chairman of the Jimmy Fund, raising funds to fight cancer which he termed "the most rewarding part of my professional life." That work merits his standing with an honorable mention.

David Fischer's Response

This was a tough one. I've always known the name Bobby Doerr without knowing much about him as a player. Even though Doerr is a Hall of Famer and has his number retired with the Sox, he never really got to shine under his own spotlight. He played for years alongside Red Sox greats Ted Williams, Johnny Pesky, and Dom DiMaggio, Joe's little brother. While Williams was the era's dominant hitter and Pesky and DiMaggio captured the hearts of Boston's fans, I now understand from your proclamation that it was the steady, genial Doerr who was the glue that held the 1940s Boston teams together. He could have used a better press agent.

The man I thought you'd select, Dustin Pedroia, is an inspirational leader: scrappy, intense, everything you want in a player. He's also been the glue holding together winning teams during this recent Red Sox run of success. To compare them, I believe Doerr edges out Pedroia in the power and run-producing offensive categories, while Pedroia has the edge over Doerr in contact and speed, like the solid table-setter that Pedroia is. Both men reliably hit in the clutch. Where Pedroia falls short in the power department, he more than makes up for on defense. Doerr was a steady defender who may have won a few Gold Gloves had the award existed back then, but Pedroia is a perennial Gold Glover—a sparkling defender with great range in all directions—and nobody turns the double play better than Pedey.

If Pedroia's knee hadn't become a chronic issue, allowing him to play more regularly these past few years, his offensive numbers might already have pushed him ahead of Doerr. But Doerr retired at thirty-three because of a back injury, robbing him of some good years, too. When all is said and done, Pedroia might accomplish enough to warrant induction into Cooperstown, but we'll have to wait and see. For our purposes it would be difficult not to select a Hall of Famer, so Doerr wins ever so slightly, and with reservations, which figures, for the Silent Captain was a player so often taken for granted.

Despite his achievements, the modest, low-key Doerr was often overshadowed by more celebrated stars of the day, including Teddy Ballgame and Joe D. This seems to have hurt him with Hall of Fame voters. When Doerr was elected in 1986, it was by the Veterans Committee, a panel that considers managers, umpires, and baseball executives, as well as players no longer eligible for selection by the usual voting of baseball writers. Perhaps Doerr was the type of player who would be appreciated more by today's standards.

A few fleeting thoughts on your honorable mentions. When I think of Jerry Remy, I think of Lou Piniella. It's 1978, the Yankees-Red Sox one-game playoff, Yanks up 5–4, bottom of the ninth, Rick Burleson on first, Remy hits a knuckling line drive to right. Piniella loses the ball in the sun but pretends to have it all the way, freezing Burleson before he catches the ball on a bounce, holding runners to first and second. Smart player, that Piniella. No wonder he went on to become a pretty darn good manager.

When I think of Mike Andrews, what immediately comes to mind is the two errors he made as a member of the Oakland A's in Game Two of the 1973 World Series against the Mets, allowing four runs to score in an extra-inning defeat. Following the game, meddling A's owner Charlie Finley forced Andrews to sign a false injury report, putting him on the disabled list and thus making him ineligible to play the rest of the series. When MLB got wind of the scam, Andrews was reinstated, but he'd had enough. He retired after the Series to pursue a career that has proven to be even more rewarding than playing in the World Series.

HEAD-TO-HEAD

Bill Nowlin: This one might turn out to be a tie, or close to one.

David Fischer: There's no tie when it comes to World Series rings. That score is five for Lazzeri, and a big fat goose egg for Doerr.

BN: All those rings for Lazzeri do mean something, and he clearly wasn't just along for the ride. Convince me more.

DF: Lazzeri posted impressive offensive numbers that should be given greater credence due to the fact that he followed Ruth and Gehrig in the lineup, because those two boppers didn't often leave runners on base.

BN: Doerr batted after Ted Williams, Jimmie Foxx, and Joe Cronin. No slouches there, either.

DF: Drilling down, Lazzeri and Doerr posted nearly identical career offensive statistics. Over an average season, Lazzeri posted a .292 batting average, 17 homers, 111 RBIs, and 31 doubles. Doerr was .288, 19 HRs, 108 RBIs, and 33 two-baggers. And, coincidentally, they both batted sixth in the lineup for most of their career. Eerie.

BN: I did have to give Doerr the edge over Pedroia due to his Hall of Fame credentials and the unresolved nature of Pedroia's career. I'm sure Pedroia is flattered to be mentioned alongside Bobby Doerr. But between Lazzeri and Doerr? I don't know. It's pretty close.

DF: I had a similar conundrum. I gave Lazzeri the edge over Cano due to the unresolved nature of Cano's career, even though my heart beats for Cano, since he's one of my all-time favorite players. This is a tough one, since we both selected a position player that wasn't even an obvious choice on his own team. Now it's your turn to convince me more.

BN: With the lifetime batting numbers being nearly identical, I think it has to come down to fielding, an important asset for any second baseman.

Doerr rates significantly better than Lazzeri when looking at the stats. For his career, Doerr handled 10,852 chances, turned 1,507 double plays, and made 214 errors for a lifetime fielding percentage of .980; Lazzeri handled 8,946 chances, turned 873 DPs, and committed 314 errors for a .965 fielding percentage. With that, I'm leaning toward Doerr on this one.

DF: Well of course you are.

BN: Gotta be able to "win" a few of these!

DF: Not so fast, my friend. Lazzeri did play some games at third base and shortstop, where throwing errors are more common when compared to second base, which may have appreciably skewed the career numbers. If you want to go by his numbers at second, Lazzeri had 8,059 chances, turned 808 DPs, and committed 263 errors for a .967 fielding percentage. But more so, Lazzeri played in the 1920s when fielders' mitts were nothing more than an overstuffed pillow.

BN: Yeah, but exactly 100 more errors in almost 2,000 fewer chances is a LOT.

DF: I see your point, but I'm not a traitor like Benedict Arnold.

BN: What team did Arnold play for? Didn't he spend a lot of time in New York?

DF: He played for both sides; I guess one could say he was not a team player!

BN: I was fortunate enough to have met Bobby Doerr on several occasions and even sat with him and Johnny Pesky during the 2012 ceremonies to celebrate the 100th anniversary of Fenway Park. He was a real gentleman in every way.

DF: A man's character has to count for something. Teammates and opponents respected Doerr. His rival on the Yankees, Tommy Henrich, said

"Doerr is one of the very few who played the game hard and retired with no enemies." That's a wonderful legacy.

BN: Did Lazzeri have many enemies? But, anyhow, you sound convinced. Maybe you're leaning toward Doerr?

DF: That's not necessarily so. I can't shake the notion of Lazzeri's jewelry from those five World Series–winning teams.

BN: Now if the Red Sox could have had Lazzeri in the 1920s, they might have finished in seventh place a few times instead of last place just about every year …

DF: Now *you* sound convinced. Maybe you're leaning toward Lazzeri?

BN: No, I like my guy.

DF: Well, I like my guy.

BN: Stalemate?

DF: Stalemate.

Winner: Tie between Bobby Doerr and Tony Lazzeri

SHORTSTOP

YANKEES SHORTSTOP: DEREK JETER

Career	H	HR	RBI	BA	Awards
1995–2014 (20-year career)	3465	260	1311	.310	1996 Rookie of the Year 14x All-Star 2000 All-Star MVP 5x Gold Glove 5x Silver Slugger 5x World Series Champ 2000 World Series MVP

Yankees All-Time Rankings:
Games Played: 2747 (1st All-Time)
Plate Appearances: 12,602 (1st All-Time)
At-Bats: 11,195 (1st All-Time)
Hits: 3465 (1st All-Time)
Singles: 2595 (1st All-Time)
Doubles: 544 (1st All-Time)
Home Runs: 260 (9th All-Time)
Extra-Base Hits: 870 (5th All-Time)
Walks: 1082 (4th All-Time)
Stolen Bases: 385 (1st All-Time)
Total Bases: 4921 (3rd All-Time)
Runs Scored: 1923 (2nd All-Time)
Runs Batted In: 1311 (6th All-Time)
Batting Average: .310 (8th All-Time)

Reason for Decision

This was an easy choice. Derek Jeter won five World Series rings in his surefire Hall of Fame career. He amassed more hits—3,465 of 'em—for the Yankees than Lou Gehrig, Babe Ruth, Joe DiMaggio, or Mickey

Mantle. Only five men in major-league history have more hits than Jeter: Pete Rose, Ty Cobb, Hank Aaron, Stan Musial, and Tris Speaker.

Jeter played in 2,743 regular-season games for the Yankees. The next most games by a player for the club is 2,401 by Mantle. The only men who played more games for only one team are Carl Yastrzemski (Red Sox), Stan Musial (Cardinals), Cal Ripken (Orioles), Brooks Robinson (Orioles), Robin Yount (Brewers), Craig Biggio (Astros), and Al Kaline (Tigers). That's an exclusive club.

Derek played 2,673 games at shortstop—and only shortstop. He never played anywhere else on the diamond, not even for one batter in an extra-inning game. He was a shortstop—the Yankees' shortstop—and long before Jeter was named the team captain in 2003, he had earned the respect of his peers. "Derek Jeter is the kind of player who one day I will get to say, 'I played with him,'" said teammate Paul O'Neill. Jeter played at the highest level for 20 wonderful years with nary a whiff of controversy. He was a role model and a matinee idol. Current players who wear uniform jersey No. 2 such as Houston's Alex Bregman and Boston's Xander Bogaerts will tell you as much.

A baby-faced Jeter reached the major leagues to stay at age twenty-one in 1996. In that season he batted .314, won the American League Rookie of the Year Award, and then led the Yankees to their first World Series championship in 18 years. Between 1998 and 2000, he was the biggest star on a team that won three straight World Series titles. In 1998, he led the AL in runs scored (127) and in 1999 led in hits (219). That season, he achieved career highs with 24 homers, 102 runs batted in, and a .349 batting average. In 2000, he became the first player to win the All-Star Game Most Valuable Player Award and World Series Most Valuable Player Award in the same season . . . and he was just getting started.

A recipient of five Silver Slugger Awards, Jeter seemingly made a career of producing one big hit after another, whether it was in the regular season or postseason. He came through in the clutch so many times that he was dubbed "Captain Clutch," and rightfully so. In 2009, he became the Yankees' all-time hits leader, surpassing Gehrig's 72-year old mark. In 2011, he became the first Yankee to record 3,000 hits—all with the Yankees—which he did in style, with a home run off Rays ace David Price. The Captain finished the day 5-for-5 with the game-winning hit, of course. In 2014, in his final game at Yankee Stadium, Jeter performed one more magic trick in the Bronx. His walk-off single drove home the winning run in a dramatic victory over the Orioles. Hollywood screenwriters couldn't have written a better script. "It's like something out of a movie," marveled Jon Sciambi on ESPN Radio.

Aside from being the best-hitting shortstop in history, Jeter is arguably the best postseason hitter of all time. He was a winner, reaching the postseason in 16 of his 20 seasons. He holds the career postseason records for hits, doubles, runs scored, and total bases. There are so many classic Jeter moments it is impossible to rank them. There was the game-tying home run in the eighth inning of Game One of the 1996 ALCS against the Orioles, a leadoff home run in Game Four of the 2000 World Series at Shea Stadium against the Mets, an extra-inning walk-off home run in the 2001 World Series against the Diamondbacks that earned him the nickname "Mr. November." The list goes on and on. Jeter is also the only player with 200 hits in the postseason. He played 158 postseason games—nearly a full regular season—and recorded 200 hits, 20 home runs, 18 stolen bases, a .308 batting average, .374 on-base percentage, and an .838 OPS. This is an astounding season of Octobers, coming against the best teams, facing the top pitchers, and under the most pressurized circumstances.

It wasn't only with his bat that he could impact a game in unimagined ways. "The Flip" in Game Three of the 2001 ALDS featured Derek's most famous highlight reel: his sprint across the field and backhanded flip relay to catcher Jorge Posada which nailed Oakland's Jeremy Giambi at the plate in the seventh inning to preserve the Yankees' 1–0 win in an elimination game, supplying the momentum to propel the team to a Series victory. "It was like Superman flying out of the sky to save the season," said New York's general manager Brian Cashman.

Jeter earned a reputation as a clutch player who has made some of the most famous plays in recent memory. When the Yankees needed a big defensive play, there was Jeter to dive into the stands, face-first, emerging with a bloody chin—as he did to catch a foul pop-up against the Boston Red Sox during the heated pennant race of 2004. When the team needed a clutch hit, there was Jeter to slap the ball the other way, slashing it to the opposite field with that inside-out swing of his. Need a stolen base? No problem, he had 358 of them and is the club's all-time leader in that category, too.

He posted a .310 lifetime batting average with a career .817 OPS. His average season over a 20-year career consisted of 204 hits, 32 doubles, 15 homers, 113 runs, 77 RBIs, and 21 stolen bases. He collected at least 179 hits in a season 15 times. He twice led the league in hits, and did so 14 years apart, with 219 in 1999 and 216 in 2012. He had over 200 hits in a season eight times. And with each single, Jeter dashed from the batters' box, as he always did, rounded first swiftly, then scooted back to the bag. Swatting a base hit to the opposite field was Jeter's signature move, as was his signature way of celebrating: he spread his arms wide and clapped hands. Inevitably, the Yankee Stadium fans would raucously chant Jeter's first and last names. *Der-ek Jee-tah! Der-ek Jee-tah!* Ah, such sweet music!

If there was one knock on Jeter, however, it was his fielding. Though he won five Gold Glove Awards, the defensive statistical measuring sticks of the modern age consistently ranked him near the bottom. It wasn't Derek's fielding that was at issue. The number of errors (or when those errors occurred) is never, ever cited as the reason why Jeter wasn't perceived to be a good fielder. It was his lack of range that was often criticized. Even so, with the bases loaded and two outs in ninth inning with the Yankees protecting a one-run lead, you prayed for a ground ball to be hit to Jeter. That's how confident you were in his ability to make the big play—especially in crunch time. Of course, he could make the sensational play, too. Even today, in my mind's eye, I can still see Jeter from deep in the third-base hole making that iconic balletic jump throw that beats a runner to first base. Give yourself a gift and watch a YouTube video of one such play Jeter made to deny Cleveland's Travis Fryman of a hit in the 1998 ALCS.

Jeter played in 14 All-Star Games and was often recognized for his individual accomplishments, but he was never a league MVP—though he finished in the Top 10 eight times. It was the so-called intangibles he possessed that made him the consummate team leader and able spokesman for a franchise. After the final game at the old Yankee Stadium in 2008, Jeter took the microphone to say goodbye to "The House That Ruth Built," and thanked the fans for their years of support while reminding everyone of the new memories soon to be made. "There are a few things with the New York Yankees that never change," he told the crowd. "That's pride, tradition, and, most of all, we have the greatest fans in the world."

The following season, to christen the new Stadium, Jeter helped lead the Yankees to their 27th World Series title, the fifth for the shortstop since he broke into the majors in 1996. Jeter hit .407 in the 2009 World Series, part of a postseason in which he batted .344. More importantly for him, he was named the winner of that year's Roberto Clemente Award for his charitable work away from the field with his Turn 2 Foundation. "From the first day I met Derek, he has not only impressed me as a great athlete but more importantly a person who has always tried to make other people's lives better," said his former teammate and manager Joe Girardi. "He has dedicated his life to being a champion on and off the field."

For Derek Jeter, Cooperstown awaits.

Honorable Mention

Phil Rizzuto took over for Frankie Crosetti as the Yankees shortstop in 1941 and played his entire 13-year career in the Bronx, with a three-year leave for military service during the Second World War. Diminutive at 5-foot-6 and 160 pounds, he was affectionately called "Scooter," and to fans of an earlier time lucky enough to see him glide after a ball in the third-base hole or flash up the middle to snare a grounder, the moniker was a perfect fit. Rizzuto played all but two of his 1,649 career games at shortstop. He was a spark plug for nine AL pennant winners and seven World Series champions, including five in a row from 1949 to 1953, and is sixth all-time in World Series games played, eighth in hits with 45, fourth in walks with 30, and tied for third in stolen bases with 10. He played in 52 World Series games—the most of any shortstop—and made just five errors. He was such an integral part of the Yankees' success that fellow Hall of Famer Ted Williams opined, "If the Red Sox would have had Phil, we would have won all those pennants." A five-time All-Star, Rizzuto was honored as the AL MVP in 1950 and as the World Series MVP in '51. Following his retirement in 1956, he moved right into the Bombers' broadcast booth and manned the microphone as the voice of the Yankees for another 40 years. His distinctive cry of "Holy cow!" was the rallying call of Yankees fans for two generations.

How do you follow a legend? In the case of **Didi Gregorious** taking over for Derek Jeter, the answer is: seamlessly. He's become the first Yankees shortstop to record three straight 20 home run seasons, and the first ever to hit 25 homers in a season—which he's now done twice. Like his predecessor, Gregorious is best in the clutch: his 2017 postseason performance is the stuff of legends. He belted a three-run homer in the first inning to bring the Yankees back from a 3–0 deficit against the Twins in the wild-card game, and his two homers against the Indians off the AL Cy Young Award winner Corey Kluber in a triumphant Game Five of the ALDS made him just the second Yankees player (after Yogi Berra) ever to hit two homers in a winner-take-all game. Didi is an acrobatic yet dependable defender with a strong throwing arm: his .987 fielding percentage led all AL shortstops in 2018—he made just six errors in 475 total chances. Surgery to replace a right elbow ligament, however, is cause for concern.

A World Series champion six times and twice an All-Star, **Frankie Crosetti** spent his entire 17-year playing career as a member of the New York Yankees—11 of those as the Opening Day starter. The Crow's career batting average was only .245, but he was adept at drawing walks and had a knack for getting hit by pitches. In 1938, he was hit 15 times—a Yankees record that stood for 46 years—and led the AL in being hit by pitches in eight seasons. He hit only 98 career home runs and just one in a World Series, but that drive—a two-run, eighth-inning homer at Wrigley Field in Game Two of the 1938 Series—was the game-winning shot over Dizzy Dean and the Cubs.

During his six seasons with the Yankees, from 1977 to 1982, **Bucky Dent** hit .239 with a .295 on-base percentage, and never hit more than eight home runs in a season. But for one month in September 1978, he earned a place in the hearts of Yankees fans forever. It began in the AL Eastern Division playoff game when he hit a go-ahead three-run homer over the Monster against the Red Sox—earning a new middle name in Boston— and culminated with his MVP performance in the World Series where he hit .414 (10-for-25) with seven RBIs in the six-game Yankees triumph. Bucky F***in' Dent was a two-time All-Star for the Yankees and their defensive anchor at shortstop on the back-to-back World Series championship teams of 1977 and '78. He has a career World Series batting average of .349 in 12 games.

Two others worthy of a brief mention are **Gil McDougald** and **Tony Kubek**. McDougald was the 1951 Rookie of the Year—over Mantle, no less!—and member of five World Series–winning teams. He was the third most valuable member of Casey Stengel's dominant 1950s clubs behind Mantle and Yogi Berra. The versatile infielder was an All-Star as a third baseman, shortstop, and second baseman, but we select him as a short-stop for our purposes here. Kubek was also a versatile player who saw time at every position on the field except catcher and pitcher, though he was primarily a shortstop during his nine years with the Yankees, from 1957 to '65. Kubek won the 1957 AL Rookie of the Year Award when he hit .297, and his 38 doubles in 1961 was the single-season record for Yankees shortstops until Derek Jeter hit 44 in 2004. He was a four-time All-Star and a part of three World Series championship teams (1957, 1961, 1962).

Bill Nowlin's Response

I had no idea Derek Jeter ranked so high in so many categories. I mean, I know he was pretty good and he made a couple of spectacular plays, including one falling into the seats down the third-base line at Fenway Park, risking life and limb to successfully catch a foul ball at a time most of the Red Sox lineup didn't seem to be putting out extra effort. But, wow! I'm almost ready to surrender now. Red Sox fans might have called him "Derek Cheater," but that was just stupid fan stuff. The real vitriol was saved for players like Alex Rodriguez. Jeter was clearly a nice guy. The only thing serious Sox fans really focused on was something you brought up—his apparent lack of range on infield defense.

In no way does it diminish your selection of Jeter, but you didn't have a whole lot of other feasible options. Rizzuto was the first alterna-tive choice who had come to mind for me. I knew he was in the Hall of Fame, of course, but I had the sense that he had never shown a lot of power. I looked it up to see that he only had 38 home runs in his entire career. He was like a Deadball Era guy; the most home runs he had in any given year was seven—and he only did that once, in 1950 (the year he was voted AL MVP). He had another year with six, one with five, one with four, and one with three. Otherwise, it was two or fewer. He did have a .351 on-base percentage (.273 batting average). Most importantly, though, his contemporaries believe him to be exceptional—he was voted an All-Star four years in succession. He was part of seven world championship teams, and helped the Yankees win nine pennants in all. His postseason offense was almost identical with his regular-season play: a .355 OBP and a .246 average, hitting two home runs. He was a key cog in all those World Series–winning teams. Even more important for his Hall of Fame credentials, however, may have been the support of Ted Williams, who reportedly had been a major advocate for him when the Veterans Committee voted him into the Hall (in 1994).

I remember when Didi Gregorious came over to the Yankees in time for the 2015 season (he only cost them Shane Greene). My thought was, "Well, he'll never be a Derek Jeter. That's a tough act to follow." Gregorious has grown in the job and become a force to be reckoned with. In the last two years (2017 and 2018), he's driven in 87 and 86 runs and homered 25 and 27 times. He is not someone I want to see step to the plate, and seems to handle the position very effectively—I'm not a defensive fielding expert but he seems to have better range than Jeter. Like Jeter, he comes across as a genuinely nice guy. Something happened to him in the 2018 ALDS against the Red Sox, though, and he's had to have Tommy John surgery and is expected to lose the first half of the 2019 season, a big blow to Yankees fans hoping to see their team match or exceed the 100 wins they had in the 2018 regular season.

Well, enough on the honorable mentions. I better get back to musing about Derek Jeter. My response is: understood. Right choice. I truly am impressed with your recitation of all he accomplished in his years on the team, knowing as well that he also did so while successfully serving as a model citizen exemplifying the "Yankee way." I'll have some more things to say about him in the Head-to-Head but, as far as your choice goes, it was a relatively simple one, certainly an easier one than I had.

RED SOX SHORTSTOP: JOE CRONIN

Career	H	HR	RBI	BA	Awards
1926–1945 (20-year career)	2285	170	1424	.301	7x All-Star Hall of Fame Inductee (1956)

Red Sox Career	H	HR	RBI	BA
1935–1945	1168	119	737	.300

Red Sox All-Time Rankings:
On-Base Percentage: .394 (8th All-Time, Tied)

Reason for Decision

This was another case in which I selected one person, but then on further reflection changed my mind. I'd initially selected Nomar Garciaparra, but I think I was mentally discounting Cronin because of his roles as Red Sox GM, president of the American League, and a board member of the National Baseball Hall of Fame, not focusing as much as I should have on his years as a ballplayer. That he was also Red Sox manager for 13 years, too, was something I had credited him, but perhaps not enough.

Managing a team while also playing shortstop couldn't have been easy, but Cronin served as a player/manager for the Red Sox from 1935 through 1945, making him the longest-serving manager in team history. As skipper, his Red Sox teams won 1,071 games. He also managed the team in 20 tie games! He won one pennant—the Red Sox winning 104 regular-season games in 1946—and saw the club take their quest for a championship all the way to Game Seven of the World Series against the Cardinals. His final year as skipper was 1947.

Cronin was a five-time All-Star for the Red Sox, who came to Boston from Washington (purchased by young owner Tom Yawkey before the 1935 season for what biographer Mark Armour deemed an "unfathomable" $250,000, calling him "the Alex Rodriguez of his time"). For the Senators, he had driven in more than 100 runs five seasons in succession. He did so three times for the Red Sox, too, three other times knocking in 95, 94, and 95. He held down the shortstop job for a full seven seasons and several partial ones.

In 1,134 career games for Boston, Cronin hit for an even .300 batting average, but drew enough bases on balls that he added almost 100 more points to his on-base percentage (.394). He had a significantly lower batting average than Nomar's .323, but the latter's on-base percentage was significantly lower at .361. It's a tough call there. One could flip a coin.

Cronin was a five-time All-Star for the Red Sox. He'd represented the Senators on two All-Star teams before he came to Boston and might have been on more of them but the All-Star Game only began in 1933 so he'd missed a few opportunities in that regard. He'd led the league in both put-outs and assists three times, though all three were with the Senators. He'd been voted the American League's Most Valuable Player in 1930, but that was before MVP became an "official" designation. By the time he came to the Red Sox, however, Cronin's fielding had become more or less average.

For the Red Sox, Cronin drove in 737 runs and scored 645 (very comparable to Garciaparra's 690 RBIs and 709 runs scored). In one stretch in 1939, he drove in one or more runs (20 in all) in 12 consecutive games. Nomar hit 178 homers to Cronin's 119, but it was a different era. One such indication: Nomar only had five sacrifice hits in his whole Red Sox career; Cronin had 89, and in 1941 led the American League with 14.

In 1942, Cronin acted wisely in his role as manager and "benched himself" in favor of rookie Johnny Pesky, who wound up leading the league in base hits and polled third in MVP voting. Cronin began to play himself as a utility infielder, but often managed a flair for the dramatic. For instance, in 1943, he hit a league-leading five home runs as a pinch-hitter. Two of them came on the same day, one three-run homer in each half of the June 17 doubleheader against St. Louis. Two days earlier, he hit another pinch-hit three-run homer. He set a team-record with 18 pinch-hits that year.

After his uniformed career was done, he served from 1948 through 1959 in the Red Sox front office as GM, treasurer, and VP, and in 1959 became the first former player to serve as president of the American League. He served through 1973. No one else in baseball has a career history like that.

Cronin was elected to the Hall of Fame in 1956 and later served on its board for many years. A charter member of the Red Sox Hall of Fame, Cronin's No. 4 was the first number retired by the Red Sox, in a joint 1984 ceremony with Ted Williams.

Honorable Mention

Nomar Garciaparra was on a trajectory. He broke in on the last day of August in 1996. He didn't do all that much in the 24 games he played that year, but he got his feet wet. And, boy, was he ready for his official rookie year! He led the American League in base hits (209) and triples (11), recorded a .306 batting average, hit 30 homers, and drove in 98 runs. He had 68 multi-hit games, leading the entire league. He was named to the All-Star team and won a Silver Slugger. He also won every single first-place vote for American League Rookie of the Year.

- In 1998, he homered 35 times and drove in 122 runs with a .323 batting average. He placed second in league MVP voting.
- In 1999, his .357 batting average led the AL.
- In 2000, he did it again—a second batting title, this time with a .372 average. He was the first right-handed hitter to earn back-to-back batting crowns since Joe DiMaggio.

He was named to the All-Star team in both 1999 and 2000, and for four years running was in the top 10 in the balloting for MVP.

Look at that trajectory starting with his rookie season: .306, then .323, then .357, and then .372. The guy could hit! At that rate—an average increase of 22 points per year—he would hit .384 in 2001 and then .416 in 2002. By 2004, he'd be hitting .460!

Well, that didn't happen. But his progression from year to year was still impressive. It's just that in 2001, he was injured (apparently in spring training), had wrist surgery on Opening Day, and only got into 21 games (batting .289), not playing his first game until July 29 and not playing at all after August 26.

In 2002, he was back—an All-Star again, leading the majors in doubles (56) and driving in 120 runs. And in 2003, he drove in 105, seventh in MVP voting and an All-Star for the sixth season.

By 2004, he was gone—traded to the Cubs in a deadline deal involving four teams. The Red Sox got Orlando Cabrera from the Expos to play shortstop and Doug Mientkiewicz from the Twins to play first base. Nomar got a ring for being part of the first world championship team the

Red Sox had fielded in 86 years, but he was in the other league at the time and watching from home as it all unfolded.

Nomar recorded an overall career .321 postseason batting average with 21 RBIs in 25 games for the Red Sox.

Rick Burleson stands out as someone who has maybe been overlooked with the passage of time. Maybe he also never got quite the attention he deserved even in his day. He played in 1,004 games at shortstop, more than any other SS save Everett Scott. He was a solid defender and a three-time All-Star for the Red Sox three years in a row: 1977–1979. "Rooster" was fiery and a key competitor on the pennant-winning Red Sox team of 1975, as well as the team which took the season to Game 163 in 1978. (Ahem, no more on that right now.) He hadn't hit for average or power as much as Cronin or Garciaparra, or the man who follows him on this list, Xander Bogaerts.

Xander Bogaerts currently has five full years under his belt. He's got the best career fielding percentage of all the shortstops listed here, though they are pretty tightly bunched. In 2018, as part of a Red Sox team which led the majors in runs scored, he drove in 103 runs thanks in part to a career-high 23 home runs. And he won himself a second world championship ring (he was part of the team in 2013 as well). He's a solid contender and has every opportunity to move up the ranks.

The Red Sox have had a lot of very good shortstops: **Rico Petrocelli**, **Vern Stephens**, and **John Valentin** all come to mind over the last half-century.

But who could forget **Everett Scott**, shortstop for world championship teams back in 1915 and 1916? Well, actually, most people have forgotten him—but they shouldn't. That's no small feat—especially for a team that had only won five world championships before the current century. In fact, Scott played more games at shortstop than any other in Red Sox history (1,093). He had more putouts and more assists than any other Red Sox shortstop, too. He was an iron man before Gehrig, playing in 1,307 consecutive games from June 20, 1916 to May 6, 1925. Problem is, that stretch embraced three seasons of playing every game for the Yankees in 1922, 1923, and 1924. And he hit a little better for the Yankees than he did for the Red Sox, so … er … let's move on. Seriously, though, he does merit an honorable mention.

Johnny Pesky rates a mention for the way his career started out, even though after his first three seasons he wound up playing more at third base than at shortstop. Those first three seasons were pretty special, though; he hit safely more than 200 times each year, leading the league all three years and leading the majors in two of the three. In his rookie year, 1942, he collected 205 base hits. After three years of military service during the Second World War, he came back and did it again, with 208 hits in 1946. Then, in 1947, he hit safely 207 times. He was a table-setter for Ted Williams, and over the course of his time with the Red Sox scored more than twice as many runs as he drove in. He was a huge fan favorite who made his home in the Boston area. And he's in the Red Sox Hall of Fame. Plus, he's got a pole named after him at Fenway Park.

David Fischer's Response
My third-grade teacher impressed upon me the important lesson of always sticking with your gut reaction, and to always trust your first instinct. You should not have wavered from Nomar Garciaparra. If I could have only one Red Sox shortstop for a season or a key series, it would definitely be Nomahhhhh. The decision is elementary.

I never saw Cronin in action, and he did put up some of the best numbers among shortstops in Boston's franchise history despite playing the tail end of his career with the Red Sox. His best season in a Red Sox uniform came in 1938 when he hit .325 with a .964 OPS, 17 home runs, 94 RBIs, and a league-leading 51 doubles. Cronin was no slouch as a player and, as you say, he holds the team record for wins as a manager with 1,071. Terry Francona is the next closest, and he isn't even close, with 744. But while the entirety of Cronin's career—on the field, in the dugout, and in the executive suite—certainly must be taken into account, it shouldn't put him over the top here. I wouldn't consider Gene Michael among the great Yankees shortstops because he was the architect of Bronx squads that won six AL pennants and four World Series titles from 1996 to 2003. Okay, I admit it's an unfair analogy, but the exaggeration helps to make my point.

When Garciaparra burst onto the scene, people began to ask who was the best young shortstop in the game? The choices were Alex Rodriguez, Derek Jeter, and Nomar. (Garciaparra was named for his father, Ramon— "Nomar" is "Ramon" spelled backward.) The question created a healthy debate and, in my opinion, Nomar at the time was every bit as good as Derek and Alex. Garciaparra could hit for average, hit with power, field, throw, and, in his prime, steal a base. There's nothing more a player can do.

No question Nomar was a fantastic hitter. His 1997 through 2000 seasons are the envy of all Hall of Fame shortstops. During those seasons it seemed like every other at-bat Nomar was whacking a ball off the Green Monster. And yet for all his power he didn't swing and miss very often. During the 1999 and 2000 seasons he was among the league's top sluggers, all the while accumulating 23 more walks (112) than strikeouts (89). He retired with a career total of one strikeout for every 10.08 at-bats, a number that Ted Williams (10.87) can relate to. The same Ted Williams that often compared Nomar with Joe DiMaggio.

Garciaparra had six amazing seasons with the Red Sox from 1997 to 2003; in those six seasons he finished eighth, second, seventh, ninth, eleventh, and seventh in MVP voting. In the six full seasons he played for Boston, 190 is the fewest hits he ever collected in a single campaign. In terms of number of hits, he reeled off seasons of 209, 195, 190, 197, 197, and 198. Of course, those hits weren't all singles. Nomar did damage. During his Red Sox career, Garciaparra posted a slash line of .323/.370/.553—hello, that's an incredible .923 OPS—and he was a five-time All-Star, Rookie of the Year, and Silver Slugger. Among Red Sox shortstops, Nomar is first in career WAR (wins above replacement) at 41.2 compared to Cronin at 29.5 despite the former having 239 fewer plate appearances for the Red Sox.

Garciaparra also enjoyed his signature Fenway Park moments. On May 10, 1999, he hit two grand slams and added a two-run homer to bring his RBI total to 10 as the Sox beat the Mariners, 12–4. On July 23, 2002, Nomar celebrated his twenty-ninth birthday by hitting three homers—two in the third inning, a grand slam in the fourth—and driving in eight runs in a win over Tampa Bay that had the Fenway crowd serenading the shortstop with birthday greetings before the game was over. It was a lovefest between city and player. From Hyde Park to Charleston and Back Bay to Dorchester, all the neighborhood kids imitated his quirky routines and rituals before getting in the batters' box. Sadly, the love affair between Boston and "Nomah" ended and, when it did, it wasn't elegant. Once his relationship with the media and teammates soured and he no longer seemed a good fit in Fenway, even the fans that once had worshipped him the way they now worship Tom Brady turned on Nomar. I always wondered if some of that ill will was sparked by Garciaparra's shirtless and ripped appearance on the cover of the March 5, 2001 issue of *Sports Illustrated* which fueled speculation of steroid usage.

Garciaparra's time in Boston was cut short by a seismic trade to the Chicago Cubs in 2004, the year the Red Sox broke the curse, and I think that was a shame. Nomar has returned to cult hero status in Boston, but he never got to celebrate a world championship or ride in a victory parade along Boylston Street. That's too bad, because Nomar produced spectacularly in the postseason, as evidenced by his .975 lifetime postseason OPS accrued in 32 divisional and league championship games.

Nomar was bound for Cooperstown until injuries derailed his journey. He had one good season in his post-Boston career: he hit .303 with 20 homers and 93 RBIs with LA in 2006. Even though the four-plus seasons following his stint in Boston did little to help his legacy, his average 162-game season still rates a .313 batting average, 42 doubles, 105 runs scored, 106 RBIs, and an .882 OPS. There are several middle infielders already in Cooperstown that would gladly take those career numbers. In fact, among shortstops with 5,000 plate appearances, Nomar has the highest OPS. Higher than Honus Wagner, Arky Vaughan, Pee Wee Reese, Phil Rizzuto, Robin Yount, Cal Ripken, Barry Larkin, Joe Cronin, and, yes, Derek Jeter.

For these reasons, I disagree with your selection of Cronin. For my money, Nomar Garciaparra is the best shortstop in Boston Red Sox history. But there's no reason for you to apologize. Nomar already has Mia Hamm as his wife; he has no need for your mea culpa.

Sorry for the horrible pun, but I'm not sorry for bringing up a subject you'd rather not discuss: Game 163 of the 1978 season. It relates to Rick Burleson, one of your honorable mentions. It wasn't a base running gaffe, but when Burleson was faked-out by Lou Piniella it changed history for both clubs. You remember it well. It was the 1978 one-game playoff between the Red Sox and Yankees. The Red Sox were trying to rally in the bottom of the ninth. With Burleson on first base, Jerry Remy hit a fly ball to Lou Piniella. Despite losing the ball in the sun, Piniella pounded his mitt, an action that forced Burleson to stay at second base. Jim Rice followed with a deep fly out which, had Burleson been on third base, likely would have tied the game. Instead the Yankees escaped with the victory. If not for Piniella's deke on Burleson, Bucky F***ing Dent never becomes a saying every Bostonian grows up knowing.

As a New Jersey guy, I'd like to elaborate on John Valentin, a graduate of Seton Hall University in South Orange, New Jersey, and the Red Sox shortstop prior to Garciaparra taking over the position. In 10 seasons with the Red Sox, from 1992 to 2001, Valentin hit .281 with a .361 on-base percentage, .460 slugging, 121 home runs, 528 RBIs, and 1,043 hits in 991 games. He posted a very respectable 32.2 WAR, third-best among Red Sox shortstops. His best season came in 1995 when he hit .298 with 27 home runs and 102 RBIs. His performance that season earned him the Silver Slugger Award and a ninth-place finish in the MVP voting. On July 8, 1994, at Fenway, during a game against Seattle, Valentin became the 10th player in major-league history to turn an unassisted triple play.

HEAD-TO-HEAD

Bill Nowlin: As I said, I really hadn't realized Derek Jeter ranked so highly. Maybe one of the reasons he never seemed to scare me that much as an opponent was based on personal observation—in Boston, where he only hit .266 lifetime at Fenway Park.

David Fischer: It matters little (even to Grady) whether you selected Cronin or my preference Garciaparra—Jeter has to come out on top. Jeter's 3,465 hits in 20 seasons for the Yankees is 1,016 more than the 2,449 total hits Cronin and Garciaparra amassed in their combined 20 seasons for the Red Sox.

BN: I don't doubt how this one is going to be resolved, but lasting a lot of years and amassing a lot of hits in one career isn't going to necessarily help in a short series between two ballclubs, like a head-to-head Yankees/Red Sox battle in the postseason. There haven't been that many of them over the years—the Yankees won in 1999 and 2003, and the Red Sox won in 2004 and 2018. The edge in games (not that it's worth a lot) is 12–11 in New York's favor. Pretty closely matched.

DF: You're avoiding the question of the individuals we're discussing in order to remind me of the fact that in their last two postseason series against the Red Sox the Yankees have dropped seven of the last eight games. I admire your attempt at misdirection (it does indeed hurt to my core), but my eyes remain focused on the prize. *Der-ek Jee-tah! Der-ek Jee-tah!*

BN: OK, I was facing a certain kind of challenge. Other than the question about his defense, did anyone ever have anything bad to say about Derek Jeter? Turns out the Internet offered me an answer. An article from 2006, by Jim Turner, titled "100 Reasons to Hate Derek Jeter." He certainly worked at it. Trouble is, a good portion of the reasons provided seemed to be reasons to appreciate him rather than the contrary, and some of them were just gripes that he hadn't won the Nobel Peace Prize yet. Reason No. 100 was interesting, though: "the Yankees haven't won the Series since Jeter was named captain."

DF: Yeah, but three years after that article appeared, the Yanks did win the Series with Jeter as captain. I don't understand the haters. Nobody complains that supermodel Cindy Crawford has a mole above her left lip.

BN: I think we know who umpire Joe West had in mind when he talked in April 2010 about Yankees-Red Sox games taking so long to play: "It's pathetic and embarrassing and a disgrace to baseball." He didn't actually name any one person. Both teams were guilty of prolonging at-bats and making multiple mound visits, but Red Sox fans tended to think that Jeter came across as something of a prima donna, the way he always stepped one foot out of the batter's box and raised one hand, calling time on every pitch.

DF: Wait a minute! That's precisely the time Nomar wasted going through a myriad of painstaking rituals before feeling comfortable every time he stepped up to the plate! His odd pre-batting behavior was a synchronized dance of glove pulling and cleat digging. Repeated four times between each pitch. Maddening.

BN: I will add something of substance regarding Jeter as shortstop. In recent years, there has been a dramatic development of defensive metrics. For the past six years, SABR's Defensive Index (SDI) has played a major role in the determination of the Rawlings Gold Glove Awards. Chris Dial's June 22, 2018, presentation at SABR's annual convention, "Gold Gloves in Advanced Metric Age," offered data that showed Jeter (since 1988) as THE worst defensive shortstop for anyone with five years of time at the position.

DF: You strike me as a visitor at the Louvre disappointed that the Mona Lisa is smaller than you imagined. While that is true, it's still the Mona Lisa! Are you ready to concede?

BN: If you leave Cindy Crawford, Mona Lisa, Mariah Carey, Adriana Lima, Tyra Banks, and Minka Kelly out of it, I'm prepared to concede that Derek Jeter's stats with the Yankees (not the Marlins) give him a solid edge over any of the Red Sox shortstops I've listed. As we've seen, though, having Orlando Cabrera at short, the Red Sox can still win a seven-game series.

Winner: Derek Jeter

THIRD BASE

RED SOX THIRD BASEMAN: WADE BOGGS

Career	H	HR	RBI	BA	Awards
1982–1999 (18-year career)	3010	118	1014	.328	12x All-Star 2x Gold Glove 5x Batting Champ 8x Silver Slugger 1996 World Series Champ Hall of Fame Inductee (2005)

Red Sox Career	H	HR	RBI	BA
1982–1992	2098	85	687	.338

Red Sox All-Time Rankings:
Games Played: 1625 (8th All-Time)
Plate Appearances: 7323 (8th All-Time)
At-Bats: 6213 (8th All-Time)
Hits: 2098 (5th All-Time)
Singles: 1544 (3rd All-Time)
Doubles: 422 (5th All-Time)
Extra-Base Hits: 554 (7th All-Time)
Walks: 1004 (5th All-Time)
Total Bases: 2869 (7th All-Time)
Runs Scored: 1067 (7th All-Time)
Batting Average: .338 (2nd All-Time)
On-Base Percentage: .428 (2nd All-Time)
On-Base Plus Slugging: .890 (9th All-Time)

Reason for Decision
His five American League batting titles were pretty convincing—including winning four in a row (1985 through 1988, which followed his first one in 1983). Four of his five titles saw him best across both leagues.

Four times he drew over 100 walks. He led in on-base percentage for six seasons.

Wade Boggs played 11 seasons for Boston, and more games at third base than any other in Red Sox history. He still holds the team record for base hits (240 in 1985), and does so by a big margin over second-place Tris Speaker (222 in 1912).

Boggs hit .349 his rookie year, but Cal Ripken won ROY honors, driving in more than twice as many runs. He would have won the batting title but for lacking enough plate appearances (.381).

Boggs hit to all fields. Watching him bat, it really did seem as though he could get a base hit any time he wanted. That was not the case, of course, but he hit .338 in his Red Sox career, second only to Ted Williams's .344. He was one point behind Jimmie Foxx with a career .428 on-base percentage; Williams topped everyone in baseball history at .482.

The Red Sox third baseman was a singles and doubles hitter, almost always producing single digits in home runs—except in 1985, when it seemed as though he just decided what would happen if he swung for the fences and homered 24 times. That was the year he drove in a career-high 89 runs. The lower RBI totals reflected him hitting leadoff in the batting order; getting on base as much as he did, however, resulted in him scoring more than 100 runs every year, from 1983 through 1989.

Though neither are tabulated by the Elias Sports Bureau, there was a widespread understanding that Boggs also led all of baseball in consumption of both chicken and beer. In fact, in 1984 he saw a book published, *Fowl Tips: My Favorite Chicken Recipes*.

Boggs later played five years for the Yankees, batting .313, and two final seasons with Tampa Bay, where he collected his 3,000th career base hit (a home run, no less). He was a 12-time All-Star, the first eight with Boston and the final four with New York. He collected eight Silver Slugger awards.

His fielding was good, with a pair of Gold Gloves to his credit. His .959 fielding percentage with Boston ranks him fourth in club history, behind Mike Lowell, Rico Petrocelli, and Johnny Pesky.

He was never a big factor in postseason play, though he hit .385 and .438 in the ALCS in 1988 and 1990, respectively. He was part of one world championship team, with some other team in 1996. Somehow Red Sox fans never really held that against him.

In 2005, Boggs was inducted into the National Baseball Hall of Fame—with a Red Sox cap. Aside from the chicken and beer, Boggs was known for a number of quirky superstitions as well, even proclaiming in his Hall of Fame acceptance speech, "Believe me, I have a few superstitions, and they work." Something worked, that's for sure, and Wade Boggs is my choice for Red Sox third baseman.

Honorable Mention

Born in the Bronx, and a Yankees fan growing up, **Frank Malzone** was a six-time All-Star who played nine full seasons for the Red Sox. He was a member of the inaugural class of the Red Sox Hall of Fame when it was first launched in 1995. He played 1,335 games at third base with a career .276 average. He was a glove man, too, winning three Gold Gloves in 1957, 1958, and 1959. Malzone drove in 103 runs in 1957, the only time he topped 100, and finished seventh in MVP voting. He accounted for 716 runs batted in over the course of those nine-plus seasons.

After Boggs and Malzone, there are five other third basemen who merit mention.

Jimmy Collins was the first third baseman the team ever had. A star for the Boston Beaneaters, he was lured over to the brand-new American League in 1901 and served as the team's first manager while also playing third base. Collins was popular with his players, as well as the fans, and he brought along several former teammates from Boston's National League team. His teams won back-to-back pennants in 1903 and 1904, and the first World Series ever played, in 1903. In 1945, Collins was inducted into the National Baseball Hall of Fame.

Larry Gardner's principal distinction is that he was a member of three world championship teams for the Red Sox—in 1912, 1915, and 1916. And that's a pretty good distinction! Gardner hit a solid .282 in his 10 seasons with the Red Sox and got on base 35 percent of the time.

Mike Lowell played five seasons for Boston and was a key member of the 2007 world championship team. Hitting .324 with 120 runs batted in that year (both career bests), he was an All-Star (he'd been a three-time All-Star with the Marlins, from whence he came with Josh Beckett) and placed fifth in league MVP balloting. He tore up the postseason with his bat, hitting .333, .333, and .400, with 15 postseason RBIs, and was named Most Valuable Player of the 2007 World Series. Lowell holds the best fielding percentage of any Red Sox third baseman.

Johnny Pesky and **Rico Petrocelli** both played a considerable number of games at third base, but both played at least a few more at shortstop—in Pesky's case, quite a few more. This unfortunately consigns both of them to something of a position in limbo when it comes to considering them as one of the best Red Sox players at their position. Rico, for instance, played 774 games at shortstop and 727 at third base. There are accolades aplenty for both, as they are deservedly members of the Red Sox Hall of Fame.

David Fischer's Response

I was confident you'd choose a player who manned the hot corner for both the Red Sox and Yankees. And no, I wasn't expecting you to tab Butch Hobson, who played 30 games for the Yankees in 1982! It's Wade Boggs, of course, no question.

Most all ballplayers are "stitious," but Wade Boggs was *super*stitious. Psychiatrists might label him obsessive compulsive, with a routine of eating chicken before every game, leaving his house at the same exact time on game days, taking batting practice at exactly 5:17, and running wind sprints at exactly 7:17. He also took exactly 150 ground balls in practice and carved the Hebrew "chai" symbol (meaning "life") in the dirt each time he stepped to the plate, even though he is not Jewish. Boggs attributed much of his success to this daily routine and refused to alter his habits, and who could blame him? The results speak for themselves. Boggs's undying allegiance to his superstitions helped lead him to one of the finest pro baseball careers of all time, and he's an appropriate player to appear on our lists for both teams.

New York fans were a tad surprised when the Yanks signed Boggs as a free agent prior to the '93 season, and were slow to warm to him.

Watching Boggs and Don Mattingly in the same lineup was a bit surreal for this Yankee fan, seeing as how I loathed Boggs back in 1986 for sitting out the last game of the season while Mattingly battled to catch him for the AL batting crown, which Boggs would eventually win .356 to .352. The image of Boggs crying in the Shea Stadium dugout after the Red Sox blew the 1986 Series was fine consolation.

But as Jerry Seinfeld says, "We root for the laundry," and Boggs was wearing the uniform of my favorite team—and producing. I guess he wasn't so bad after all. Boggs even has his own singular Yankee October moment. While Game Four of the '96 Series is best remembered for Jim Leyritz's three-run homer that tied the score at six, it was Boggs's patient at-bat that gave the Bombers the lead in the 10th inning. With two outs and the bases loaded, he was called upon as a pinch-hitter. Displaying his trademark plate discipline, he dug out of a 1-2 hole to work a six-pitch walk from Atlanta's Steve Avery, which scored Tim Raines with the go-ahead run. The Yanks added another run to win, 8–6, tying the Series and swaying momentum back to the Yankees from the Braves.

That led to the iconic image of a joyous Boggs riding that police horse along the outfield track at Yankee Stadium. As comedian and diehard Red Sox fan Denis Leary says, "If you had told my father that, one day, Wade Boggs would win the World Series with the Yankees, his head would have blown up." Now that's an image this Yankee fan can savor.

YANKEES THIRD BASEMAN: ALEX RODRIGUEZ

Career	H	HR	RBI	BA	Awards
1994–2013, 2015–16 (22-year career)	3115	696	2086	.295	14x All-Star 2x Gold Glove 1996 Batting Champ 10x Silver Slugger 3x MVP 3x POY 2009 World Series Champ

Yankees Career	H	HR	RBI	BA
2004–2013, 2015–2016	1580	351	1096	.283

Yankees All-Time Rankings:
Home Runs: 351 (6th All-Time)
Total Bases: 2914 (10th All-Time)
Runs Scored: 1012 (10th All-Time)
Slugging Percentage: .523 (6th All-Time)
On-Base Plus Slugging: .900 (7th All-Time)

Reason for Decision

The decision came down to Alex Rodriguez and Graig Nettles. Each played about 1,500 games over 11 full seasons for the Yankees. Rodriguez has the more impressive stats in virtually every offensive category: better in batting average (.283 to .253), on-base average (.378 to .329), slugging percentage (.523 to .433), home runs (351 to 250), and runs batted in (1,096 to 834). At the time of his retirement, Nettles held the mark for most homers by an AL third baseman … that is, until A-Rod broke it.

A-Rod won two MVP awards as a Yankee (three total), both at third, and Nettles's best showing in MVP voting was fifth place in '77. A-Rod was a seven-time All-Star as a Yankee (14 times total), Nettles five. As a Yankee, Rodriguez led the league in homers twice, RBIs once, runs scored twice, slugging three times, and OPS twice. Nettles led the league in homers once. During his time in the Bronx, A-Rod hit 30 or more HRs and drove in 100 or more runs in seven straight seasons; Nettles did this once in his entire career.

Even though he had won two Gold Gloves as a shortstop with the Texas Rangers, Alex agreed to switch positions and become a third baseman when he joined the Yankees, which allowed Derek Jeter to remain at short. Alex was the best shortstop in the majors, but he knew the Yankees would be a better team with him and Jeter playing together. So like his hero, the Baltimore Orioles star Cal Ripken Jr., he moved to third. But Ripken moved to third when he had gotten older and slower. Rodriguez was still in the prime of his career. His position switch was the selfless act of a team player.

In 2007, A-Rod hit 54 homers and won his third (overall) MVP award. His mark of 54 homers is the most ever hit in a season by a third baseman. Rodriguez now holds the records for most home runs in a single season at two positions, shortstop and third base.

A-Rod's postseason hitting was not spectacular, save for his clutch performance in the 2009 postseason leading to his one world championship. We concede Nettles was the better fielder, but A-Rod, a converted shortstop with excellent range and a strong arm, ranks first here as the best all-around third baseman in Yankee history.

After much discussion, we decided that use of performance-enhancing drugs wouldn't be a major factor affecting our rankings. Decisions would be based on players' performances while with the team, and if two players were equal in that ranking, the player who wasn't tainted by drug use would get the nod. And so, if I were going to discount A-Rod's achievements because he's a drug cheat, I'd need to discount Nettles for loading his bat with Super Balls. In any case, these two players aren't equal; A-Rod is the otherworldly talent, regardless of what you think of him as a person.

Honorable Mention

Graig Nettles was a five-time All-Star who hit 250 home runs in 11 seasons in the Bronx, including a league-leading 32 in 1976. In his best season of '77, he set career highs with 37 homers and 107 RBIs, and won the first of two consecutive Gold Glove awards. He was the offensive and defensive anchor for the Bombers' 1976–1981 run that included two world titles, two AL pennants, and five division titles. He's an easy choice for No. 2 here. His sparkling fielding in Game Three of the '78 WS saved the Yankees' bacon, and he was named MVP of the 1981 ALCS after hitting .500 with a home run and nine RBIs in the three-game series, driving in three runs in each game.

Red Rolfe's playing career lasted only nine full seasons with the Yankees, from 1934 to '42. During that brief period, his impressive resume includes six pennant winners, five world championships, and four All-Star selections. Rolfe scored over 100 runs in seven consecutive seasons from 1935 to '41, averaging 121 runs a year. His best year was 1939, when he led the league in hits (213), doubles (46), and runs scored (139). From August 9 to 25 of that season he scored at least one run in 18 consecutive games, a modern record (equaled by Cleveland's Kenny Lofton in 2000). Rolfe batted a respectable .289 with an on-base percentage of .360 for his career.

Scott Brosius wore pinstripes for only four seasons that all ended in the World Series, winning three in a row from 1998 to 2000. In '98, he batted .300 with 19 homers and 98 RBIs, made the All-Star team, and was awarded the Series MVP. The Yanks won again in '99, aided in part by Brosius's only Gold Glove and two homers against the Red Sox in the ALCS. He hit another homer in the 2000 Series against the Mets, and in Game Five of the 2001 Series, he tied the game in the bottom of the ninth with a homer, leading to a Yankees win. In the postseason he hit eight homers and drove in 30 runs. Although he was only thirty-four and had just batted .287, he retired after the 2001 World Series.

Wade Boggs was already a Hall of Famer-in-waiting for what he'd done with the Red Sox, but after arriving in the Bronx in 1993 he batted .302, .342, .324, .311, and .292 in his five seasons in New York, won both of his Gold Gloves as a Yankee, and made four of his 12 All-Star appearances in pinstripes. He was the starting third baseman on the 1996 world champions, celebrating on horseback.

Clete Boyer held down the third-base position on five straight pennant winners, from 1960 to '64, winning titles in 1961 and '62. A remarkably gifted fielder at his peak, he was second-to-none (actually to Brooks Robinson) and performed brilliantly in the '61 Fall Classic. He wasn't a great hitter, but did hit 95 homers as a Yankee, and probably would have hit a lot more had he not been a right-handed hitter aiming for Death Valley at the pre-renovated old Stadium. In '64, he and his brother, Ken, became the only brothers to both homer in a World Series game.

Bill Nowlin's Response

The Red Sox really wanted to sign Alex Rodriguez. He would have been a hero in Boston the minute he signed, because when a trade was worked out with the Texas Rangers it was well-known (or well-publicized) at the time that he was willing to restructure his contract for one that paid him millions and millions of dollars less for the privilege of playing in Boston. Giving up well over $10 million so he could play for the Red Sox? Wow! How to win over local fans! Who does that?

Well, the answer was: nobody does that, not with the Players Association refusing to allow one of its members to settle for so much less money. It was something the union couldn't abide. The deal was scotched, and the Yankees slipped in and signed him. Red Sox GM Theo Epstein was furious. Some Sox fans (perhaps a little disingenuously) took heart in the nickname A-Rod had picked up with the Mariners and the Rangers: he was dubbed "The Cooler." He had great stats, but both teams not only didn't jell—but seemed to cool off.

A-Rod has one World Series ring. Red Sox teams he played against have three. He drove in six runs in the 2009 ALDS, six runs in the 2009 ALCS, and six runs in the 2009 World Series. Hideki Matsui was named Series MVP, but A-Rod was no "cooler" at all in 2009. The last seven seasons he was on a Yankees payroll, he was generally mediocre, averaging 36 RBIs per year (this calculation factors in 2014, when he was suspended for the entire year and 2017, when he just wasn't wanted). If you only counted the years he did play, he only averaged 51. A-Rod was with the Yankees for 12 years; the first seven were excellent. He wasn't going to leave baseball at age thirty-four, but things really fell apart starting in 2011.

HEAD-TO-HEAD

Bill Nowlin: We've each got Boggs here, either as first choice or honorable mention.

David Fischer: He's deserving of the recognition. A Hall of Famer, and one of the lucky Red Sox players who lost a World Series with Boston but then got to experience what it's like to win a world championship as a member of the New York Yankees.

BN: But even had A-Rod been sporting Red Sox laundry and put up the same stats, I wonder if I would have picked him.

DF: A-Rod's career offensive totals rank him among the greatest of all time, and he posted some impressive seasons as a Yankee. I think you'd gladly add that kind of titanic production to your Boston lineup.

BN: With A-Rod, it's not just about the play. It's about the player. He comes with a ton of baggage.

DF: You'll get no argument from me on that score. His Yankee career was filled with controversy, distractions, and self-inflicted drama. All of which took away focus from what his team was trying to accomplish: win games.

BN: Wade Boggs was focused, that's for sure. He dealt with his own controversy, but never seemed to let it cause a distraction.

DF: He was a player Yankees fans admired and respected, but we didn't like him—until he came to our side and helped us win games.

BN: Dislike is irrational, not to mention hatred. Most Red Sox fans never disliked Derek Jeter, or Brett Gardner, and certainly not Mariano Rivera. But Alex Rodriguez? That's another story.

DF: You wouldn't be singing that song if the Players Association had allowed A-Rod to join the Red Sox.

BN: It wasn't just that we felt jilted. It wasn't his fault the Players Association prevented him from playing in Boston. But there's just that irrational *something* that made him easy for many people to dislike.

DF: Even Yankees fans were cool to him. It was a love-hate relationship. But still, I can't help but wonder how history might have changed these franchises had A-Rod been a member of the Red Sox.

BN: He might have been riding around Fenway Park on a horse a time or two, and he might have had Jorge Posada's glove thrust in his face.

DF: Hypothetically, A-Rod's first season as a Red Sox could have ended in a disastrous postseason collapse in the 2004 ALCS, when Boston—not New York—would have become the only team ever to lose a best-of-seven playoff series after being up 3–0 in games.

BN: Over the years, the Red Sox have had perhaps a fair share of teams that suffered postseason exits, though they weren't all quick ones. They tended to either get wiped out pretty quickly, like in 2017 to name a recent year, or maybe more painfully extend to a Game Seven that left them wanting.

DF: I can't imagine A-Rod as the difference-maker. One World Series title is an accomplishment not to be taken for granted, but as you remind us, "The Cooler" was an integral part—and reason—for many underachieving Yankee teams that suffered quick postseason exits.

BN: Sounds like you're beginning to sour on your guy.

DF: New York fans, and the Yankees organization, soured on him. Especially at the end, when he was caught up in all the lies about PEDs.

BN: His legacy certainly is tainted by PEDs. Without doubt, he was an extraordinary talent, but was he a winner?

DF: I'd say no. In all, A-Rod appeared as a Yankee in 14 postseason series, and won just six of them—three of which occurred during the team's 2009 World Series title run. And at the end of his career, he lost postseason at-bats because manager Joe Girardi was either benching or pinch-hitting for him.

BN: Both are great players, but different players. One set the table, the other cleaned up—but as it turned out, he wasn't clean. I pick Boggs.

Intangibles, likeability, team chemistry, PEDs—all factors must be considered.

DF: As a young journalist, I was assigned by *Yankees Magazine* to write a feature story on Boggs when he came to the team. I found him to be one of the nicest, most sincere, most professional athletes I've ever interviewed. I'll never forget that. On the other hand, A-Rod always seemed to act as if he knew people were watching him. There is genuine fakeness to his demeanor and, truth be told, despite his superhuman talent, I wouldn't want A-Rod in my clubhouse.

Winner: Wade Boggs

LEFT FIELD

RED SOX LEFT FIELDER: TED WILLIAMS

Career	H	HR	RBI	BA	Awards
1939–1942, 1946–1960 (19-year career)	2654	521	1839	.344	19x All-Star 2x MVP 6x Batting Champ Triple Crown (1942, 1947) 5x POY Hall of Fame Inductee (1966)

Red Sox All-Time Rankings:
Games Played: 2292 (3rd All-Time)
Plate Appearances: 9788 (3rd All-Time)
At-Bats: 7706 (4th All-Time)
Hits: 2654 (2nd All-Time)
Singles: 1537 (4th All-Time)
Doubles: 525 (2nd All-Time)
Triples: 71 (9th All-Time)
Home Runs: 521 (1st All-Time)
Extra-Base Hits: 1117 (2nd All-Time)
Walks: 2021 (1st All-Time)
Total Bases: 4884 (2nd All-Time)
Runs Scored: 1798 (2nd All-Time)
Runs Batted In: 1839 (2nd All-Time)
Batting Average: .344 (1st All-Time)
On-Base Percentage: .482 (1st All-Time)
Slugging Percentage: .634 (1st All-Time)
On-Base Plus Slugging: 1.116 (1st All-Time)

Reason for Decision

"The Greatest Hitter Who Ever Lived"—any debate puts Ted Williams among a list of candidates you can count on the fingers of one hand. This was the easiest call in the entire book for me.

The stats one could reel off go on and on, and I'll get to a number of them. If I had to pick one, though, it would be on-base percentage. Ted Williams was a four-decade player, with a career spanning the years 1939–1960. Over the course of his 19 years of playing, his career on-base percentage was .482. Stop and think for just a moment what that means. The first goal of a batter is to get on base. In 9,788 plate appearances, Williams got on base almost half the time—48.2 percent. He ranks tops in all of baseball history. (Babe Ruth came in second, at .474.)

Part of the reason was his extraordinary discipline at the plate ("get a good ball to hit" was his mantra). Williams also owns the highest walks percentage of all time—20.75 percent. But he didn't just walk—he hit, too, for a career .344 batting average. There have been a handful (five, since the 1900s) who hit for a higher average, but Williams hit for power as well as average. Only Babe Ruth topped him in career slugging percentage. And Ruth struck out a lot more—he whiffed in 12.5 percent of his plate appearances, while for Williams it was just 7.2 percent. Strikeouts never help your team.

Ted Williams was a 19-time All-Star. We will note that he missed almost five full seasons due to wartime service in World War II and the Korean War, in the latter flying 39 combat missions, several with Marine Corps squadron mate (and future astronaut) John Glenn.

He set a rookie record in 1939 with 145 RBIs, one that has yet to be matched even in the days of the 162-game season. Two years later, in 1941, he hit for a batting average of .406—in the 77 seasons since then, no one has hit .400. And the year "The Kid" did it, sacrifice flies were counted as outs, so the bar to .400 was that much higher. He followed up his 1941 season with a Triple Crown win in 1942, leading not just the AL but all of baseball in homers, RBIs, and batting average. He then lost three years to military service, only to come back and win his first MVP award in 1946 followed by yet another Triple Crown in 1947. He's the only American League player to win two Triple Crowns, and only Rogers Hornsby won two in the NL. He "only" led the league in batting in 1948, but followed that with his second MVP award in 1949. He might have won a third Triple Crown in 1949; he led in HRs and RBIs, but lost the batting title to George Kell—by one ten-thousandth of a point.

Williams was on his way to a career year that might have been like none other to that point in time in 1950—he had 83 RBIs before the All-Star Break—when he broke his elbow in the All-Star Game, costing him most of the rest of the season. He came in with 97 RBIs, the first of his nine seasons in the big leagues that he didn't drive in at least 100.

Some might argue that Williams's most impressive season as a hitter came late in his career, in 1957—the year he turned thirty-nine years old. He hit .388 and, had he been a little younger and thus a little more fleet of foot, might have legged out six more hits and had another .400 season.

And, famously, he hit a home run in his last career at-bat.

As a fielder, Ted Williams was none too shabby, with 140 outfield assists to his credit, leading to 30 double plays. None other than Dom DiMaggio, who played so many seasons next to Ted in center field, argued that Williams was a very good fielder who knew how to play Fenway's tricky left-field wall better than most.

Williams was elected to the Hall of Fame in 1966 and famously turned a portion of his speech (his handwritten speech can be seen at the Hall) into a plea that the great Negro League players would one day be recognized in the Hall of Fame. They had been excluded from major-league baseball before Jackie Robinson broke the "color barrier" in 1947. When Pumpsie Green became the first African American ballplayer on the Boston Red Sox, Williams hadn't said anything but made it a point to be seen with Green as his throwing partner as they loosened up on the field before games. Entirely unappreciated until 2002, when this author published an article in the *Boston Globe Magazine* a few weeks before Ted's death, Williams was actually the first Latino in the National Baseball Hall of Fame. His maternal grandparents had both been Mexican immigrants.

Ted Williams's book *The Science of Hitting* remains a bible of baseball for many, nearly a half-century after its publication.

For decades, his chosen cause was the Jimmy Fund, to fight cancer in children. He was chairman of the Jimmy Fund for numerous years, and a trustee from 1954–1981, serving as an honorary trustee thereafter until his 2002 death.

Honorable Mention

Carl Yastrzemski and **Jim Rice** are the other two names which immediately come to mind. Yaz, though, I decided to put at first base. Unlike

Rice and Williams, Yaz played more than 750 games at first base. Jim Rice played 1,503 games in left field and was a DH in 530 more. He's a Hall of Fame ballplayer, often cited as the most feared batter in baseball for a full decade (1975–1986). He drove in more than 100 runs in eight of those twelve years, twice leading the league while also leading it three times in home runs. He was MVP in 1978 when the Red Sox came up one game short of winning the division title due to some fluky long fly ball. In five other seasons, he placed among the top five in MVP balloting.

In 1975, his rookie year, Rice came in second only to teammate Fred Lynn. There's a good chance the Red Sox might have won the World Series that year had not Rice had his hand broken by a pitch in September. Rice was an eight-time All-Star and hit for a career .298 average while driving in 1,415 runs.

One could also mention some other notable left fielders for Boston over the years: **Mike Greenwell, Duffy Lewis**, and **Manny Ramirez. Andrew Benintendi** is off to a very good start in his first couple of seasons, but of course it takes years to build up the kind of resume one needs to rate more than a mention in passing.

David Fischer's Response

In their long history, the Boston Red Sox have boasted a bunch of excellent left fielders, from Lewis to Williams to Yaz to Rice to Greenwell to Manny and now Benintendi, who with his smooth swing is likely to be a fixture in front of the Green Monster for many years to come. In his short career, Benintendi has done damage against the Yankees, and particularly in Yankee Stadium, where his lefty stroke often finds the short porch in right field. While Boston's left-field lineage is mighty potent, there is no debate that Ted Williams is the best of them all. Not merely Boston's best left fielder, but a case can be made for The Splendid Splinter as the best left fielder in baseball history. In his storied career, Williams was never afraid to be himself. He refused to tip his cap to fans for most of his 19 seasons in Boston and maintained a contentious relationship with reporters, which surely cost him at least one MVP award—in a year he won the Triple Crown. Yet Williams's fearlessness showed in other, more noble ways. I'm glad you noted his Hall of Fame speech; that was a groundbreaking statement, and it led to the induction of Satchel Paige, Buck Leonard, and Josh Gibson as among the first Negro Leagues players enshrined in Cooperstown. Not only did he hit baseballs, he flew Marine Corps jets during the Korean War alongside John Glenn. Williams's career statistics are doubly impressive when you consider that he missed nearly five full seasons to two wars. Since he averaged 32 home runs a year through 1951, it's reasonable to speculate that he lost 150 homers while in the service. And he still came within 300-odd hits of attaining 3,000. Remarkable.

While Teddy Ballgame was the best hitter who ever lived, Jim Rice was indeed the most feared hitter of his time. Rice was the rare power threat who could mash 35 home runs and collect 200 hits a season. His strength was legendary—he once broke his bat on a check swing! Rice's 1978 MVP season was one for the ages. He collected 406 total bases, the most since Joe DiMaggio in 1937. That season he hit 46 homers, drove in 139 runs, collected 213 hits, scored 121 runs, and led the league with 15 triples. I take exception to your statement that the Yankees kept Rice and the Sox out of the playoffs that year due to a fluky long fly ball. Dent's fly ball was not long!

YANKEES LEFT FIELDER: ROY WHITE

Career	H	HR	RBI	BA	Awards
1965–1979 (15-year career)	1803	160	758	.271	2x All-Star 2x World Series Champ

Yankees All-Time Rankings:
Games Played: 1881 (7th All-Time)
Plate Appearances: 7735 (7th All-Time)
At-Bats: 6650 (9th All-Time)
Walks: 934 (8th All-Time)
Stolen Bases: 233 (6th All-Time)

Reason for Decision

Roy White played more than 1,500 games in left field for the Yankees, from 1965 to 1979, far more than any other player at the position. For poor timing, only Don Mattingly can commiserate with him. White arrived just as the old dynasty was collapsing, and he played on some forgettable teams during those dreadful CBS ownership years. But White held his own against the league's left fielders during that span. Over his career, he averaged 155 hits per season, 80 walks, 26 doubles, 14 homers, 65 RBIs, 83 runs scored, 20 steals, a .271 batting average, and a .360 on-base percentage.

White finally got to play on some excellent Yankees teams toward the end of his career, appearing in three World Series and winning two (1977 and 1978). And he played well when it counted, raising his game in the postseason: a .278 batting average with a .387 on-base percentage in 25 games. His first-inning homer off Hall of Famer Don Sutton in Game Three of the 1978 Series when the Yanks trailed the Dodgers two games to none was a clutch wake-up call to his teammates, and in Game Four he walked and scored the winning run in the 10th inning to tie the Series at two games apiece; a Series the Yankees would eventually win in six. In that 1978 World Series, Roy hit .333 (8-for-24) with nine runs scored, a homer, four RBIs, and two stolen bases. If not for Bucky Dent's stellar postseason performance, White might have been the Series MVP.

A team-oriented player and fundamentally sound, White led the AL in walks in 1972 and runs scored in 1976. He never batted .300 for a season, or hit 25 homers, or had 100 RBIs. He was not a spectacular player—far from it. But he was steady and consistent over a 15-year career, the entirety spent in the Bronx. As such, he ranks among the club's all-time Top 10 in games played (1,881), walks (934), plate appearances (7,735), at-bats (6,650), and sacrifice flies (69). He also stole 233 bases, sixth best, and was caught 117 times, tied with Babe Ruth for the most in team history. (Who knew the Babe was so frisky on the basepaths?)

White was a two-time All-Star, but his ability to draw walks and reach base safely, underappreciated during his playing days, might garner more attention today. Also of value was his ability as a switch-hitter; and with very distinct stances from either side of the plate. His right-handed stance was of the conventional variety, he stood pigeon-toed batting left handed, a bit hunched over the plate, with his hands held low almost resting the bat on his back hip. Long before the batting stance guy went viral, all the kids growing up in my neighborhood playing Wiffle ball could imitate Roy White's unique left-handed set-up.

White also was an excellent defensive left fielder, with enough speed and range to have played center, if not for Bobby Murcer's presence at that spot through the mid-1970s. White's throwing arm was the subject of much ridicule, but he countered this lack of velocity by charging base hits with vigor and always throwing accurately to the proper base. White also owns the distinction of having played left field in the old Yankee Stadium and the remodeled one that opened in 1976. He was one of the few who mastered the difficult sun that embarrassed many a left fielder over the years. "The old Yankee Stadium left field was notorious for the sun," he once told me. "From three o'clock on in the afternoon the sun was straight, dead-on in the left fielder's eyes. There was no home-field advantage for anybody with that sun."

Honorable Mention

A five-time All-Star, **Charlie Keller**, known as King Kong (though not to his face), completed an outstanding outfield alongside Joe DiMaggio in center and Tommy Henrich in right during the 1940s. In four World Series, three of them as winners, Keller hit .306 with five homers and drove in 18 runs in 19 World Series games. His regular-season career on-base percentage of .410 ranks fourth highest in team history, behind only Ruth, Gehrig, and Mantle, and his .928 OPS is fifth best, trailing only Ruth, Gehrig, DiMaggio, and Mantle. That's a darn good list.

Bob Meusel played left field from 1920 to 1929, contributing to six AL pennant winners and three World Series–winning teams. In ten seasons he knocked in 1,005 runs. He ranks seventh all-time on the Yankees with a .311 batting average. In 1925, he led the AL with 33 homers and 134 RBIs, one of five seasons with 100 or more runs driven home.

Others deserving of a mention: **Brett Gardner** and **Lou Piniella**.

Bill Nowlin's Response

My first reaction was a snarky one: Roy who? Faced with so many great Yankees over so many decades, it's nice to be able to do something like that once in a while. But that wasn't a dignified enough response so while I will just confess to the impulse here, I didn't actually assert it. I might have rated Keller higher, but, hey, you're the Yankees guy.

More seriously, reading what you wrote about White, he has an impressive resume, starting with being a two-time All-Star. And even if he wasn't with the Yankees during their peak years, he played in three World Series and was part of the winning team in two of them. As noted, he played, all told, in 25 postseason games. To be selected by your manager to play that many games in postseason play is pretty darned impressive.

And I'll tell you as a Red Sox fan in 2018, I still get a little extra nervous every time Brett Gardner comes to the plate against the Red Sox. He's one of those guys—kind of like Brock Holt at times—who seems to come through when it's most needed, except that Gardner is a regular and seems to do this against the Red Sox in particular.

HEAD-TO-HEAD

David Fischer: Roy White was no slam-dunk selection. Charlie Keller and Bob Meusel would seem the more obvious choices, as each man was an AL All-Star and member of multiple world championship teams. But upon intense introspection, I decided to choose White. He played more games at the position than any other Yankee, and he had a solid career in all phases of the game. That has to count for something.

Bill Nowlin: It certainly does. It counts for a lot—and it's your choice as to which Yankee you nominate for the position. One never knows what might happen in a true head-to-head, of course. I'm ready to pit Ted Williams against him and see how it all plays out.

DF: That's just it. You can pit Ted Williams against anybody who ever played left field for the Yankees, and the winner is always going to be "the greatest hitter who ever lived." Unless you count Babe Ruth, who started over 850 games in left field for the Yankees. But that wouldn't be fair, selecting the same player at two positions.

BN: As noted elsewhere, I could have put in Babe Ruth as the left-handed pitcher for the Red Sox, too! And it wouldn't be difficult at all to consider him for DH—even though the position wasn't created until more than 24 years after his death. Now if we were to play "Ted Williams with a broken elbow" against Roy White, that might even things up a bit. In the first inning of the 1950 All-Star Game, Williams crashed into the left-field wall at Comiskey Park and broke his left elbow. Two days later, seven bone fragments were removed in surgery. But he didn't know it was broken at the time, and he just kept playing. In the fifth inning, he singled to right field and drove in Larry Doby with what was then a go-ahead run. After eight full innings, Williams was removed from the game and Dom DiMaggio took over for him in left. Ted had gone 1-for-4 with a run batted in.

DF: It's true. Ted Williams beats Roy White with a broken arm tied behind his back! In all seriousness, this is not to begrudge White his rightful place in Yankees history or to demean his talents. Besides Bobby Murcer (and later Thurman Munson), White was the only player worth rooting for on some awful Yankees teams of the late 1960s and early 1970s. He mastered the sun and shadows of Yankee Stadium's treacherous left field like no other at his position. In 15 seasons he recorded 86 outfield assists and he made just 43 errors for a lifetime fielding percentage of .988—a heck of a lot better than the league average of .980 posted by his outfield contemporaries. Also of note, White's regal, graceful playing style gave him an air of dignity sorely lacking among pinstriped players at the time. White possessed many of the skills that are missing from today's players: baseball fundamentals. He was a good situational hitter, as evidenced by twice leading the AL in sacrifice flies. In addition, I have to mention the Roy White knishes sold at Yankee Stadium that was once a popular concession stand item.

BN: By the way, you note White's ability to play left field at Yankee Stadium before and after the 1976 renovation. We didn't have the fielding metrics then that we have today, but center fielder Dom DiMaggio played alongside Ted Williams for many years, and Dominic—considered a superb fielder—has said that Williams played a very good left field. He knew how to play the Wall. Hence, those 140 outfield assists.

Winner: Ted Williams

CENTER FIELD

RED SOX CENTER FIELDER: TRIS SPEAKER

Career	H	HR	RBI	BA	Awards
1907–1928 (22-year career)	3514	117	1531	.345	1916 Batting Champ 1912 MVP 3x World Series Champ Hall of Fame Inductee (1937)

Red Sox Career	H	HR	RBI	BA
1907–1915	1327	39	542	.337

Red Sox All-Time Rankings:
Triples: 106 (2nd All-Time)
Stolen Bases: 267 (2nd All-Time)
Batting Average: .337 (3rd All-Time)
On-Base Percentage: .414 (4th All-Time)
On-Base Plus Slugging: .896 (8th All-Time)

Reason for Decision

I knew it was going to come down to Speaker vs. Dom DiMaggio, and I thought it could be kind of fun if one of us selected Dominic and the other selected Joe DiMaggio. But in the end, I had to go with Tris Speaker.

Speaker has the fifth-highest lifetime batting averages of all time for players since 1900 (.3447), just edging out Ted Williams (.3444), earned over the course of a 22-year career. His 792 doubles rank first all-time among major leaguers. He was a member of three world championship teams. As an outfielder, he recorded a stunning 449 outfield assists. As a center fielder, he took part in 145 double plays—almost twice as many as second-place Ty Cobb (74) and 86 more than third-place Willie Mays. He's also been in the Hall of Fame since 1937.

Speaker didn't have quite as long a tenure with the Red Sox. He played seven full seasons (1909–1915), following two partial seasons when he was just breaking in. And his best years were really with the Cleveland Indians, 11 of them. But it wasn't really Speaker's fault that Red Sox owner Joseph Lannin wanted to cut his pay in half after the World Series win in 1915, and was then traded to Cleveland when he refused to accept the pay cut. All he had done was hit .332 that year and help them win the World Series over the Phillies. Lannin said he'd seen Speaker's average decline three years in a row: from .383 in 1912 to .363, then .338, and finally .322. But the real reason was that Lannin had been forced to give Speaker a huge pay increase to entice him to stay with the Red Sox rather than "jump" to the Federal League in 1914. That league only lasted two years and Lannin simply wanted to cut salary. Speaker held out, got traded, and then hit .386 for the Indians in 1916.

All in all, he hit .337 for the Red Sox and .355 for the Indians. He'd been part of Boston's championship teams in 1912 and 1915, and won his third World Series with Cleveland in 1920.

Forget about the Indians, though, for now. For the Red Sox, he still ranks high among all outfielders in both offense and defense. Over the seven full seasons he was with the Sox, he averaged just over 34 doubles each year, just under 15 triples, and 38 stolen bases. Wins above replacement? His WAR for Boston was 55.8.

Honorable Mention

First choice among the other contenders is indeed **Dom DiMaggio**. "The Little Professor" in a sense had to play in the shadow of both his left fielder, Ted Williams, and his brother, Joe DiMaggio. He played his entire career for the Red Sox, one that saw him play 10 full seasons but lose three years to military service in the Second World War. He was a seven-time All-Star and is a charter member of the Red Sox Hall of Fame. "Our" DiMaggio's 1,399 games for the Red Sox saw him hit .298 (.383 on-base percentage) and put up a WAR of 32. He covered a lot of ground in center field and recorded 147 assists and 32 double plays. In back-to-back seasons of 1950 and 1951, he led the league in runs scored. In the one World Series he played (1946), he drove in three runs and scored two, and had he been playing center field during the fateful eighth inning of Game Seven in St. Louis, Enos Slaughter never would have dared try to make a mad dash from first base to home on a routine single to center. (He had hurt himself in the top of the eighth, legging out a double.)

During the years he played—1940–1942 and 1946–1952—he got more base hits that any other player in the major leagues. The four who followed him are all in the Hall of Fame: Enos Slaughter, Stan Musial, Ted Williams, and Pee Wee Reese.

He is one of only four players in the twentieth century to average more than 100 runs scored per season over the length of his career (the others are Lou Gehrig, Joe DiMaggio, and Barry Bonds).

Fred Lynn merits honorable mention as well. In 1975, he was both the Rookie of the Year and the MVP of the American League, while also winning a Gold Glove. He was a six-time All-Star for the Red Sox, drove in three runs in the 1975 ALCS and five more in the World Series against Cincinnati. Without his three-run homer in the first inning of Game Six, Carlton Fisk would not likely have been in position to hit his game-winning homer in the 12th. Lynn hit .308 in his years with the Red Sox, driving in 521 runs. His four Gold Gloves testify to his excellence on defense; he nearly killed himself crashing into a then-unpadded wall in that same Game Six of the '75 Series. After the 1980 season, the Red Sox weren't willing to pay him what he thought he was worth so he was traded to the Angels—a shame, in that Fred Lynn was the kind of player meant to play in Fenway Park. Interestingly, Lynn's WAR of 32.1 for his time with the Red Sox edges out Dom D. by 0.1.

Jimmy Piersall gets our third honorable mention. After overcoming serious issues with depression, acknowledged in the book and film *Fear Strikes Out*, Piersall played eight years with the Red Sox and was an All-Star in 1954 and 1956. He put up very good numbers in all regards, particularly on defense, and still ranks ninth among all outfielders in team history for career putouts. He is admittedly a personal favorite since he was the first Red Sox player I ever met, getting an autograph from him sometime in the middle 1950s at Michelson's Shoe Store in Lexington, Massachusetts.

Some other center fielders of note include **Ellis Burks**, **Jacoby Ellsbury**, **Ira Flagstead**, and **Reggie Smith**. And you'll rarely find anyone make such spectacular catches as current center fielder **Jackie Bradley Jr**.

David Fischer's Response

The Brothers DiMaggio in a head-to-head battle would have made for interesting book fodder but, alas, that dream did not come to fruition. Chalk it up to our integrity!

As a kid, I remember reading stories about Boston's Golden Outfield: center fielder Tris Speaker, left fielder Duffy Lewis, and right fielder Harry Hooper. The three helped the Red Sox win two World Series titles, in 1912 and 1915. Ty Cobb and Babe Ruth both said the Golden Outfield was the best they had ever seen. Two of the three, Speaker and Hooper, have been enshrined in the Baseball Hall of Fame, a cool thirty-four years apart.

You'll get no argument from me on selecting Tris Speaker. Undeniably, his best season was his MVP effort in 1912 when he hit .383 and led the AL in doubles (53), home runs (10), and on-base percentage (.464), to go along with 222 hits, 136 runs, 52 stolen bases, 12 triples, and 90 RBIs. Not many players are capable of hitting 50 doubles and stealing 50 bases in the same season. That year, Speaker compiled three hitting streaks of 20 or more games (30, 23, and 22). What a remarkable achievement!

An effective batter—3,514 hits is a ton of base knocks—Speaker was also equally known for his fielding skills, earning praise for his speed, range, and accurate throwing arm. He was especially noted for playing very shallow in center field, which helped him set a career record for outfield assists and double plays. His defensive positioning so close to the infield also allowed him to regularly get involved in rundown plays on the base paths. Experience taught Speaker the importance of playing shallow: "I still see more games lost by singles that drop just over the infield than a triple over the outfielder's head," he said. "I learned early that I could save more games by cutting off some of those singles than I would lose by having an occasional extra-base hit go over my head."

The bespectacled Dominic DiMaggio is a worthy runner-up to the legendary Speaker. Due to the fact that he lived and played in the shadow of his brother Joe and his teammate Ted Williams, Dom may have been the most underrated player of his day. "Your" DiMaggio—not Ted, not Carl, not Wade, not Nomar—holds the Boston franchise record for longest hitting streak, with 34 consecutive games in 1949.

Leon Culberson was the outfielder who replaced the injured Dom DiMaggio in Game Seven of the 1946 World Series. Culberson was slow to retrieve the ball hit to left-center field by Harry Walker of the Cardinals. Then he relayed it to Johnny Pesky, who may or may not have hesitated before throwing home, which allowed Slaughter to make his famous "mad dash" that is a staple of the World Series highlight reel.

Two players honorably mentioned evoke emotional reactions to my core that are polar opposites. I wish Fred Lynn played for the Yankees, but he didn't. And I wish Jacoby Ellsbury didn't play for the Yankees, but he does (sometimes).

Fred Lynn could have been in pinstripes if not for a promise he made to his father. The Yankees drafted him out of El Monte High School in Southern California in the third round of the 1970 amateur draft, but he did not sign with them. Instead, he preferred to be the first person in his family to attend college. Lynn went to USC on a football scholarship—one of his teammates was Lynn Swann—while also playing baseball. The Sox noticed, and grabbed him in the second round of the '73 draft. He burst onto the national scene by hitting three home runs and driving in 10 runs in a game against the Tigers in Detroit on June 18, 1975. Years later, he hit the first grand slam in an All-Star Game. Lynn was a graceful and dignified player. I admired his home run trot. He jogged with his chest puffed out, and with a confident bounce in his step. He would've made a fine Yankee, and with the vast Stadium outfield expanse, he would've had plenty of room to roam without fear of crashing into a wall.

Then there's Jacoby Ellsbury. He had a very fine season for the Red Sox in 2011, deservedly finishing second in the MVP balloting that year. Sadly, the Yankees are currently paying him a millionaire's ransom based on a few good seasons in Beantown. Ellsbury's contract may be the worst free agent signing in Yankees history. He's been snake-bitten by injuries and seemingly forever on the disabled list with a bruised reputation. He hasn't yet earned a sarcastic nickname like "Fragile Freddie" as did Lynn, but Jake makes me pine for another ex-Red Sox center fielder who came to the Yankees and actually played—and played well: Johnny Damon.

YANKEES CENTER FIELDER: MICKEY MANTLE

Career	H	HR	RBI	BA	Awards
1951–1968 (18-year career)	2415	536	1509	.298	20x All-Star 1962 Gold Glove 1962 Batting Champ 3x MVP 1956 POY Triple Crown (1956) 7x World Series Champ Hall of Fame Inductee (1974)

Yankees All-Time Rankings:
Games Played: 2401 (2nd All-Time)
Plate Appearances: 9907 (2nd All-Time)
At-Bats: 8102 (2nd All-Time)
Hits: 2415 (4th All-Time)
Singles: 1463 (5th All-Time)
Doubles: 344 (9th All-Time)
Triples: 72 (9th All-Time, Tied)
Home Runs: 536 (2nd All-Time)
Extra-Base Hits: 952 (3rd All-Time)
Walks: 1733 (2nd All-Time)
Stolen Bases: 153 (10th All-Time)
Total Bases: 4511 (4th All-Time)
Runs Scored: 1676 (4th All-Time)
Runs Batted In: 1509 (4th All-Time)
On-Base Percentage: .451 (3rd All-Time)
Slugging Percentage: .557 (4th All-Time)
On-Base Plus Slugging: .977 (3rd All-Time, Tied)

Reason for Decision

Of all the glamour positions in sports, no position in any sport can compare to playing center field for the New York Yankees. It is hallowed ground. Starting with Earle Combs and then Joe DiMaggio, who passed the baton to Mickey Mantle, the Yankees boasted a Hall of Fame center fielder every year (except when DiMaggio was in the military) from 1924 to 1966, Mantle's last year in the outfield. And those who followed weren't too shabby, either.

The near-impossible decision came down to DiMaggio or Mantle. Two immortal players, both Hall of Famers, numbers retired, with plaques in Monument Park. They both were World Series heroes and three-time MVPs. Whose signature feat is more impressive? DiMaggio's unbreakable 56-game hitting streak in 1941 or Mantle's Triple Crown in 1956? Each was the leading sports celebrity of his era. Joe D. was revered and briefly married to the voluptuous movie star Marilyn Monroe; the Mick's tape-measure home runs made him a popular cover boy for national magazines. Each man was an icon, mentioned in literature and in song lyrics. Both successfully pitched products on TV. Choosing one legend over the other could start an argument among Yankees fans. I agonized for weeks over this decision. I even played mind games, such as flirting with the idea of making Mantle my designated hitter, only to succumb to reality: the Mick was never a DH, and wishing won't make it so. I had to man up. And Mantle is my man. Here's why:

Mantle played more games in center than DiMaggio (1,742 to 1,634), he hit more home runs (536 to 361), he had more hits (2,415 to 2,214), he scored more runs (1,676 to 1,390), and Mantle led the league in runs scored five times while DiMaggio did so only once. Mantle was issued more walks (1,733 to 790) and led the league in walks five times, something DiMaggio never did. Mantle had a higher career on-base percentage (.421 to .398) and led the league three times in on-base percentage, which DiMaggio never did. Mantle led the league four times in slugging percentage; DiMaggio twice. While Mantle and DiMaggio posted identical OPS figures of .977, DiMaggio never led the league in OPS, though Mantle did six times. Each led the league in total bases three times, but Mantle hit for more career total bases (4,511 to 3,948). Mantle stole more bases (153 to 30) and reached double figures in steals six times, a mark DiMaggio never reached.

Joe D. bested Mickey in a few significant statistical categories. DiMaggio had a higher career batting average (.325 to .298) and drove in more runs (1,537 to 1,509—though all those walks to Mantle may explain the difference). DiMaggio had a higher slugging percentage (.579 to .557). DiMaggio struck out only 369 times to 1,710 for Mantle, who led the league in strikeouts five times. DiMaggio hit more doubles (389 to 344) and triples (131 to 72). DiMaggio topped 200 hits twice, while Mantle never did (again, all those walks are the reason).

DiMaggio played 13 seasons, missing the 1943, '44, and '45 seasons during World War II. He was named to the AL All-Star team all 13 seasons. He batted over .300 in 11 seasons and had nine seasons of 100 or more RBIs. He was a member of 10 pennant-winning teams, nine of which won the World Series. Those 361 homers were, at the time he retired in 1951 (because he "no longer had it"), the fifth most all-time behind Babe Ruth, Jimmie Foxx, Mel Ott, and Lou Gehrig. But today, he ranks just 83rd in career homers. Mantle's 536 career homers were third on the all-time list at the time of his retirement in 1968; he currently ranks 18th. DiMag was graceful and carried himself with a regal demeanor. He was regarded as the best defensive outfielder of his generation, like Tris Speaker before him. The Mick wasn't on Joe's level as a fielder, but as his catch to preserve Don Larsen's perfect game in the 1956 Series proved, he was still a pretty darn good outfielder.

Mantle was the biggest star of the 1950 and '60s, the centerpiece of a team that won seven world championships. He hit for average and power, had extraordinary speed (until his legs were ravaged by injuries), and is the best switch-hitter in baseball history. Beginning in 1952, his second season, Mantle went on a run of 11 consecutive seasons of 20 or more homers (usually many more). During that stretch, ending in '62, he won three MVP awards, six World Series rings (he retired with seven), four home run titles, and led the league in runs and walks five times apiece. During Mantle's peak seasons from 1954 to '62, he was a better player than DiMaggio. But Mantle's final four seasons from 1965 to '68 were disappointing. DiMaggio's only subpar season was his final season, 1951, the year their careers overlapped.

If you're a member of the New York Yankees, what matters most is your performance during October in the World Series. Mantle's World Series exploits are what set him apart. Mantle played in 12 Series and DiMaggio played in 10. DiMaggio's Fall Classic batting average was .271 compared to Mantle's .257. Pitchers in October walked Mantle 43 times to 19 for DiMaggio. That gave Mantle an on-base percentage of .374 compared to .338 for DiMaggio. Mantle also had a higher slugging percentage (.535 to .422), which gave him a substantial OPS advantage (.908 to .760). Mantle had 40 World Series RBIs, 10 more than DiMaggio. Mantle scored more World Series runs (42 to 27), had more World Series hits (59 to 54), and hit more World Series home runs (18 to 8). Mantle appeared in more Series games than DiMaggio (65 to 51), which explain his advantage in career totals, but has no bearing on the averages. In the opinion of this reporter, no player contributed more to his teams winning World Series titles than Mantle. He holds Series records in home runs (18), RBIs (40), runs (42), total bases (123), and walks (43). DiMaggio doesn't hold any World Series career batting records.

Still not convinced? Let's explore the intangibles for each man. Since his death in 1999, biographers have depicted DiMaggio has a petulant, selfish jerk. Mantle, who died in 1995, abused alcohol and was a lousy husband and father. Those are awful personality traits, to be sure. Yet for all his failings, Mantle's teammates raved that he was the best teammate they ever had. Both were respected players. But Mickey's peers loved him, and that should never be discounted.

Honorable Mention

Bernie Williams played 1,856 games in center for the Yankees, more than Mantle or DiMaggio. He hit cleanup for four World Series–winning teams in his 16-year career for the Yankees, from 1991 to 2006. Though never regarded as a serious contender to be enshrined in Cooperstown, he had a lifetime batting average of .297 and compiled eight straight .300 seasons, including the 1998 batting title (.339). He collected 2,336 hits, including 449 doubles (second on the all-time Yankees list behind Gehrig), 55 triples, 287 homers, 1,257 RBIs (including five 100-RBI seasons), 1,366 runs, and 147 stolen bases. The switch-hitting Williams was a five-time All-Star and four-time Gold Glove winner. While those numbers are not quite Hall of Fame-worthy, some Yankees fans held out hope that Williams's postseason numbers would be factored into his overall equation. With 12 trips to the postseason, he is the all-time leader in postseason RBIs (80) and ranks second in postseason home runs (22), runs scored (83), hits (128), doubles (29), total bases (223), and third in games played (121) and walks (71). He's also the only Yankee to hit two walk-off homers in postseason play, both in Game Ones of an ALCS: in 1996 in the

11th inning vs. Baltimore off Randy Myers (he was the ALCS MVP), and in 1999 in the 10th inning vs. Boston off Rod Beck.

Earle Combs played 1,157 games in center field for the Yankees from 1924 to 1935. A lifetime .325 hitter, he averaged over 200 hits, 132 runs scored, and 75 walks per season during his career. His career on-base percentage was .397. For eight consecutive years, he scored more than 100 runs and hit more than 30 doubles. Combs led the AL in triples three times, picking up 154 for his career. In 1927, Combs whacked 23 triples and batted .356 with a league-leading 231 hits—a Yankees team record that stood until Don Mattingly broke it in 1986. Combs was a member of three world championship teams (1926, 1927, 1932) and was at his best at World Series time: .350 batting average and .451 on-base percentage in 16 games. He was elected to the National Baseball Hall of Fame by the Veterans Committee in 1970.

He's regarded as the best leadoff batter in big-league history. He's a Hall of Famer who is the all-time leader in runs scored and stolen bases. In the four full seasons he wore pinstripes from 1985 to '88, **Rickey Henderson** was selected to four All-Star Games. In 1985, he led the AL with 146 runs scored and 80 stolen bases. He also hit .314 that year, slugging 24 homers and walking 99 times. He became the first player in major-league history to reach the 20-home run plateau and steal 80 bases in the same season. The following season, Henderson again led the AL with 130 runs scored and 87 stolen bases while also hitting 28 home runs (a career high). In his four-plus seasons, he amassed an astonishing 326 stolen bases to rank second best in franchise history.

Bobby Murcer had the misfortune to join the Yankees right after the old dynasty collapsed, in 1965, and to be traded away just as the new dynasty was being built, in 1974. During that time he was a four-time All-Star. In 1971, he batted .331 and led the AL with a .427 on-base percentage. The next year he led the league in total bases (314) and runs scored (102), while winning a Gold Glove. Bobby returned to the Bronx in 1979. That August, he gave a eulogy for his teammate Thurman Munson and, in that night's game, drove in all the Yankees runs with a three-run homer and a walk-off two-run single to propel the Yankees to a 5–4 win over Baltimore in one of the most emotional games in Yankees history. He was a member of the 1981 team that lost to the Dodgers in the World Series, then served as a Yankees broadcaster from 1983 to 2008.

Bill Nowlin's Response

I had no idea how you were going to decide between the two most obvious choices. And I definitely am glad it was your choice to make and not mine. At one point, I recall sending you an e-mail suggesting we should maybe create a "bench player" category just so there would be someplace to put whichever one didn't rank first.

I notice that you didn't accord Joe D. an "honorable mention." I don't know if that was deliberate on your part, but I think it was a wise decision. That would have been too much of a demotion. He really was almost a co-equal with Mantle.

I say "almost" because you did convince me, and rapidly so. I had simply never put their two sets of accomplishments side by side the way you truly had to do. I knew DiMaggio hadn't played as many years or as many games, but I also knew that was because of the intrusion of the Second World War. I knew that Mantle's legs eventually gave out on him, costing him a lot of "leg hits"—thrown out at first on a grounder and throw he might have otherwise beat out for a single. We see his batting average drop precipitously over his last four seasons, and his stolen bases number go down as well.

I knew that Joe DiMaggio liked being introduced as "Baseball's Greatest Living Player"—insisted on it, actually. I know that the one time I met Mickey Mantle, he was very nice to me. (I had the sense he had enjoyed a few drinks and was in a mellow mood.)

Both Joe D. and Mantle come up quickly in any discussion of my hero, Ted Williams. They each had careers that overlapped 10 years with Williams, so they were each inevitably compared to him. And then there's the story of the time—reputedly around 1948 or 1949—that Red Sox owner Tom Yawkey and Yankees co-owner Dan Topping agreed to trade the two, late one night after the consumption of a number of beverages. Yawkey had second thoughts when he woke up and the deal was never consummated. Just as well from a Red Sox perspective; Williams had many more years to play than did Joe D.—though it's tempting to think how many more homers Ted would have hit if he had that short right-field porch in Yankee Stadium as part of his home ballpark.

Really, though, you convinced me, and even before you got to the World Series section. It may seem sacrilegious to some, but I think you made the right call.

Now, on your honorable mentions, some more outstanding players there, too, but of course only Combs and Rickey Henderson have been accorded Hall of Fame status. Henderson played one year for the Red Sox, too, albeit not a very good one. He stole eight bases that year, and I found it amusing that every time he stole one he set a new major-league record for total stolen bases. Combs, well … nobody remembers him. Being a little more serious, wow, lifetime .325 batting average over 12 seasons, all with the Yankees, and he got on base almost 40 percent of the time (as you have noted). Agreed, he's well worth an honorable mention. The Veterans Committee thought he was worth HOF induction, and it's nice that they did so several years before he died.

There has been mention of both Damon and Ellsbury going on from the Red Sox to the Yankees. Jacoby Ellsbury was an exciting player for the Red Sox—70 stolen bases in 2009, obliterating the previous team record—and with a .297 batting average over seven seasons. He's got two World Series rings, both with Boston. The Sox were right with their timing on that one; when he hit his window for free agency, they pretty much just let him go—just as they had with Pedro Martinez right after the 2004 season. Pedro had one good year with the "other New York team," but that was about it.

Johnny Damon was in something of a similar boat; the Sox made him an offer, but the Yankees offered *so* much more that the Red Sox elected not to compete. They let Damon go, too, but in his case, the Yankees got good value (albeit at a much higher cost in salary). His four years with the Yankees and his four years with the Red Sox produced very similar numbers—and Damon has one World Series ring with each team.

HEAD-TO-HEAD

David Fischer: When I decided to choose Mantle over DiMaggio, admittedly, I wasn't sure you'd be convinced by the decision. But I have a hunch such powers of persuasion won't be required in order to sway you to side with Mantle over Speaker.

Bill Nowlin Hmmm. "The Grey Eagle" versus "The Commerce Comet"? Speaker had a nephew who played in the majors—Tex Jeanes. He's got something there Mantle never had. And he might have been a better bargain— his salary for his years with the Red Sox is reported as totaling $44,000 over nine years. Mantle was paid over $1 million.

DF: It's irrelevant what they got paid. Speaker and Mantle played in different eras and, besides, what Mantle contributed was priceless. Tex Jeanes had 73 at-bats over five seasons in the big leagues. His claim to fame was that he was the American League's sixth-youngest player in 1921. He had five at-bats for Cleveland. But we digress.

BN: Digression can be a form of diversion. I have a feeling I might lose this one. Sticking with salaries for just a bit longer, I'd note that our friend Jacoby Ellsbury was paid $20 million for seven seasons with the Red Sox. The Yankees paid him more than $21 million each year from 2014 through 2018. He hit .297 for the Red Sox, driving in 314 runs. He hit .264 for the Yankees, driving in 198. And he didn't appear in even one game in 2018. Actually, I always liked him (when he was a Red Sox player), and I do feel kind of sad for him. He certainly didn't want to sit out all of 2018.

OK, let's get back to Mantle vs. Speaker. Since so many people focus on it these days, I thought I'd look up their respective WARs. Mantle's was 110.3 but Speaker's was markedly better at 134.1. What do you say to that?

DF: This talk about salary reminds me of a great DiMaggio anecdote. Asked in 1981, after the Yankees had signed Dave Winfield to a then-record 10-year, $23 million deal, what he thought he would be worth as a free agent, DiMaggio said: "If I were sitting down with [Yankees owner]

George Steinbrenner and based on what Dave Winfield got for his statistics, I'd have to say, 'George, you and I are about to become partners.'"

Here's what I say about comparing their respective WARs. Speaker's total WAR breaks down to 55.8 during his nine seasons with Boston and 74.2 during his 11 seasons with Cleveland. (He posted a combined 4.1 WAR in his final two seasons with Washington and Philadelphia.) While playing for the Red Sox, Speaker averaged a WAR of 6.2 per season, while Mantle averaged a WAR of 6.13 per season with the Yankees—nearly identical, and that includes Mantle's final years when he was but a shell of his former self. Speaker's WAR with Boston was the start of his prime years. That said, with an average season WAR so similar, I would favor the home run hitter over the doubles machine. I also feel that Speaker's finest seasons were spent with Cleveland, and that's saying something, because he was great with Boston. His WAR with Cleveland was 6.745 per season, markedly better than his time spent in Boston. If we are to compare Boston's Speaker with New York's Mantle, it doesn't take a tape measure to gauge Mantle's superiority. That's my opinion, and I'm sticking with it.

BN: Fair enough. I had noticed that, unlike many (most?) players, Speaker seemed to get distinctly better after hitting age twenty-eight. Maybe he felt he had something to prove to Red Sox ownership for shuffling him off. But if that was his initial motivation, he kept it going for a decade. Ranking sixth all-time for batting average continues to impress me. He didn't hit as many home runs as Mantle, of course, though in his day that wasn't such a "thing." He did, however, only lead the league once in home runs. I hear you. As a threat on offense, in today's game, I'd pick Mantle, too.

Winner: Mickey Mantle

RIGHT FIELD

RED SOX RIGHT FIELDER: HARRY HOOPER

Career	H	HR	RBI	BA	Awards
1909–1925 (17-year career)	2466	160	816	.281	4x World Series Champ Hall of Fame Inductee (1971)

Red Sox Career	H	HR	RBI	BA
1909–1920	1707	30	496	.272

Red Sox All-Time Rankings:
Games Played: 1647 (7th All-Time)
Plate Appearances: 7334 (7th All-Time)
At-Bats: 6270 (7th All-Time)
Hits: 1707 (9th All-Time)
Singles: 1301 (7th All-Time)
Triples: 130 (1st All-Time)
Walks: 826 (6th All-Time)
Stolen Bases: 300 (1st All-Time)
Runs Scored: 988 (9th All-Time)

Reason for Decision

At the very last minute, I switched from Dwight Evans and decided to select Harry Hooper. Although Hooper was inducted into the National Baseball Hall of Fame by a Veterans Committee vote back in 1971, he was even then not well known. His candidacy is hampered by the fact that he played so long ago. It came down to Hooper or Evans. In the end, there was one fact that simply overrode any other: Hooper was the Red Sox right fielder on four world championship teams: 1912, 1915, 1916, and 1918. No other Red Sox player at *any* position can claim such a distinction.

Hooper played at a time when scoring was low and home runs were a rarity. In 1916 and 1918, he led the Red Sox in runs scored, but those are about the only two times he stood out on offense. He was never tops on the club in RBIs or batting average, but he was there for every one of the Red Sox World Series wins in that decade of dominance. None other than New York Giants manager John McGraw said Hooper was "one of the most dangerous hitters in a pinch the game has ever known."

Hooper did have a lot of ground to cover, playing half his games in Fenway's right field, yet he was considered a truly superb fielder. Their numbers were perhaps more comparable than they might at first seem. Hooper had 260 outfield assists; Evans had 151. He kicked off 56 double plays; Evans had 40. Opposition coaches knew of Evans's great arm and fewer base runners put themselves in a position to get thrown out.

It's astonishing what similar totals Hooper and Evans posted on offense:

Base hits: Hooper, 2,466; Evans, 2,446

Runs: Hooper, 1,429; Evans, 1,470

Batting Average: Hooper, .281; Evans, .272

On-Base Percentage: Hooper, .368; Evans, .369

Evans had 50 at-bats in World Series play (1975 and 1986) and hit an even .300 combined, with 14 RBIs. In his 92 World Series at-bats, Hooper hit .293.

RBI totals can be deceptive in many ways. In the 1916 World Series, for instance, Hooper drove in only three runs—but the Red Sox as a team only scored 12 times in the entire World Series, yet won four of five games.

Honorable Mention

Dwight Evans is a borderline Hall of Famer. He's certainly in the Red Sox Hall of Fame (and a beloved alumnus who made his home in the Greater Boston area). Despite one final year with the Orioles, Evans played 19 of his 20 seasons with the Red Sox. Only Ted Williams played more games as a Red Sox outfielder; Evans played 2,079 games.

As noted above, runners rarely ever tried to take an extra base on a ball hit to Evans in right field as he had a gun of an arm. Four times he drove in over 100 runs. Only in the strike-shortened 1981 season did he

RIGHT FIELD • 93

lead the league in home runs (all it took was 22, but that was still more than anyone else). Evans's home run totals were deceptive, but they added up. A common trivia question back around the turn of this century asked: Who hit more home runs in the American League than any other player during the 1980s? From 1980 through 1989, the answer was "Dewey"— with 256 homers in the decade-long stretch. He also led the American League in extra-base hits over the same decade.

Jackie Jensen started his career with the Yankees but was traded to the Senators and then from Washington to the Red Sox. He played in Boston for seven seasons (1954 through 1959, and then in 1961), averaging 105.7 runs batted in over the stretch. He led the American League in RBIs three times and was AL MVP in 1958 with 35 homers and 122 RBIs. He would no doubt have played longer but a morbid, paralyzing fear of flying grounded him, and being away from his family so much was dispiriting. He retired twice, once after the 1959 season and then (after sitting out 1960) again after the 1961 campaign.

In **Mookie Betts**, we face another right fielder who has the potential to excel and even climb to the head of the pack. He's put up three spectacular seasons on offense. In 2018, he led the league in both batting average (.346) and slugging percentage (.640), the first Sox player to lead in both categories since Ted Williams in 1947. Betts helped win a world championship in 2018 and was also named the American League MVP. He won a Silver Slugger in 2018, too, and has proven to be one of the best fielders in the game with back-to-back-to-back Gold Gloves in 2016, 2017, and 2018. Betts became only the second player in major-league history to win a Gold Glove, Silver Slugger, MVP, and a world championship all in the same year. He led the majors with 10.9 WAR, which ties him with Ted Williams's 1946 season for the second-highest WAR ever recorded by a Red Sox player. In fact, the only Sox player with a higher WAR was Carl Yastrzemski in 1967 (12.5), when he won the Triple Crown. Two things would be necessary for Mookie's ascension: he'll have to continue performing at the high standards he has already set, and he'll also have to sign with the Red Sox again when he reaches free agency in 2021. That is by no means a certainty, with him already (as this book goes to print) being considered (with Mike Trout) as one of the two top position players in the game. The Red Sox don't seem short on funding, and one has to assume they've already tried to sign him to a long-term deal. Red Sox fans hope such a deal can be struck.

David Fischer's Response

Bill, your last-minute decision to switch from Evans to Hooper as Boston's right fielder feels much like my thought process in selecting Lazzeri over Cano as New York's second baseman. We both thought long and hard, wavered, and finally made a difficult decision from which there is no turning back! In both cases, we selected Hall of Fame players with multiple World Series rings from 100 years ago over the modern-day players that are extremely likeable and graceful performers and whose talents we witnessed in person and on television. That is certainly not the case with Hooper and Lazzeri, for whom purple prose must suffice. And yet I believe we both made the correct call. Hooper, as you point out, was not very well known upon his induction into Cooperstown, and the same is true today. However, there is no denying his value as a leadoff batter and table-setter for those great championship Red Sox teams of the 1910s. No matter the era, any player who averages 100 runs scored and at least 170 hits per season over an extended career will earn a roster spot on my all-time team, so I agree with Hooper over Evans even though I marveled at the latter's ability during the hotly contested Yankees-Red Sox battles of the 1970s and '80s.

When Evans first came up, I didn't think very much of him as a hitter. However, he quickly figured it out and made himself into a productive offensive force. Over the years he got better and better, and some of his best seasons were toward the end of his career. I credit Dewey's ability to make adjustments, his knowledge of the opposing pitchers and how they planned to attack him, and his marvelous use of the entire field, from foul line to foul line. Then, of course, there is Evans's exceptional throwing arm. He was accurate, always hit the cutoff man, and was particularly adept at racing toward the right field foul line to snare a ball heading toward the corner, pivoting on a dime, and throwing a strike to third base.

Jackie Jensen, the golden boy from California, was a superb two-sport athlete who played football in the Rose Bowl and baseball in the World Series—with the Yankees, thank you very much—as a defensive replacement for one game of the 1950 World Series. Mookie Betts is indeed in the conversation with Mike Trout as the best player in the game today. In time, he very well may surpass Hooper as Boston's all-time best right fielder.

YANKEES RIGHT FIELDER: BABE RUTH

Career	H	HR	RBI	BA	Awards
1914–1935 (22-year career)	2873	714	2214	.342	2x All-Star 1916 ERA Champ 1924 Batting Champ 1923 MVP 7x World Series Champ Hall of Fame Inductee (1936)

Yankees Career	H	HR	RBI	BA
1920–1934	2518	659	1978	.349

Yankees All-Time Rankings:
Games Played: 2084 (5th All-Time)
Plate Appearances: 9199 (4th All-Time)
At-Bats: 7217 (6th All-Time)
Hits: 2518 (3rd All-Time)
Doubles: 424 (5th All-Time)
Triples: 106 (6th All-Time)
Home Runs: 659 (1st All-Time)
Extra-Base Hits: 1189 (2nd All-Time)
Walks: 1852 (1st All-Time)
Total Bases: 5131 (1st All-Time)
Runs Scored: 1959 (1st All-Time)
Runs Batted In: 1978 (2nd All-Time)
Batting Average: .349 (1st All-Time)
On-Base Percentage: .484 (1st All-Time)
Slugging Percentage: .711 (1st All-Time)
On-Base Plus Slugging: 1.195 (1st All-Time)

Reason for Decision

Babe Ruth had several nicknames, "The Sultan of Swat" and "The Bambino" among them. He will always be known as the man who made the home run famous. In the early 1900s, baseball was dominated by pitching and speedy baserunners. Frank "Home Run" Baker earned his nickname by leading the AL with 11, 10, 12, and 9 homers from 1911 to 1914. When Ruth hit 29 in 1919, he stunned the baseball world. No major-league player had ever hit more than 27 homers in a season. The next-highest home run total that year was 12. The following year he hit 54—more homers than any *team* in the league—and, just like that, the home run became the dominant aspect of the game. Fans flocked to every AL ballpark to watch the Babe knock one out of the yard; he rarely disappointed. He became the first baseball star to be known by everyone in the United States. Even people who weren't baseball fans knew his name. His fame soon spread to Europe and the Far East.

History looks on Babe Ruth as the "savior" of baseball. He emerged into international fame when the game needed him most. Baseball was still reeling from the "Black Sox" scandal of the 1919; that several White Sox players had been paid to throw the World Series. Fans had lost faith in the national pastime and it took Babe Ruth and his incredible home run stroke to restore the nation's trust in the game.

Ironically, Babe Ruth began his career as a pitcher. He was so talented that, had he remained a pitcher for his entire career, he probably would have made it into the Hall of Fame for his skill on the mound. He pitched for the Red Sox from 1914 to 1919, posting an 89–46 record. He threw 29 2/3 consecutive scoreless innings in the 1916 and 1918 World Series.

By 1918 he had switched to the outfield and become a full-time slugger. The future looked bright in Boston. The Red Sox had won five of the first 14 World Series, including the first one in 1903, when they were still the Boston Americans. They won the Series again in 1918. Then, following the 1919 season, Red Sox owner Harry Frazee, infuriated by Ruth's refusal to abide by team rules and his incessant salary demands, sold Babe to the Yankees for $125,000. The Yankees went on to become the greatest dynasty in the history of sports, and the Red Sox didn't appear in another World Series until 1946 and wouldn't win one until 2004. Superstitious Red Sox fans came to believe in the "Curse of the Bambino."

Ruth's on-the-field record speaks for itself: leading the league in homers 12 times, walks 11 times, on-base percentage 10 times, runs scored eight times, RBIs five times, slugging percentage and OPS 13 times, and his major-league-record 72 games in which he hit two or more home runs. He also holds records with a career .690 slugging average and 1.164 OPS. He led the Yankees to seven pennants and Yankee Stadium, opened in 1923, came to be known as "the House That Ruth Built."

His off-the-field exploits are well known, too. He had a huge appetite for food and drink, and would often show up for a game after an all-night party binge. He was also a natural-born actor who loved the spotlight. But the Babe never forgot his youth. The man who was born George Herman Ruth Jr. in Baltimore, Maryland, in 1895, did not have an easy life. At age seven he was sent to St. Mary's Industrial School for Boys, a combination reform school and orphanage, where he lived until he was eighteen. That no doubt contributed to the Babe's legendary compassion for children. He often visited them in hospitals, promising to hit home runs for them, then followed through on his word.

Ruth remains one of the best-known celebrities of the twentieth century, and it was no surprise that in 1936 he was among the first five players, the Five Immortals, to be inducted into the new Baseball Hall of Fame.

Honorable Mention

As half of the fabled M&M Boys (with Mickey Mantle), **Roger Maris** hit 61 homers in 1961, breaking Babe Ruth's once-thought-unbreakable record of 60 in a season—one in which Maris played 161 games of a 162-game schedule, compared to Ruth's 151 games of a 154-game schedule. But why quibble? Asterisk be damned, a record is a record. Maris of course won the MVP that season, but not many folks realize he also won the award the year before. As a Yankee, Maris led the league in homers, RBIs (twice), slugging, runs scored, and total bases. He was also a splendid defensive right fielder. How is he not in the Hall of Fame?

Though he played just five seasons with the Yankees, **Reggie Jackson** made the most of his time in the Bronx Zoo. He led the league with 41 home runs in 1980 and drove in 100 or more runs twice. But "Mr. October" made his bones in the postseason: five homers, including three in the clinching game, eight RBIs, nine hits, 10 runs scored, and the MVP Award in the 1977 World Series. In the 1978 Series he hit two dingers among his nine hits while driving in eight runs. Reggie hit .300 or better for the Yankees in five postseason series with 12 homers. That's being the straw that stirs the drink.

Dave Winfield played eight full seasons with the Yankees, five in right and three in left. He was an All-Star every year, won three Gold Gloves, and topped 100 RBIs six times. His .340 batting average in 1984 was second-best in the AL to teammate Don Mattingly. It's a shame his one World Series appearance with the Yankees in 1981 resulted in a disappointing 1-for-22 performance. The "Mr. May" sobriquet was unfair.

Also deserving of recognition are **Paul O'Neill**, **Hank Bauer**, and **Tommy Henrich**, in that order. O'Neill (1,254) played fewer games than Bauer (1,406) and Henrich (1,284), but was the better hitter among the three. O'Neill recorded 100 or more RBIs in four consecutive seasons; Henrich had one and Bauer none. O'Neill also won a batting crown with a .359 average in 1994—one of six straight seasons he batted .300; Henrich and Bauer had five such seasons combined. O'Neill hit 185 homers with the Yankees to 183 for Henrich and 158 for Bauer, and "The Warrior" collected 1,426 hits in pinstripes, compared to 1,326 for Bauer and 1,297 for Henrich. Henrich holds an advantage in All-Star appearances with five, to four for O'Neill and three for Bauer. Bauer led the trio in World Series championships, playing a vital role on seven World Series–winners to four each for Henrich and O'Neill.

Bill Nowlin's Response

Hmmm, who was really better: Harry Hooper or Babe Ruth? Which player would you rather have on your team? Faced with the choice, 99 of 100 might stammer and ask, "Harry who?" Well, I had to pick someone. In a short series, you never know what might happen. But looking to the Head-to-Head section, I'm going to be challenged to come up with decent arguments. Maybe I should just give up now—but I won't. Hooper was a great ballplayer, and by all accounts a very good man.

When Ruth hit his 29 homers in 1919, he was still a member of the Red Sox. And their *left* fielder. But there was more than one reason that Frazee sold him to the Yankees. He was becoming more and more of a problem, disciplinary and otherwise. It was by no means clear that Ruth was a team player; Frazee was ridding the Red Sox of a headache. In the process, Frazee picked up a bunch of cash from the Yankees, including an additional sum understood to be $300,000, for which the Yankees owners were given a mortgage on Fenway Park that stood until paid off by Tom Yawkey in 1933. Over time, Frazee also dealt the Yankees about a dozen other players, including future Hall of Famer Herb Pennock.

There's no question that New York City presents a bigger stage than Boston. It suited Ruth more and he settled in and made himself famous in a way that probably couldn't have happened in Boston.

I don't know how to measure his range as an outfielder and thus to know how to rate him in that regard. In terms of fielding percentage, he made 83 errors in 2,390 chances (.965), not bad but not appreciably different from Hooper's .967.

It's too bad George Steinbrenner couldn't have chosen the path of accommodation rather than enmity in his relations with Dave Winfield, but there's no way Winfield would edge out Ruth for our purpose here. There's no way I could, or would want to, fault your choice of Babe Ruth for right field.

HEAD-TO-HEAD

David Fischer: One almost has to feel sorry for Harry Hooper, for he did nothing to deserve this fate. Comparing Hooper's skills—or anyone's for that matter—to Ruth is like entering a gunfight with a wooden stick. The Babe is top ten is MLB history in the following categories: third in home runs, tenth in batting average, second in RBIs, first in all-time slugging percentage, second in all-time on-base percentage; first in all-time OPS, fourth in all-time runs list, seventh in all-time total bases, third in all-time walks … I'm plum tuckered out already!

Bill Nowlin: Yeah, so? What else did Ruth do? I mean, besides his pitching. Let me see. Ah, he leads Hooper by a big margin in strikeouts. They had almost the same number of career at-bats: Hooper had more (10,623) than Ruth (10,255), but Ruth struck out more than twice as often—Ruth whiffed 1,330 times to Hooper's 582. Hooper struck out in fewer than 5.7 percent of his at-bats. But 13 percent of the time Ruth came up to bat, he struck out. What good is that? How did that help his team?

DF: Why stop there? You're selling Hooper short. He also leads Ruth in stolen bases (375 to 123) and sacrifice hits (247 to 113). Thank heavens there was no record keeping back then of number of times grounding into double plays, for I fear that Hooper, with his great speed, didn't rap into many 6-4-3s. Although I am led to believe from watching the old home movies that Ruth's launch angle was such that he didn't hit many ground balls, so perhaps that career stat would be a push.

BN: You're making my case for me! I'll grant you one thing—something else not tabulated in modern-day statistics: I believe it may well be the case that Babe Ruth led the majors in curfew violations. For his part, Hooper was a graduate of St. Mary's College and honored by none other than the United States Government by being appointed a postmaster in Capitola, California.

DF: While Babe Ruth was not appointed a postmaster of his hometown, he goes Hooper one better. To commemorate the 50th anniversary of the All-Star Game, the US Postal Service honored the Babe with a 20-cent stamp on July 6, 1983. So even though both Hooper and Ruth were featured on episodes of *The Simpsons*—seriously!— the Babe is an American icon, known the world over. Only surfer dudes living near Santa Cruz know Hooper Beach.

In conclusion, your honor, Ruth licks Hooper like a postage stamp. In fact, you can combine the career home runs and RBIs of your first selection Hooper and your second selection Dwight Evans and their totals do not add up to Ruth's career totals. Hooper and Evans combined to hit 460 home runs. Ruth hit 714. Hooper and Evans combined to drive in 2,200 runs. Ruth drove in 2,213. As Bart Simpson would say, "Don't have a cow, man!"

BN: There's absolutely nothing more I can say. I knew it was going to be futile. Anything can happen in a short series. But when one of America's more eloquent philosophers speaks, all dialogue necessarily comes to a halt. (You may or may not know this, but a few years ago, I co-edited *Nuclear-Powered Baseball* for SABR, a book centered around a famous

Simpsons episode. I wrote Homer's bio for the book.) I concede: if the Red Sox could get Babe Ruth back from the Yankees, he'd be my right fielder over Hoop.

Winner: Babe Ruth

DESIGNATED HITTER

RED SOX DESIGNATED HITTER: DAVID ORTIZ

Career	H	HR	RBI	BA	Awards
1997–2016 (20-year career)	2472	541	1768	.286	10x All-Star 7x Silver Slugger 2004 ALCS MVP 3x World Series Champ 2013 World Series MVP

Red Sox Career	H	HR	RBI	BA
2003–2016	2079	483	1530	.290

Red Sox All-Time Rankings:
Games Played: 1953 (5th All-Time)
Plate Appearances: 8398 (5th All-Time)
At-Bats: 7163 (5th All-Time)
Hits: 2079 (6th All-Time)
Doubles: 524 (3rd All-Time)
Home Runs: 483 (2nd All-Time)
Extra-Base Hits: 1023 (3rd All-Time)
Walks: 1133 (4th All-Time)
Total Bases: 4084 (5th All-Time)
Runs Scored: 1204 (5th All-Time)
Runs Batted In: 1530 (3rd All-Time)
Slugging Percentage: .570 (4th All-Time)
On-Base Plus Slugging: .956 (4th All-Time)

Reason for Decision

This is one of those no-brainers. Was there ever a greater DH for any team, at any point, in baseball history? In selecting who to choose for the Red Sox, there's no question that the choice is No. 34, "Big Papi"—David Ortiz. Heck, within just months of retiring at the end of the 2016 season he already had a bridge in Boston named after him, as well as a Boston street. And the Red Sox waived any five-year rule by retiring his number almost instantly.

Ortiz came to the Red Sox in 2003 as something of a castoff, a player the Twins elected not to retain. They didn't even attempt to re-sign him. Sox GM Theo Epstein snapped him up and he drove in 101 runs that first year, homering 31 times. Starting in 2004, he was named to the All-Star team five years in a row and was later named five more times.

He helped the Red Sox in the 2003 postseason, but it was 2004 which cemented him as a force to be reckoned with. First, he hit a two-run homer in the bottom of the 10th inning of Game Three of the Division Series to send the Red Sox back to the ALCS, once more facing the Yankees who had vanquished them the year before (no more on that here). The 2004 ALCS did not start well, to say the least, for the Sox and their fans. They dropped the first two games to New York, and then were slaughtered in Game Three, 19–8. Or was it 101–2? That was about as bad as it gets. The story has been told at length a million times, but it was David Ortiz who struck the deciding hit in Game Four with a two-run homer in the bottom of the 12th inning. Game Five ran even longer, but once again it was Big Papi who came through. He'd already driven in two runs earlier in the game, but it was tied, 4–4, in the bottom of the 14th. With two outs and runners on first and second, Ortiz dropped a bloop single into center field, scoring Johnny Damon from second base with the winning run. The Red Sox were not to be denied from that point forward; they won the next six games in a row, too, eliminating New York and then sweeping the World Series from the St. Louis Cardinals. Ortiz drove in 11 runs in the ALCS alone and was named the MVP.

As a DH, Ortiz led the majors with 148 RBIs in 2005 and led the American League the following year with 137 RBIs, built in large part around a franchise-record 54 home runs. It was a little more exciting to see Big Papi step to the plate than to see one of the Red Sox pitchers do so.

His 117 RBIs helped the Red Sox get into the 2007 World Series, where he hit .333 with four RBIs.

In 2013, after a fiery speech from Fenway's mound in the wake of the Boston Marathon bombing, Ortiz hit another 30 homers, drove in 103 runs, and was named World Series MVP as the Sox again squared off against the Cardinals. All he did was hit .688 in six games (that's a batting average, not a slugging percentage); his OPS was 1.948. He didn't get a single hit in Game Six—they walked him four times.

Ortiz hit 483 homers as a Red Sox player, a total eclipsed only by Ted Williams's 521. Only Yaz and Ted drove in more runs than Ortiz's 1,530.

Even when interleague play forced him to forego the DH role, he excelled at first base with a career fielding percentage of .990 in 2,169 chances, a better fielding percentage than any Red Sox first baseman.

But it's his work as DH that marked him in Red Sox history, a three-time world champion and one of the most beloved figures in Boston sports history.

Honorable Mention

Of course, there was no such thing as a designated hitter before the American League adopted the idea beginning with the 1973 season. Orlando Cepeda was the first Red Sox DH. He's in the Hall of Fame, but he only played one season for the Red Sox. He was good that year, but that doesn't earn him a ranking here.

I looked at Carl Yastrzemski first just to see what his stats as a DH had to say. While he was an honorable man, a .246 average just didn't do it for me, either.

Let's look at a few possibilities, listed alphabetically.

Don Baylor played two years as DH, leading the majors in hit-by-pitch both years. He homered 31 times and drove in 94 in '86, and won a Silver Slugger, but only drove in 63 runs in '87. Welcome as his contribution was, it doesn't make the cut here.

Jose Canseco really only DH'd two seasons for the Red Sox: 1995 (.306 with 24 homers and 81 RBIs, which was very good) and 1996 (.282, 23 HR, 72 RBIs, which was good but not great).

Cecil Cooper started with the Sox three years before the DH was instituted. He only played DH in 161 games (one less than a full season) spread over 1974, 1975, and 1976. The best of those years was '75; he was a DH in 54 games and hit .318/10/25. The Red Sox won the pennant; he hit .400 in the ALCS against Oakland but only drove in one run. In the World Series, he played first base. Again, he drove in one run.

Mike "Hit Man" Easler was another two-season DH. He put up excellent numbers in 1984 (.313, with 27 homers and 91 runs batted in), but tailed off in 1985 (.259, with 14 homers and 48 runs batted in).

Reggie Jefferson only started 286 games as DH for Boston, and only in the years 1997 and 1999 did he start more than 50. In 1997, while DH'ing, he hit .325 with 13 homers and 62 RBIs, while in 1999 he hit just .272/4/15.

Mo Vaughn only started 170 games as a DH. We really shouldn't be giving serious consideration to players for barely playing a season's worth of games at a given position.

I skipped over one player who, had Ortiz not come along, may have stood as the best designated history in Red Sox history: **Manny Ramirez**. In 2001, he served as DH in 87 games and hit .333 with 23 homers while driving in 80 runs. In 2002, he DH'd in 51 games, hit .356, homered 11 times, and drove in 40. From 2003 through 2008, until he was traded to get him off the team, he was a DH in 94 other games. So, he accumulated enough games and certainly hit well enough. But when it comes down to it, there's just no one the Red Sox ever had at the "position" to rival Big Papi.

David Fischer's Response

If only Red Sox ace Pedro Martinez hadn't spotted David Ortiz, his longtime Santo Domingo buddy, in a local restaurant one day back in December 2002. The Minnesota Twins had just released Ortiz. Knowing the type of teammate Ortiz could be, Pedro declared, "You're going to play for us!" Pedro called Boston GM Theo Epstein, and the rest is history, much to the dismay of Yankees fans.

No Yankees fan ever enjoyed the sight of David Ortiz's arrival in the batter's box, when he tucked the bat under his armpit, spit into the palm of his right batting glove, and clapped his hands before digging in to face the pitcher. The reason was clear: Big Papi crushed baseballs and the dreams of Yankees fans. On October 18, 2004, at 1:22 a.m., he belted a 12th-inning homer in the ALCS that rivaled the excitement of Carlton Fisk's World Series clout in 1975. In the evening game that followed, on the same calendar day, Ortiz came through again, delivering a 14th-inning walk-off single. It was an epic at-bat: Big Papi had fouled off *five* two-strike pitches before blooping a winning single to center, keeping the Sox alive. It turned out that the Red Sox needed a hero of David's physical and mental strength to eradicate the "Curse of the Bambino," which had plagued the franchise for 86 years.

The Red Sox stormed to the 2004 World Series title, and Ortiz became baseball's new Mr. October. His clutch postseason hitting resulted in World Series triumphs in 2007 and '13, the year he personified "Boston Strong" following the Boston Marathon bombings. In 2015, he surpassed 500 home runs and showed no letup in his production. The next season he topped 100 RBIs for the fourth straight year. He led the league in doubles, RBIs, slugging percentage, and OPS in 2016 and then retired while still considered as one of the most feared sluggers in the game. Too bad those painful feet couldn't allow him to continue playing. Even staunch Yankees fans were sorry to see him go.

For years, there was much discussion on New York sports talk radio about throwing a pitch under Big Papi's chin; to move his feet, to make him uncomfortable in the batter's box. But there was no intimidating Big Papi, and each time he crossed home plate after hitting a homer he looked up and pointed both index fingers to the sky in tribute to his mother, Angela Rosa Arias, who died in a car crash in January 2002 at the age of forty-six. You have to admire a man of his stature, and I did admire Ortiz for his ability to perform in the clutch. He cemented his postseason legend in Game Two of the 2013 ALCS with a grand slam that tied the game and keyed a dramatic comeback victory for the Red Sox, changing the face of the series and likely saving their season.

Big Papi was the consummate leader. In the 2013 World Series, with the Red Sox trailing two games to one, Ortiz went 3-for-3 with a double, an intentional walk, and two runs scored. He also delivered an impassioned speech to his teammates in the sixth inning, down by a score of 1–0, when he felt the players lacked energy. His motivational words inspired the Red Sox, who responded with a three-run rally to take a lead they never surrendered. "It was like twenty-four kindergartners looking up at their teacher," said teammate Jonny Gomes. "He got everyone's attention."

Haters will mention the leaked 2009 report alleging that Ortiz's sample test from 2003 showed a positive indication for a substance that is now banned—but wasn't banned at the time. That's sour grapes, because he never failed one test administered under MLB's Joint Drug Agreement. Of course, Manny Ramirez is another matter. Too bad "Manny being Manny" will be remembered for the unsavory end to his career instead of what he was: a dangerous right-handed batter and with Ortiz, a feared one-two punch.

You'll get no fight from me. Big Papi was the best DH ever, with Seattle's Edgar Martinez a worthy second. He also hit Mariano Rivera very well, but I've already evoked enough bad memories without rehashing those nightmares.[1]

---

[1] In 38 at-bats against Rivera, Ortiz went 13-for-38 (.342) with a homer and four runs batted in, to go along with two walks and six strikeouts.

YANKEES DESIGNATED HITTER: HIDEKI MATSUI

Career	H	HR	RBI	BA	Awards
2003–2012 (10-year career)	1253	175	760	.282	2x All-Star 2009 World Series Champ 2009 World Series MVP

Yankees Career	H	HR	RBI	BA
2003–2009	977	140	597	.292

Reason for Decision

In the first home game he ever played at Yankee Stadium, on Opening Day in 2003, Hideki Matsui hit a grand slam. In the final home game he played at Yankee Stadium in 2009, he went 3-for-4 with a homer and six RBIs to clinch the Yankees' 27th World Series championship. In the seven years between those magical moments, Matsui added to an impressive collection of clutch hits, prompting Derek Jeter to proclaim: "He's always been one of my favorite teammates, and he always will be."

Matsui was twenty-nine years old and already a three-time MVP of Japan's Central League when he signed with the Yankees prior to the 2003 season. "Godzilla" first came to the majors as an outfielder. He finished that first year as a leading candidate for AL Rookie of the Year with a .287 batting average, 16 homers, 42 doubles, and 106 RBIs. Shockingly, the winner was Angel Berroa of the Kansas City Royals. "I guess I just looked too old for a rookie," Matsui said.

The Yankees held off the Red Sox for first place in the AL East that season. The Yankees and Twins split the first two games in the best-of-five division series. In Game Three, Matsui hammered a Kyle Lohse fastball into the Metrodome's upper deck in right field for a two-run homer. The Yanks won, 3–1, and then closed out the Twins the next day. The Red Sox were up next in the ALCS. The series was a nail-biter from the first pitch through Aaron Boone's walk-off homer to win Game Seven. Along the way, Matsui's double off Pedro Martinez in Game Three drove home a crucial run to break a tie in an eventual 4–3 Yankees victory. And he victimized the Boston ace with another double to ignite New York's dramatic eighth-inning rally in the deciding Game Seven, perhaps the greatest game ever played at the old Stadium.

He continued his hot hitting in the World Series against the Florida

Marlins. After the Yankees lost Game One, Matsui sparked his team in the first inning of Game Two, getting the green light on a 3–0 count and delivering a long three-run homer off Mark Redman, becoming the first Japanese player to hit a home run in World Series history. In Game Three, with the scored tied at 1–1 in the eighth, Hideki stroked a two-out single to left field off southpaw Dontrelle Willis to score Jeter and put the Yankees ahead, 2–1. The resilient Marlins fought back to win the next three games and capture the championship, but Matsui had proven himself to be a reliable hitter in pressure situations.

In 2004, Hideki improved in almost every statistical category, finishing with a .298 batting average, 31 home runs, 108 RBIs, 109 runs, and 88 walks. In the ALDS against Minnesota, he finished with seven hits—including a double and a homer—and three RBIs in the four-game series. In the ALCS against Boston, he spearheaded the offense in the Game One win over Curt Schilling, going 3-for-5 with a pair of doubles and five RBIs. In the Game Three laugher, when the Yanks clobbered the Sox, 19–8, Hideki was the star with two doubles, two homers, a single, five RBIs, and five runs scored. He continued his offensive assault in Game Four with a double and a triple, but Mariano Rivera blew the save and the Red Sox stayed alive. Boston rode that momentum to another victory, and another, and another. It wasn't Godzilla's fault: in the 2004 postseason he was a menace, hitting .412 with three homers and 13 RBIs in 11 games.

Matsui had another outstanding season in 2005 with a .305 batting average, 23 homers, and 116 RBIs, becoming the first Yankee since Joe DiMaggio to knock in 100 or more runs in each of his first three major-league seasons. He suffered a broken wrist making a sliding catch against the Red Sox in a May 2006 game and immediately underwent surgery, ending a playing streak of 518 games, sidelining him for much of that season. The following year he finished with 25 homers and 103 RBIs, both second on the club to A-Rod.

By 2009, Matsui had transitioned to a full-time DH role, finishing the regular season with 28 homers and 90 RBIs. During postseason series victories over the Twins and Angels, Hideki drove in five runs and drew eight walks in nine games. After the Yankees lost Game One of the World Series to Cliff Lee and the Phillies, in the crucial Game Two, Matsui hit what proved to be the game-winning home run off Pedro Martinez in the bottom of the sixth as the Yankees knotted the Series at one. As the Series moved to Philadelphia, where there would be no designated hitter under National League rules, Matsui knew he would be manager Joe Girardi's first pinch-hitter. Sure enough, in the top of the eighth inning of Game Three, Matsui was called upon with two outs and the Yanks leading, 7–4. He would come through again, clubbing a solo homer for the Yankees' eighth and final run in an 8–5 victory.

But Game Six was Matsui's signature moment. Facing Martinez again, he opened the Yankees' scoring with a two-run homer in the bottom of the second. An inning later, he laced a single to center to drive in two more runs. In the fifth, Hideki collected two more RBIs with a double off J. A. Happ that made the score 7–1. The Yankees went on to capture their 27th championship, and Matsui was the first DH to win MVP honors in a World Series. In his 14 plate appearances, he collected eight hits and a walk for a .615 batting average, .643 on-base percentage, and an amazing 1.385 slugging percentage. He hit three homers and drove in eight runs, including a single-game World Series record of six RBIs, which was first accomplished by Bobby Richardson for the Yankees in 1960.

The Yankees have not employed a full-time DH for any extended period of time in their history, but no other Yankees DH has been a World Series MVP, so Matsui is an easy call.

Honorable Mention

Don Baylor won two Silver Slugger Awards (in 1983 and '85) in his three seasons as DH for the Yankees. The muscular Baylor was consistent: 21 HRs and 85 RBIs in 1983; 27 HRs and 89 RBIs in '84; and 23 HRs and 91 RBIs in '85. He also led the American League in being hit by pitches with 23 in 1984 and 24 in '85.

Danny Tartabull served as the Yankees' primary DH in 1993 and '94. He hit there in 88 games in 1993 and 78 in '94, both of which were productive seasons. He belted 20 of his 31 homers and drove in 70 of his 102 runs in 1993 as DH. The next year, he hit 13 of his 19 homers in that spot.

Others to consider: During his 20-year career, **Ruben Sierra** hit 306 home runs for nine different teams. While a member of the Bombers in 2004, he slugged 17 homers and recorded 30 extra-base hits in 307 at-bats as the DH. **Jack Clark** DH'd for the Yankees in 1988 at age thirty-two, hitting 27 HRs with 93 RBIs. Of course, April 6, 1973, was the debut of the designated hitter in the American League, with the Yankees' **Ron Blomberg** going down in history as the first player to take an at-bat as a DH. He walked with the bases loaded against the Boston Red Sox on Opening Day at Fenway Park.

Bill Nowlin's Response

I'd agree: maybe Matsui "wuz robbed" of the Rookie of the Year Award in 2003. That Matsui had a full 10 seasons of major-league ball behind him (albeit for the Yomiuri Giants in Japan's Central League) no doubt played into the decision for a number of writers—though nine seasons of Japanese big-league ball hadn't prevented Ichiro Suzuki from being named ROY just two years earlier. Matsui was a "rookie" in MLB but already had 332 homers in the Japanese majors. He did come in second in ROY balloting. At least he was recognized as an All-Star that year, and his sophomore season as well.

I was wondering who you were going to choose as the Yankees' DH. They've certainly had a surfeit of scary-good hitters, but I couldn't immediately think of one who stood out as such. That's probably just my ignorance, but I see you took me off the hook a bit in that regard by noting that the Yankees never really had a long-time DH. When I saw you'd chosen Matsui, I thought, "Of course!"

Isn't it interesting that, other than Ortiz, neither the Yankees nor the Red Sox have had a DH for more than about three years?

I'll go with it being an easy call for Matsui. After all, by definition, World Series MVPs only come along once a year. The year 2009 was Matsui's sixth trip to the postseason with the Yankees. He'd done particularly well in 2004, hitting (as noted) .412 in both the ALDS and the ALCS. But his performance in 2009 took it to another level.

He was the Yankees' designated hitter in 493 games, more than three full years' worth. Red Sox fans could never rest easy when Matsui stepped to the plate.

HEAD-TO-HEAD

Bill Nowlin: I find it interesting that both Matsui and Ortiz were pretty good defenders at the field positions they played when needed, for instance in interleague games or the World Series. Matsui played the outfield in 692 games (5,948 1/3 innings)—all three positions, but almost 90 percent of the time in left field. Ortiz played 278 games at first base, some 2,162 innings. Both had very good fielding percentages—.983 for Matsui and .990 for Ortiz. And—sorry, Jeff Suppan—engraved in my mind forever is the alertness Ortiz showed playing first base in Game Three of the 2004 World Series. After taking a routine throw from second baseman Mark Bellhorn to retire the batter at first base, Ortiz spotted Suppan having rounded third base a little too optimistically, took five or six crow-hop steps toward third base, and fired the ball across the diamond in time for Bill Mueller to put the tag on a chagrined pitcher, who otherwise would have been on third base with one out as the potential tying run in a 1–0 game.

David Fischer: Matsui was a serviceable left fielder until his balky knees made it difficult for him to cover much ground in the "death valley" that is left field and left-center field at Yankee Stadium. It was Matsui's bat that made him an international superstar. What characterized his seven-year stint in New York was an overall excellent and disciplined plate approach coupled with the ability to put the ball in play with more regularity than one would expect from a hitter with above-average power. In the 916 games he played for the Yankees, Matsui hit 140 homers with 597 RBIs, walked 416 times, and yet struck out only 485 times. That's nearly DiMaggio-esque.

BN: Borderline sacrilege! Joe D. struck out in 5.4 percent of his at-bats. Matsui struck out in 14.5 percent of his. (Ortiz in 19.7 percent, but I shouldn't be helping bolster your case.)

I will say that Matsui's performance in the 2009 World Series was truly exceptional—.615 over the course of the six games against the Phillies, with three home runs and eight runs batted in. After all, who hits over .600 in six World Series games?

Oh, wait, David Ortiz did—in 2013, hitting .688.

It's tempting to say that Matsui's performance was truly "Ortiz-esque." Looking more carefully, though, the two had fairly comparable World Series stats. Matsui hit three homers in his six games and drove in eight runs. Ortiz hit two homers and drove in six. Matsui's OPS was an other-worldly 2.027 … in a World Series! Ortiz had a still-stratospheric 1.948 OPS. Balancing the stats a bit, Ortiz went to the plate 25 times and scored seven runs. Matsui had 14 plate appearances and scored three.

DF: Matsui's plate appearances were limited to pinch-hitting in the three games played in Philadelphia under the National League rules—yet his impact on the World Series is etched in history. So, too, is Ortiz's impact on three World Series wins, and he was a postseason MVP of a World Series and an ALCS. There's no denying that Big Papi slays Godzilla, but we knew that from the start.

Looking ahead, if current DH Giancarlo Stanton were to continue at this pace—he hit 38 homers with 100 RBIs in his first year wearing pinstripes—over the length of his contract (which runs through 2028), he's a good bet to become the all-time best for the Yankees at this one-dimensional position. But for all his tape-measure home runs, Stanton has yet to prove he can hit in pressure situations, and nobody in recent memory is better than Ortiz at the plate with the game on the line.

By the way, I like that we both recognized the late Don Baylor, one of the game's great leaders. He played on three different World Series teams in three consecutive seasons: the Red Sox in 1986, the Twins in 1987, and the A's in 1988—winning with Minnesota in '87.

Winner: David Ortiz

RIGHT-HANDED STARTER

RED SOX RIGHT-HANDED STARTER: PEDRO MARTINEZ

Career	G	IP	W–L	ERA	Awards
1992–2009 (18-year career)	476	2827 1/3	219–100	2.93	8x All-Star 1999 All-Star Game MVP 5x ERA Champ 3x Cy Young Award Winner Triple Crown (1999) 2004 World Series Champ Hall of Fame Inductee (2015)

Red Sox Career	G	IP	W–L	ERA
1998–2004	203	1383 2/3	117–37	2.52

Red Sox All-Time Rankings:
Strikeouts: 1683 (3rd All-Time)
Wins: 117 (6th All-Time, Tie)
Win–Loss Percentage: .760 (1st All-Time)
Earned Run Average: 2.52 (10th All-Time)
Strikeouts Per 9 IP: 10.947 (1st All-Time)
Hits Per 9 IP: 6.791 (2nd All-Time)
Walks Per 9 IP: 2.010 (6th All-Time)
Walks & Hits Per IP: 0.978 (2nd All-Time)
Strikeouts to Walks: 5.447 (1st All-Time)

Reason for Decision

I'll start off by acknowledging that—fair or not—the two more recent righties got more consideration than the ones who pitched more than 100 years ago. This was a tough call, but with a number of these calls there is a strong subjective element. We'll return to that topic when looking at the first of the honorable mentions. For now, let's focus on the positive. GM Dan Duquette went all out to get, and sign, Pedro Martinez to the Red Sox. In 1997, Martinez won the National League Cy Young Award with a league-leading 1.90 ERA, earning 25 of 28 first-place votes. He'd also been an All-Star for the second of eight times. He was 19–7 in 1998, his first year in Boston, and then went on to have two of the best seasons any pitcher has ever had.

In 1999, he was 23–4 with a 2.07 ERA, striking out a team-record 313 batters while only walking 37, averaging 13.2 strikeouts per nine innings. He was the unanimous choice for the Cy Young Award that year, with a WAR of 9.8. He followed that with a 2000 season that also saw him win the Cy Young, receiving 100 percent of the first-place votes. His record was 18–6, leading the majors in earned run average (1.74) and an even better strikeout-to-walk ratio (8.88).

Of the 21 games when a Red Sox pitcher has struck out 15 or more batters, Pedro Martinez holds 10 of them. He also threw two one-hitters.

Twice more he led both leagues in ERA, in 2002 and 2003. He was 4–1 in postseason pitching for the Red Sox and looked set to bank a fifth win in Game Seven of the 2003 ALCS against the Yankees—he'd left the mound with a 5–2 lead through seven innings, accepting congratulations from his teammates in the dugout, only to have manager Grady Little ask him to go out and pitch the eighth. That backfired, big time. He gave up four hits and three runs and finally got removed—but New York had tied the game, and went on to win it and head to the World Series.

In 2004, he finally got to the World Series and threw seven shutout innings in Game Three, the first game the Sox played in St. Louis.

Martinez's winning percentage of .760 (117–27) is the best in Red Sox history. Smoky Joe Wood was second with .674 (116–56).

When Pedro pitched, it was always an event—and it is no small matter that he drew lots of Latinos to the ballpark, many proudly parading the aisles with Dominican flags. There were few fans who didn't like Pedro. And nearly 15 years after he departed, Pedro remains involved with the Red Sox.

Honorable Mention

Roger Clemens, "The Rocket," had great stats, too. He is, among other things, tied for the most wins in Red Sox history—192, tied with none other than Cy Young. Clemens himself won three Cy Young Awards with the Red Sox. He still holds the major-league record for strikeouts in a nine-inning game (20) which he achieved twice, once in 1986 and once in 1996. He leads the team in strikeouts with 2,590, in part reflecting the 13 seasons he pitched for Boston.

Clemens did win one more Cy Young with Boston than did Pedro, but he also won four others with different AL East teams, and that didn't sit well. He said he wanted to pitch closer to home (Texas), and then signed with Toronto. And then he went to the (gasp) Yankees. And Boston fans have long memories. They recalled Clemens complaining about having to carry his own luggage. His last four seasons with the Red Sox, he was only 40–39.

There's also the cloud that hangs over Clemens's head. Steroids. Just a couple of months after he retired, in the words of Rick Bush, "all sorts of skeletons fell out of Clemens's closet upon the release of the Mitchell Report." It's been a dozen years since he retired and despite unquestionable first-ballot Hall of Fame stats, he hasn't been elected. In fact, in his first year of eligibility he was named on only 37.6 percent of those ballots.

Smoky Joe Wood had *two* World Championships on his resume. In 1912, he had the best won–loss record of any Red Sox pitcher: he was 34–5 with a 1.91 ERA in a season that saw him throw 10 shutouts. In 1915, he had an even better earned run average: 1.49. His record was 15–5. The only reason he didn't win a Cy Young Award or two was because the award wasn't initiated until 1956. He also threw a no-hitter in 1911.

In the 1912 World Series, Smoky Joe won three games for the Red Sox. An arm injury kept him from taking part in the 1915 World Series or playing at all in 1916. Wood later converted to become an outfielder for the Cleveland Indians, and proved to also be a very good hitter, with a career .297 batting average over six seasons for the Tribe.

Cy Young didn't win a Cy Young Award, either, for the same reason Joe Wood did not. But he probably would have, in each of the first three years of the franchise: 1901, 1902, and 1903. He threw two no-hitters, one a perfect game on May 5, 1904. In fact, Young faced 76 consecutive hitters without giving up a hit over 25 1/3 innings, as part of a stretch in which he threw 45 2/3 consecutive scoreless innings. During that stretch, Young threw four straight shutouts, three of the wins by the score of just 1–0.

As noted above, Young won 192 games for Boston, tied with Clemens for tops in team history. Interestingly, the first seven of his eight seasons for Boston pre-dated the club adopting the name "Red Sox." It was a different era, for sure—his first four seasons with Boston, he won more than 25 games each year, the first two of them winning 33 and 32.

Clearly, the Red Sox have had some dominant right-handers over the years. I had to select one, and chose Pedro Martinez.

David Fischer's Response

Respect and adoration are two very different animals. I respect Pedro and, in his prime, there was not a more intimidating right-hander—with the possible exception of the Rocket. But to speak frankly, I hate them both. My dislike for Clemens even extended to when he was pitching for the Yankees. But the hatred for Pedro remains palpable to this day, due to the nature of the rivalry at a time when both teams were competing for the division title. Pedro irked Yankees fans by saying he'd like to wake up Babe Ruth and drill him in the posterior. Then, in a game in July 2003 at the Stadium, he purposely drilled both Derek Jeter and Alfonso Soriano in the first inning, sending both players to the hospital for X-rays. Later in that year's ALCS he purposely threw over the head of Karim Garcia at Fenway, sparking a bench-clearing brawl that culminated in Pedro throwing seventy-two-year-old bench coach and former Red Sox manager Don Zimmer to the ground. Very shabby behavior on Petey's part, although Zim apologized for his role in the set-to. In September 2004, the Yankees tagged Pedro for eight runs in five innings, prompting him to "call the Yankees my Daddy." The Yankees enjoyed some success against Pedro: he was 11–11 against the Yankees while with Boston. I will admit he pitched one of the greatest games I've ever seen in person: a stellar 17-strikeout one-hitter at Yankee Stadium, with the Yankees' lone hit being a Chili Davis home run in the second inning. A truly dominant performance I won't soon forget. For that performance alone, I'd pick Martinez, too.

While Martinez was an arrogant, cocky headhunter, you got the sense he was a terrific teammate—a trait that he cements with his insightful and humorous commentary as an analyst on the MLB Network. And while Clemens was an arrogant, cocky headhunter, you got the sense he was someone to avoid at all costs—a trait that he cements with his unwavering lies and deceit.

A tad surprised Curt Schilling and his bloody sock did not make your list. Oh, and by the way, I hate him, too.

YANKEES RIGHT-HANDED STARTER: RED RUFFING

Career	G	IP	W–L	ERA	Awards
1924–1942, 1945–1947 (22-year career)	624	4344	273–225	3.80	6x All-Star 6x World Series Champ Hall of Fame Inductee (1967)

Yankees Career	G	IP	W–L	ERA
1930–1942, 1945–1946	426	3168 2/3	231–124	3.47

Yankees All-Time Rankings:
Games Pitched: 426 (7th All-Time)
Games Started: 391 (3rd All-Time)
Complete Games: 261 (1st All-Time)
Shutouts: 40 (2nd All-Time, Tie)
Innings Pitched: 3168 2/3 (2nd All-Time)
Batters Faced: 13,353 (1st All-Time)
Strikeouts: 1526 (5th All-Time)
Wins: 231 (2nd All-Time)

Reason for Decision

Red Ruffing overcame a childhood accident in which he lost four toes on his left foot to become a Hall of Fame pitching great for the New York Yankees. Although the coal-mining injury dashed his hopes of becoming an outfielder, Ruffing took the mound and won 273 major-league games for the Boston Red Sox and New York Yankees. His 231 wins as a Yankee ranks second on the team's all-time list. He is also third in games started (391), and second in innings pitched (3,168 2/3) and shutouts (40), and has the seventh most appearances in team history (426). "The foot bothered me [during] my career," said Ruffing. "I had to land on the side of my left foot in my follow through."

Ruffing joined the Red Sox at the age of nineteen and struggled for last-place Boston clubs from 1924 to 1930, putting together a 39–96 record. Then he was traded to New York, still just twenty-six years old. Ruffing's turnaround was immediate. He went 15–5 in his first season with the Yankees. In the next 14 seasons, the Yankees won seven pennants and six World Series. Ruffing went 231–124, including four straight 20-win seasons from 1936 to 1939, helping the Yankees win four straight championships during those years. "If I were asked to choose the best pitcher I've ever caught," said Hall of Fame catcher Bill Dickey, "I would have to say Ruffing."

In World Series play, Ruffing was 7–2 with a 2.63 earned run average. The highlight of his World Series career was his run from 1937 to 1941: five Series games, five wins, five complete games. He allowed just six runs in 45 innings. He nearly achieved pitching immortality against the St. Louis Cardinals in Game One in 1942, coming four outs away from hurling the first no-hitter in Series history.

Ruffing was one of the best-hitting pitchers ever to play the game. He put together a .269 lifetime batting average, driving in more runs (273) than any pitcher in major-league history, and his 36 lifetime home runs ranks third among pitchers all-time. He batted over .300 eight times, including .364 in 1930. On September 18 of that season he hit two home runs in one game, a feat he would repeat on June 17, 1936. He was a 20-game winner in 1939 and batted better than .300, becoming one of the few pitchers in major-league history to accomplish both feats in the same season.

Honorable Mention

Waite Hoyt averaged 18 wins and 253 innings over an eight-year stretch from 1921 to 1928. His best years with the Yankees were in 1927 and '28, when he was 22–7 with a 2.64 ERA, and then 23–7 with a 3.36 ERA. He was at his best in World Series play and got ample opportunities as the Yankees won six pennants and three World Series titles (1923, '27, and '28) during his time in the Bronx. In his first season in New York, he won 19 games and pitched three complete games in the World Series without allowing an earned run. Hoyt posted an impressive 157–98 record with the Yankees, a win total good enough for ninth place on the team's all-time list.

Allie Reynolds pitched eight seasons for the Yankees, winning six World Series titles including five in a row from 1949 to 1953. He compiled a 131–60 record with a 3.30 ERA. Known as "Super Chief" because he was one-quarter Creek Indian, he pitched two no-hitters in 1951. In World Series play, Reynolds was 7–2 with four saves and a 2.79 earned run average. Said manager Casey Stengel of Reynolds's dual ability to start and relieve: "He's two pitchers rolled into one." Despite pitching only eight seasons for the Yankees, Reynolds still ranks in the team's all-time Top 10 in wins, win–loss percentage (.686), and shutouts (27).

Mel Stottlemyre won 164 games, seventh most in franchise history, with a 2.97 ERA for the Yankees during the late 1960s and early 1970s when the team was mired in the second division. Even so, he still posted three 20-win seasons. A durable and consistent pitcher, he ranks fourth in starts (356) and innings pitched (2,661 1/3), and eighth on the team's list for strikeouts (1,257). He completed 152 games (eighth on the all-time list), including 24 of his 39 starts in 1969, a year in which he logged 303 innings. He also tossed 40 shutouts, tied for second best. He retired in 1974 at the age of thirty-two due to a shoulder injury, then won four rings as a Yankees pitching coach in the 1990s.

Timing is everything. **Mike Mussina** might just be the best Yankees pitcher never to win a World Series ring. He pitched for the Bombers from 2001 to 2008—one year after their championship in 2000 and one year before their 2009 title. In those eight seasons he compiled a 123–72 record with a 3.88 ERA and 1,278 strikeouts, the seventh-most whiffs in franchise history. A master of control, his 4.109 strikeout to walk ratio is fourth best. "The Moose" was one out away from a perfect game against the Red Sox in 2001, and he reached 20 wins for the only time in his career in his final season. He finished with 270 career wins and only 153 losses (including his time with Baltimore), a winning percentage that made him a Hall of Famer.

In a career that spanned from 1937 to 1947, **Spud Chandler** helped the Yankees win three World Series (1941, '43, and '47) and won the 1943 AL MVP award with a 20–4 mark and a 1.64 ERA. He was 109–43 with a 2.84 ERA during his splendid Yankees career.

Vic Raschi pitched eight seasons with the Yankees, from 1946 to '53, with a 120–50 record and a 3.58 ERA. During the team's five straight World

Series titles from 1949 to '53, he went 90–40, including three 21-win seasons in a row from 1949 to '51. Impressive.

Bill Nowlin's Response

Six honorable mentions to my three? I could toss in a few more, too! You did mention Curt Schilling. A good point. I could understand you hating him. He did, after all, help beat the Yankees in Game Seven of the 2001 World Series when he was with the Diamondbacks. And he beat the Yankees in Game Six—the "bloody sock game" of the 2004 ALCS. His 11–2 record (with a 2.23 ERA) in postseason play stands as arguably the best record of anyone in playoff baseball. But it wasn't all against the Yankees. He was 1–1 against the Yankees because of the six runs he gave up in Game Three of the same ALCS in 2004. If he'd won that game, there wouldn't have been such a turnaround beginning with Game Four; rather than being down, 0–3, the Red Sox would have been playing Game Four with just a 1–2 deficit. All the drama that followed wouldn't have been that dramatic. Hating him? OK, understood. He hasn't got many fans in the Rhode Island legislature, and he lost favor with many liberals in New England with his political commentary. Enough on Big Schill, though.

Now, to Red Ruffing. You hate Pedro, you hate Roger, and you hate Schill. Reflexively, that makes me want to hate Red. Like Roger Clemens, he pitched for both the Red Sox and then the Yankees. What did he do for the Red Sox? He won 39 games and lost 96, fewer than 29 percent of his decisions. For the Yankees, he won more than 65 percent of his decisions (231–124). In both 1928 and 1929, pitching for the Red Sox, he led the league in losses. Thanks a lot, Red.

You want to make the argument that the Red Sox stunk in those years, 1924 through 1930, when he wore a Boston uniform? They finished seventh his first year (1924) and then finished in last place every other year Ruffing was on the team. Well, OK, it does take a team. But Ruffing pitched better for the Yankees, with an ERA that was more than a full run better than when he pitched for the Red Sox (his ERA was 3.47 for the Yankees and 4.61 for the Red Sox). And the Red Sox graciously donated him to the Yankees—all they asked for was Ced Durst and $50,000. Head-to-head, pitching for the Yankees, Ruffing was 29–16 against the Red Sox, but when he was a member of the Red Sox, his record against the Yankees was 1–16. What's up with that?

In a more serious vein, what a lucky guy Charles Herbert Ruffing was. It was his good fortune to join a dominant Yankees team at a time he could help extend and maintain that dominance. In his 15 years with the Yankees, the team finished in first seven times. He never would have made any hall of fame based on his Red Sox record. With the Yankees, he rode into the National Baseball Hall of Fame.

HEAD-TO-HEAD

Bill Nowlin: I'll kick it off. Pedro was better. He pitched under a spotlight Ruffing never had. Every game was on TV. He was not only representing the Red Sox, but also the Dominican Republic when he pitched. And just citing a couple of good old-fashioned stats, Pedro won 76 percent of the games he pitched for the Red Sox while Red won 65.1 percent of the games he pitched for the Yankees. Ruffing's NYY ERA was 3.47; Martinez's BOS ERA was almost a full run less: 2.52.

David Fischer: There's no debate: Pedro's seven years with the Red Sox were dominant seasons in any era. Yet those seasons took their toll on the spindle-thin Dominican. Over the next five years with the Mets and Phillies, Pedro's innings went from 217 to 132 to 28 to 109 to 44 and then he retired. Ruffing, however, pitched 15 years with the Yankees and his career was peaking as he entered his mid-thirties, an age when most pitchers are struggling to hang around.

BN: Yeah, Pedro faded, for sure. The Red Sox were apparently perspicacious in not working hard to re-sign him. We're comparing Ruffing as a Yankee to Martinez as a member of the Red Sox, right? So what Red did with the Red Sox and what Pedro did (or didn't do) for the Mets is of some interest, but a little off topic. Neither would have made the Hall of Fame if we focused on their work for their "other" teams.

DF: OK, let's focus on Pedro's work for the Red Sox and Red's work for the Yankees. Red completed 261 of the 391 games he started for the

Yankees, a rate of 66 percent. Pedro completed only 22 of the 201 games he started for the Red Sox, a rate of 11 percent. Red also was credited with nine saves for the Yankees—and Pedro had none for the Red Sox. To be sure, Red was the better hitter!

BN: You're stretching! In Red's day, pitchers were expected to complete games. By the time Pedro pitched, going for complete games was discouraged. Yep, Ruffing was better as a batter. He was also a little better in terms of career fielding percentage. But look at some pitching stats: Pedro struck out 1,683 batters for the Red Sox, while Red struck out 1,526 for the Yankees—BUT look at the walks. Red walked 1,066 opponents, and Pedro only walked 309. That gives Pedro a 5.45 strikeout to walk ratio, while Red's is 1.43. If you look at strikeouts per nine innings, Pedro struck out 10.9 batters per nine innings, but Red only struck out 4.3. Overall, there's WHIP (walks and hits per inning pitched): Red was 1.282 while Pedro was less than one (.978).

DF: Red and Pedro pitched in very different eras, a fact that cannot be discounted. Red toiled during the 1930s, which was a decade of dominance for the offense. Taking that into account, Red's sub-4.00 ERA in each season from 1932 to 1941 *is* actually a pretty impressive stretch. But I am no longer able to pretend to support any Yankees right-handed starter over Pedro Martinez. There's a valid reason Petey received 91.1 percent of the votes in his first year on the Hall of Fame ballot. He was a transcendent talent.

Winner: Pedro Martinez

LEFT-HANDED STARTER

YANKEES LEFT-HANDED STARTER: WHITEY FORD

Career	G	IP	W–L	ERA	Awards
1950, 1953–67 (16-year career)	498	3170 1/3	236–106	2.75	10x All-Star 2x ERA Champ 1961 Cy Young Award 6x World Series Champ 1961 World Series MVP Hall of Fame Inductee (1974)

Yankees All-Time Rankings:
Games Pitched: 498 (4th All-Time)
Games Started: 438 (1st All-Time, Tie)
Complete Games: 156 (6th All-Time, Tie)
Shutouts: 45 (1st All-Time)
Innings Pitched: 3170 1/3 (1st All-Time)
Batters Faced: 13,036 (2nd All-Time)
Strikeouts: 1956 (2nd All-Time)
Wins: 236 (1st All-Time)
Win–Loss Percentage: .690 (7th All-Time)
Earned Run Average: 2.75 (10th All-Time)
Hits Per 9 IP: 7.852 (9th All-Time)

Reason for Decision

Edward Charles "Whitey" Ford was the ace of the pitching staff on the great Yankees teams of the 1950s and early 1960s. The only Yankees pitcher from that era to make it into the Hall of Fame, Ford changed his pitch speeds expertly, mixing up a solid fastball, a sharp breaking curve, and a very effective change-up. A top-notch fielder, Ford also had one of the league's great pickoff moves.

Whitey joined the Yankees in 1950 and won his first nine games on his way to a 9–1 rookie record, along with a 2.81 ERA. Ford helped the

Yankees win the pennant his first season. That year, in his first of many World Series, he pitched 8 2/3 innings without allowing an earned run, winning Game Four of a four-game Yankees sweep over the Philadelphia Phillies.

Ford spent 1951 and 1952 in military service. He returned in 1953 and went 18–6, followed by a 16–8 record in 1954. His 18–7 record in 1955 tied him for most wins in the AL. He led the league with 18 complete games and finished second in ERA (2.63), earning his first All-Star selection. He returned to the All-Star Game the following year, going 19–6 during the season to lead the AL in win percentage (.760) and ERA (2.47). He also won the ERA title in 1958 with a 2.01 average.

Casey Stengel, who managed the Yankees from the time Ford arrived until 1960, limited his starts, resting him four or five days between appearances and saving him for use against the better teams in the league. When Ralph Houk took over as the Yankees manager in 1961, he moved Ford into a regular four-man rotation and the durable lefty thrived on the bigger workload. In 1961, Ford led the AL in starts (39) and innings pitched (283), and won his only Cy Young Award (when pitchers in both leagues competed for only one award), posting a spectacular 25–4 record. He also led the majors in wins and winning percentage (.862). In 1963 he again led the league in wins (24), winning percentage (.774), starts (37), and innings pitched (269). Ford finally retired as a player in 1967. His .690 career winning percentage is the highest among any twentieth-century pitcher with 200 or more wins. His consistently low ERA stayed below 3.00 in 11 of his 16 major-league seasons, never rising higher than 3.24 throughout his career. Known as the "Chairman of the Board" for his wizardry on the mound, Ford led the AL in victories three times and in ERA and shutouts twice.

Ford compiled his most impressive career stats during World Series play. He holds a number of Fall Classic pitching records, including most Series (11), most games (22), most innings (146), most strikeouts (94), and most wins (10). In 1960 and '61 he started four World Series games, won them all, and allowed no runs. On his way to his fourth straight World Series shutout in Game Four of the 1961 Series, Ford injured his ankle and had to leave the game. He departed with a streak of 32 consecutive scoreless innings, having broken Babe Ruth's World Series pitching record of 29 2/3 scoreless innings in a row. Ford continued his streak in the 1962 Series, ending up with 33 2/3 consecutive scoreless innings—still the World Series record for a starting pitcher. The Yankees won 11 pennants and six World Series during Ford's years with the club, and it would have been eight if his country hadn't called him away from the team in 1951 and '52.

Also known by the nickname "Slick," Ford was accused of throwing a spitter and mudball on occasion. Whether he did or not—and he did, by his own admission—just the thought of such gamesmanship kept hitters guessing, which meant that Whitey had the upper hand. The smooth lefty leads all Yankees hurlers in wins (236) and is tied with another lefty stalwart, Andy Pettitte, for most career starts (438). Ford tossed 156 complete games, sixth best in franchise history—and 45 of them were shutouts, the most ever by a Yankees pitcher. He also logged the most innings (3,170 1/3) and ranks second in career strikeouts (1,956). In their storied history the Yankees have sent to the mound many a quality left-handed starting pitcher, but nobody was better than Whitey Ford.

Honorable Mention

Andy Pettitte was a five-time World Series champion who pitched 15 seasons with the Yankees between 1995 and 2013. For the Yankees, he went 219–127 with a 3.94 ERA in 447 games, and never had a losing record. Pettitte pitched 2,796 1/3 innings and holds the franchise strikeout record with 2,020 and is number three in team wins behind Whitey Ford and Red Ruffing. His Yankees postseason record of 18–10 is unmatched. His career does involve the controversial use of human growth hormone to help recover from injury, a fact that may keep his Hall of Fame candidacy on the borderline.

Lefty Gomez was known as much for his colorful, eccentric personality and his good humor and wit as he was for his pitching ability. The seven-time All-Star and Hall of Fame inductee was the ace of a Yankees pitching staff that won five World Series titles during the 1930s. He compiled a career mark of 189–102—fourth-most victories in club history. In 1934, Gomez achieved a pitching Triple Crown: he led the AL in wins (26), ERA (2.33), and strikeouts (158). He duplicated that feat in 1937 with 21 wins, a 2.33 ERA, and 194 Ks. His perfect 6–0 record in World Series games is still a major-league record.

Ron Guidry was the ace of the Yankees pitching staff when the team won consecutive World Series championships in 1977 and '78. Over those two seasons he went 41–10 with 25 complete games and 14 shutouts. In 1978, he was 25–3 with a 1.74 ERA, the unanimous choice for the Cy Young Award and second in MVP balloting (to Boston's Jim Rice). His 18-strikeout performance in June 1978 is the club's single-game record. Guidry—also known as the "Louisiana Lightning" and "Gator"—spent his entire career with the Yankees, posting a 170–92 record with a 3.29 ERA from 1975 to '88.

During his 11-year stint with the Yankees, from 1923 to 1933, **Herb Pennock** posted an excellent 162–90 record. He is listed among the team's Top 10 in wins, games started, innings pitched, and complete games. Known as a big-game pitcher, Pennock was a member of four World Series–winning teams and five AL pennant winners with the Yankees. He boasted a perfect 5–0 record in World Series play and pitched to an enviable 1.95 earned run average.

Some fans thought his loss to the Red Sox in Game Four of the 2018 ALDS might be the final outing for **CC Sabathia** with the Yankees, but the club re-signed him for the 2019 season. To date, his Yankees record stands at 129–80 with a 3.74 ERA in 284 regular-season starts over 10 seasons and he's 8–4 with a 3.45 ERA in the postseason. He led the AL in regular-season victories in back-to-back seasons in 2009 and '10 and was selected as the MVP of the 2009 ALCS after two dominant performances against the Angels en route to a world championship.

Bill Nowlin's Response

I read that the Red Sox tried to sign Ford, but the Yankees were the team he followed as a kid and offered more money than Boston did. It's rare Tom Yawkey let anyone outbid him for a player he really wanted, so Yawkey must have been given bad advice. That's on the Red Sox scouts of the day.

So, let's see. I'm supposed to say bad things about Whitey Ford? The guy Elston Howard called the Chairman of the Board? I think there was maybe a kid once upon a time whose feelings got hurt because Ford didn't sign an autograph for him. Maybe. I definitely read he got fined once for coming in a few minutes after curfew ... which cost him five bucks.

Did he use swear words sometimes? I don't know. I have my suspicions.

Maybe it's a low blow for me to mention it here, but in his SABR biography of Ford, C. Paul Rogers III catalogues instances in which Ford himself (after his retirement) admitted cheating—throwing mudballs, having a special ring he wore that allowed him to cut the ball, doctoring the baseball in other ways, and the like.

I'm scuffling, admittedly. Should I complain that he wouldn't have won as many games in 1961 if he didn't have Roger Maris and Mickey Mantle on the team? Everyone seeks advantages, and in a way one can admire those who are adept enough to get away with it.

Really, I just wish Ford *had* signed with the Red Sox.

For that matter, I wish the Red Sox had kept Herb Pennock. They had him first, and traded him to the Yankees. He was even on two world championship teams for the Red Sox—1915 and 1916—though in wins and losses he was 0–2 for the two years combined and never saw any postseason play.

Pettitte cheated, too—taking steroids—and he also admitted it. I always liked him as a pitcher, though, and liked the fact that he came clean about his HGH use.

CC? Looking at his splits, I see the Red Sox did slightly better against him than most other teams, but he was still 18–13 versus Boston over the years. In the postseason, though, he was 0–3 (thank you very much), losing two games when working for the Indians in the 2007 ALCS and giving up just enough runs for the Sox to win the final game of the 2018 ALDS.

I can't fault your choice of Ford. He was a great pitcher, and a very deserving member of the Hall of Fame.

RED SOX LEFT-HANDED STARTER: JON LESTER

Career	G	IP	W–L	ERA	Awards
2006–present (13-year career)	381	2366	177–98	3.50	5x All-Star 2016 NLCS MVP 3x World Series Champ

Red Sox Career	G	IP	W–L	ERA
2006–2014	242	1519 1/3	110–63	3.64

Red Sox All-Time Rankings:
Games Started: 241 (4th All-Time)
Strikeouts: 1386 (4th All-Time)
Wins: 110 (9th All-Time)
Strikeouts Per 9 IP: 8.210 (4th All-Time)

Reason for Decision

There were several worthy candidates here. In the end, it was the stats that did it—though the differences were not major ones. Jon Lester was 110–63 for the Red Sox—not quite as many wins as Mel Parnell's 123, but his .636 winning percentage was better than any of the pitchers listed here except George Ruth. Lester was a three-time All-Star for the Red Sox (2010, 2011, and 2014). He was also a World Series winner in both 2007 and 2013, with a 3–0 record and a Series ERA even better than Mr. Ruth: 0.43.

Lester's career was interrupted early on, when the Red Sox rookie was diagnosed with a rare form of non-Hodgkin's lymphoma near the end of August 2006. He'd won his first five games, then gone to 7–2 that season before having to leave the team to fight cancer. Lester's next game was 11 months later, on July 23, 2007. He won that day, and then three more (for a 4–0 season; the Red Sox won nine of his 11 starts in what remained of the season. And then, in as fine a feel-good story as one could ask for, he started and won the clinching game of the 2007 World Series over the Colorado Rockies, 4–3 (all three runs were unearned).

In January 2008, Lester was named recipient of the Tony Conigliaro Award as the major leaguer who had best exemplified overcoming adversity to continue to play the game.

He never won 20 games in a given season, but was 19–9 in 2010 and averaged more than 16 wins per season from 2008 through 2011. One of his first wins in that stretch was his May 19, 2008 no-hitter at Fenway Park against the Kansas City Royals. In 2010, he placed fourth in Cy Young Award voting.

After a 15–8 regular season, Lester won his second World Series ring in 2013, beating the St. Louis Cardinals by the score of 8–1 in Game One and a 3–1 score in Game Five. Only the one run in Game Five was earned.

Lester was traded on the July 31 deadline date in 2014 to the Oakland A's, but then signed as a free agent with the Chicago Cubs.

With 1,386 Ks, Lester still ranks first all-time in strikeouts as a lefty for the Red Sox.

Lester helped win another world championship—this time for the Cubs in 2016. He'd had his best year in the regular season (19–5, 2.44 ERA), and then won Game Five—ending a 108-year drought for Cubs fans. In 2018, his 18 victories led the National League in wins (he was 18–6, 3.32). To think, for the money the Red Sox paid—say, David Price—they could have kept Lester and had an awful lot left over.

Cubs and cancer aside, Jon Lester was an excellent pitcher for the BoSox and the choice here for starting left-hander on our all-time team.

Honorable Mention

Robert Moses "Lefty" Grove was a five-time All-Star for the Red Sox, with a record of 105–62 (a .629 winning percentage) during his eight seasons in Boston. (His Red Sox ERA was 3.34.) He'd spent nine seasons with the Philadelphia Athletics before being acquired in December 1933 by Tom Yawkey's Red Sox. He'd been an All-Star that year, too, making it six All-Star appearances in all.

And there's little doubt that he would have been an All-Star at least five more years as well—except there was no such designation prior to the first All-Star Game in 1933. One can safely bet that his 31–4 record (2.06 ERA) in 1931 would have gotten him an All-Star berth. He was the AL MVP that year, and led the American League in either wins or ERA (or both) in all five seasons in Boston, from 1928 through 1932.

There's no doubt his better years were with Connie Mack's Athletics. He was 195–79 (a .712 winning percentage) with a 2.88 ERA. He pitched in eight World Series games for the A's, with a 4–2 record, a 1.75 ERA, and two world championship rings.

All told, he won 300 games, and was 300–141 with a 3.06 ERA for his career.

Is it fair to select Grove on the basis of his full career, as opposed to just his statistics for the Red Sox? I'd give him the edge over the other three, anyhow, even if not. He's been in the National Baseball Hall of Fame since 1947.

Mel Parnell was known as Marvelous Mel … because he was both. Parnell pitched his entire career for the Red Sox, from 1947 through 1956, and put up some good numbers. He won 123 games, lost 75 (a .621 winning percentage, working for some very good teams but also some very lackluster Sox teams), and his career ERA was 3.50. His best year was 1949, when his 25–9 record and 27 complete games both led the majors and his 2.77 ERA led the American League. Unfortunately, the Red Sox lost the pennant during the last possible game both in 1948 and 1949, and Parnell never pitched in a World Series. He was a two-time All-Star and pitched a no-hitter on July 14, 1956, his very last season.

Hubert Benjamin "Dutch" Leonard pitched for the Red Sox from 1913–1918, a contributor to three pennant-winning teams in 1915, 1916, and 1918. He was 90–64 for the Red Sox over those six seasons with a career 2.13 earned run average. In the only two games he got to pitch in the World Series—Game Three in 1915 and Game Four in 1916—he threw complete games, winning both (by scores of 2–1 over the Phillies and 6–2 over Brooklyn), giving up only one earned run in each. He might have pitched in the 1918 World Series as well, but the World War was in progress and he left the team to join a Naval shipyard.

Astute readers may have noticed that the very same **Babe Ruth** is already appearing as first choice for the New York Yankees. That renders him ineligible here, but it should be noted nonetheless (as it was in the right-fielder section) that he began his career as a pitcher for the Red Sox. He won 89 games and lost only 46, with a career 2.19 ERA—which is far from shabby. He was 3–0 in World Series play with an even better 0.87 earned run average. And he set a record with 29 2/3 consecutive scoreless innings pitched in World Series action. This was later topped by Edward Ford (see above).

David Fischer's Response

I was surprised to see Jon Lester as your choice. I thought the top selection would be Lefty Grove, with Lester and Mel Parnell battling it out for second place. A cursory look at the numbers tends to support Grove as the better choice over Lester. Grove's WAR of 44.7 leads the Boston franchise among all left-handed pitchers, far ahead of Lester's second-place WAR of 30.4. And while Grove did achieve greatness while pitching for Philadelphia, he is the only pitcher to notch his 300th victory in a Red Sox uniform. After struggling with a sore arm in his first season, Grove returned to stardom for the next five seasons. From 1935 to 1939, he averaged 17 wins per season for the Sox, with a 2.83 ERA. In four of those five seasons, he led the American League in ERA. Grove also led the league in WHIP twice, and made the All-Star Game in each of those five seasons.

Jon Lester is a fine pitcher, and he succeeded in the AL East against good-hitting teams, pitching in hitter-friendly ballparks, facing lineups that included a designated hitter, and during the offensive explosion defined by the steroid era. As I dig deeper into the statistics, the spotlight shines even brighter for Lester. He leads his Red Sox competition in games started (241 for Lester, 232 for Parnell, and 190 for Grove). Lester pitched fewer innings (1,519 to 1,752 for Parnell and 1,539 for Grove) but struck out more batters (1,386 to 743 for Grove and 732 for Parnell). He also had the lowest WHIP (1.287 to 1.321 for Grove and 1.411 for Parnell); the most strikeouts per nine innings (8.2 to 4.3 for Grove and 3.8 for Parnell); and second lowest walks per nine innings (3.1 to 2.6 for Grove and 3.9 for Parnell). Most importantly, however, Lester was 3–0 in World Series contests, allowing just a single run in 21 innings pitched. The Red Sox could always count on Lester to pitch well in the clutch, and for that reason you've convinced me. I agree with your selection of Jon Lester as best left-handed starting pitcher in Boston Red Sox history.

One can only wonder how history might have changed for Parnell—and the Red Sox—had manager Joe McCarthy not bypassed him and selected a thirty-six-year-old journeyman right-hander, Denny

Galehouse, to pitch the one-game playoff against the Cleveland Indians to decide the AL pennant in 1948. Galehouse was soundly beaten, 8–3. Parnell's best season was in 1949, as you state, a season so good he placed fourth in the MVP voting. If there were a Cy Young Award back then, he'd have been a shoo-in. But Parnell pitched poorly against the Yankees in the penultimate game of the season at Yankee Stadium when a Boston victory would have clinched the pennant for the Red Sox. Boston lost that game and the season finale, too, as the Yankees went on to capture the first of their five consecutive World Series titles under manager Casey Stengel. Unfortunately, Parnell's career was cut short. Following his 21-win season in 1953, he broke his arm and never fully recovered. He only won 12 games over the next three seasons before calling it quits following an operation on his elbow. However, in his final season, Parnell had a little magic left in his left arm. That season, he threw a no-hitter at Fenway Park against the Chicago White Sox.

In 1914, Dutch Leonard posted the lowest ERA, still to this day, in modern baseball history. That season he was 19–5 with a league leading 0.96 ERA and a 0.88 WHIP. Regardless of the era, that is an all-time great season.

That Ruth kid you mention posted terrific pitching numbers. What ever happened to him?

HEAD-TO-HEAD

Bill Nowlin: Glad you came around regarding Lester. As I started to read your response, your second sentence made me gulp: "Oh, oh, I forgot about WAR."

David Fischer: Although the composer was not referencing baseball, like the song says: "WAR. What is it good for? Absolutely nothing."

BN: Maybe I'm an unimaginative curmudgeon of some sort, but I've yet to be persuaded that WAR is not a purely subjective stat. I need someone to sit me down and convince me.

DF: The best I can say about WAR is that is allows us to compare players and rank them over different eras, but I prefer the eye test and the old-fashioned statistics. That said, Whitey Ford's career WAR is 56.9, well ahead of Lester's career WAR of 43.4—and I don't think Lester will catch Ford.

BN: I'm afraid if it's Lester against Whitey Ford, I might have to roll over and play dead. That wouldn't be right, though. Gotta put up a good fight—after all, Whitey lost 106 games. Who's to say if our two top teams squared off against each other, he wouldn't lose another?

DF: Both Ford and Lester have reputations as big-game pitchers, and our two top teams squaring off against each other would definitely be considered a big game, so both likely would pitch well. I simply believe Ford would pitch better against an All-Star caliber Red Sox squad.

BN: Heck, Ford was 24–11 lifetime against those crummy Red Sox teams he faced from 1953 through 1966. Only twice did Boston finish as high as third place during that stretch. For the years 1960 through 1966, they averaged worse than seventh place.

DF: Okay, those Boston teams Ford faced were not All-Star caliber. Conversely, the Yankees teams Lester faced were always postseason contenders.

BN: True. Through 2018, Lester was 13–6 against the Yankees, a nearly identical winning percentage to Ford's (.684 to .686). Almost even odds, but Lester was facing some tough Yankees teams—only twice did they finish as *low* as third place.

DF: When the Yankees and Red Sox face off, it doesn't seem to matter how the teams are faring in that particular season—it's always a fiercely contested battle. I admire you for not rolling over and playing dead; you did put up a good fight. However, this is Whitey Ford, and as Mickey Mantle said, "Line up all the pitchers in the world in front of me, and give me first choice, and I'd pick Whitey." So do I.

Winner: Whitey Ford

RELIEF PITCHER

RED SOX RELIEF PITCHER: BOB STANLEY

Career	G	IP	W–L	SV	Awards
1977–1989 (13-year career)	637	1707	115–97	132	2x All-Star

Red Sox All-Time Rankings:
Games Played: 637 (1st All-Time)
Games Finished: 377 (1st All-Time)
Innings Pitched: 1707 (6th All-Time)
Batters Faced: 7238 (6th All-Time)
Wins: 115 (8th All-Time)
Saves: 132 (2nd All-Time)

Reason for Decision

Bob Stanley started his 13-year Red Sox career in 1977 as a versatile pitcher; that year he started 13 games, finished 13, and relieved in 15 others. He was 15–2 (with a 2.60 ERA) in his second season, but with only three starts. In his third year, 30 of his 40 games were as a starter. He started 17 of 52 in 1980 but then became almost exclusively a reliever—until, seemingly out of the blue in 1987, he started 20 games, relieving in 14 others. All told, he relieved in 552 games for the Red Sox.

"The Steamer" finished 377 of those relief appearances, but that didn't necessarily make him a "closer." Aside from the 175 games in which he neither started nor finished, one finds that Stanley was often pitching multiple innings in the games he did finish. The year in which he finished the most games was 1983, when he appeared in 64 and finished 53 of them (with no starts). That makes him appear to be what we, today, call a closer. But Stanley worked 145 1/3 innings that year, making his average number of innings pitched in each relief appearance come to 2.27 innings pitched. That's not the way we have come to think of a final-inning, nail-it-down specialist closer.

He did save 132 games in his career with the Red Sox—second only to Jonathan Papelbon—but that fact shouldn't consign him to being considered only a closer. His value to the team clearly included his ability to pitch multiple innings at a time when called upon to do so. And he was called upon often—more than any other pitcher in Red Sox history. His 637 games rank him first, ahead of Tim Wakefield (590).

Stanley had a winning record with the Red Sox (115–97) and a career 3.64 ERA.

In the postseason, 1986 was the only year that Boston went deep. Stanley pitched in three ALCS games against the Angels and in five of the seven World Series games against the New York Mets. He didn't let up a run in any of the five World Series appearances, spanning 6 1/3 innings, though we would be remiss if we did not note the blown save he was charged with in Game Six when his wild pitch allowed the Mets to tie the game. They won it a few moments later on an error at first base. Boston had every opportunity to win Game Seven, but did not.

That he was a native of New England (Portland, Maine) probably didn't hurt him in Boston, though in fact he'd left Maine for New Jersey at the age of two. He was a popular figure among Sox fans, in his earlier years, though—like many Sox players—a target of some boos when he came up short in later seasons. Stanley was a two-time All-Star and twice placed in the top seven in the Cy Young voting.

Honorable Mention

Mike Timlin ranks fourth all-time, through 2018, in games pitched for the Red Sox, with 394. Only Bob Stanley, Tim Wakefield, and Jonathan Papelbon appeared in more games. Unlike any of the others listed here, Timlin owns a World Series ring. In fact, he owns two of them: 2004 and 2007. And he might well have been in another World Series in 2003; he helped take the team all the way to Game Seven of the ALCS. He pitched six seasons for the Red Sox and in five of those six seasons—2003, 2004, 2005, 2007, and 2008—the Red Sox made it to the postseason. Timlin's record was 30–22 with 27 saves, but his work was most often as a middle reliever (275 of his 394 appearances). His career ERA in Boston was 3.76. He struck out 273 opponents and only walked 98.

Averaging more than 65 games a year during the regular season, he was special in the postseason. In the aforementioned 2003, Timlin worked 4 1/3 innings in three Division Series games, not allowing a hit nor walking a batter while striking out five. Against the Yankees in the ALCS, he appeared in five games for a total of 5 1/3 innings, giving up just one hit and nary a run. It was Alan Embree and Timlin who closed the door in Game Seven after Grady Little had sent a weary Pedro Martinez out to be pummeled for three runs that tied the game in the bottom of the eighth. Come postseason 2004, he didn't shine but was still a workhorse, appearing in 11 of the team's 14 postseason games. He pitched in six games in the 2007 postseason, earning a hold in both Game Three and Game Four of the World Series against the Rockies.

Known as "The Monster" because of his massive size—6-foot-6 and listed at a generously slim 230 pounds—**Dick Radatz** was a supernova. He burst on the scene in 1962, striking out 13 of the first 27 batters he faced. He didn't allow an earned run in his first dozen games. Radatz placed third in Rookie of the Year voting that year, and was an All-Star in both 1963 and 1964. In 1962 and 1964 he was named "Fireman of the Year" by *The Sporting News*.

Radatz never started a game in the big leagues and burned out quickly due to overuse.

In that first year, 1962, he led the league in appearances (62) and in saves (24). In 1963, Radatz—exclusively a reliever—went 15–6 with an earned run average of 1.97. In 1964, he was 16–9 (2.29); his 29 saves led the majors. In 1965, he may have begun to tire; he was 9–11 with 22 saves and a 3.91 ERA. In each of those four years, he faced more than 500 batters. He won only three more games for the rest of his career and booked only 23 more saves. In 1962 and 1964, he led the league in games finished, typically (these days) a stat for a closer. But he, like Bob Stanley, often pitched more than one inning. Over the course of his Red Sox career, Radatz averaged 1.95 innings pitched per game. He still holds the major-league record for the most strikeouts in one season by a relief pitcher: 181, in 1964. There's no telling how he might have extended his career had his managers paced his performances more carefully.

Ellis Kinder was known as "Old Folks" because he started his big-league career at an advanced age—thirty-one years old—for the St. Louis Browns. He came to Boston in 1948, working mostly as a starter but always with a few relief appearances mixed in. Each year, he worked more in relief than he had the year before. In 1949, he was 23–6 but relieved in 10 of his 43 games. In 1950, he relieved in 25 games and in 61 in 1951. His 16 saves that year led the majors. In 1953, then thirty-eight years old, Kinder led the majors in games (69), games finished (51), and saves (27). His Red Sox career lasted eight years, his last year in Boston at age forty when he led the majors with 38 games finished. He ranks seventh in games among all Red Sox pitchers with 365. His Red Sox record was 86–52 (3.28), though that embraces his time as a starter as well as the reliever he became. Among Red Sox pitchers with over 1,000 innings to their credit, Kinder ranks 12th, and his 91 saves see him ranked fifth. Though a closer and not a reliever, **Craig Kimbrel** has racked up 108 saves in just three years with the Red Sox, vaulting over Kinder.

Another name to note, **Junichi Tazawa** ranks 11th all-time in game appearances for the Red Sox. He pitched seven years in Boston, often overshadowed by others but getting his work done. He was 17–20 with a 3.58 ERA while striking out 308 batters and only walking 71. Tazawa was 5–4 (3.16) in 2013, and pitched in 13 games of that year's 16 post-season games with a combined earned run average of just 1.23 (allowing only six hits, no walks, and one run). He was credited with the win in the clinching Game Six of the League Championship Series against Detroit and earned six holds in other postseason games.

It seems like a brief note should be made of the most impressive Red Sox relief outing of all time. On June 23, 1917, the Senators were at Fenway Park. Babe Ruth started the game and walked the first batter, then got in an animated dispute with plate umpire Brick Owens. Ruth got ejected, and **Ernie Shore** came on in relief. There was nobody out and a runner on first. With Shore pitching, said baserunner tried to steal second but was thrown out. Shore retired the next 26 batters in succession. It was, essentially, a perfect game, and probably the best relief effort in the history of baseball.

David Fischer's Response

Let's get one thing straight at the outset: Bob Stanley did *not* throw a wild pitch. Rich Gedman allowed a passed ball. At least that is the opinion of this humble reporter. Stanley possessed a wicked sinking fastball, used to great effect, resulting in a plethora of ground balls. However, much to Stanley's detriment, Boston never was known to back him up with a particularly athletic or sure-handed infield during his pitching career. Marty Barrett was a good little player—but didn't have much range at second base. There was always a merry-go-round of shortstops such as Jackie Gutierrez, Rey Quinones, Spike Owen, Jody Reed, and Luis Rivera. At first base, after Bill Buckner there was a parade of Nick Esasky, Todd Benzinger, and Carlos Quintana. Not many Gold Glove Awards among the bunch. And this was before Wade Boggs became a competent third baseman in New York. The Boston boo-birds may have had every right to jeer The Steamer but, in my memory, there were a ton of seeing-eye ground balls that went for base hits against him.

I admit to being a huge Timlin fan and am happy to see his name listed here.

Tazawa's major-league debut came against the Yankees on August 7, 2009—in the 15th inning of an epic five-hour, 33-minute game. After giving up a leadoff single to Derek Jeter, Tazawa left a breaking ball up in the zone to Alex Rodriguez, who hit a two-run homer to left-center field for a 2–0 Yankees victory. Give Tazawa his due: he was not scarred or traumatized by that outing and went on to a post a solid career.

YANKEES RELIEF PITCHER: DELLIN BETANCES

Career	G	IP	W–L	SV	Awards
2011–present (7-year career)	357	381	21–22	36	4x All-Star

Reason for Decision

Dellin Betances burst onto the scene in 2014 and immediately set the Yankees single-season strikeout record for a reliever with 135 Ks. And there's been no stopping him ever since. The right-hander was selected to represent the AL All-Star team in four consecutive years (2014–2017), a rare and deserving accomplishment for an eighth-inning set-up man. Just look and marvel at his marquee numbers during the past five seasons:

2014: 90 innings pitched, 135 Ks, 46 hits

2015: 84 innings pitched, 131 Ks, 45 hits

2016: 73 innings pitched, 126 Ks, 54 hits

2017: 59 2/3 innings pitched, 100 Ks, 29 hits

2018: 66 2/3 innings pitched, 115 Ks, 44 hits

Towering above the pitching rubber at 6-foot-8, Betances is one of the most feared pitchers in all of baseball. He possesses two devastating pitches: an overpowering 100 mph fastball and a wicked knee-buckling curveball. He is a nightmare for right-handed batters who have to protect against the fastball, only to look foolish when he breaks off one of those curves. And he's no picnic for lefties, either.

When the Yankees are in a jam and need a strikeout, Betances is the man they call upon. In 2018, he recorded at least one strikeout in 44 consecutive appearances over 120 days, setting an AL single-season record for a relief pitcher and finishing just one appearance shy of the major-league record set by Corey Knebel in 2017. Over the course of his strike-out streak, Betances tallied 76 strikeouts and posted a 1.69 ERA while holding opposing batters to a .158 average. The big righty recorded at least two strikeouts in 26 of the 44 games and struck out the side six times.

Dellin continued dealin' in 2018. During an unbelievably dominant stretch from May 23 to August 11, he allowed just two runs and 12 hits over 33 2/3 innings, while striking out 58 batters. The thirty-year-old looked completely unhittable for those 11 weeks, and what makes him so valuable is his ability to raise his efficiency when the stakes are high: when runners are on base and in scoring position.

Betances is the first relief pitcher in major-league history to strike out 100 or more batters in five straight seasons. Already in his brief career he can boast an enviable 1.045 WHIP to go along with a dominating 5.4 hits per nine innings and an otherworldly 14.6 K/9. The Yankees' bullpen of late is widely considered to be one of the best in the business, and Betances has proven to be one of his skipper's most trusted arms in an arsenal full of dangerous weapons.

Honorable Mention

Good relievers come and go, but **David Roberston** has been a consistent performer since joining the Yankees in 2008. Employing a sharp, downward breaking curveball to enhance a mid-90s fastball that keeps its line, D-Rob has become one of the game's top setup men, able to wiggle out of jams and keep his composure even with traffic on the basepaths. In addition, he proved to be a dependable closer, converting 39 of 44 save chances in 2014 in place of Mariano Rivera, before becoming a free agent and signing with the White Sox. When Robertson returned to the Bronx in 2018, Yankees fans couldn't have been happier. He is the only pitcher in major-league history to average at least 10 strikeouts per nine innings in each of his first 11 big-league seasons. The durable righty has thrown at least 60 innings each year since 2010 and has appeared in 501 games with the Yankees, third best on the all-time list. As a member of the Yankees, he posted a 38–22 record with a 2.75 ERA, a 1.157 WHIP, 12 K/9, and a 3.26 strikeout-to-walk ratio. Impressive statistics, but none tops this: he pitched 498 innings and allowed just 372 hits as a member of the Yanks. In January 2019, he signed a free-agent contract to go pitch for Philadelphia. I am sorry to see him go.

In six seasons with the Yankees, from 1997 to 2002, **Mike Stanton** appeared in 456 games, the fifth-highest total in team history. He sported a 31–14 record with a 3.77 ERA over that span. The lefty reliever was an unsung hero for Bombers teams that won three straight World Series from 1998 to 2000. He was the reliable bridge manager Joe Torre needed in order to get the ball to Mariano Rivera to close out the game.

Johnny Murphy was an integral pitcher for the Yankees dynasty of the 1930s and early '40s. The save was not yet an official statistic but, retroactively, Murphy led the AL in saves four times in five seasons from 1938 to '42. The righty was a three-time All-Star and member of six world championship teams. His World Series numbers are impressive: 2–0 record, 1.10 ERA, and four saves in eight games. In four separate Fall Classics, he allowed no runs.

Joe Page led the league in saves in 1947 and 1949; in both seasons he finished among the top four MVP vote getters. He picked up 14 relief wins to go along with 17 saves in 1947. In that year's World Series, he saved the first game, took the loss in Game Six, and came back to win the clincher, holding the Dodgers to one hit in five scoreless innings. In 1949 he was even better, saving 27 games to go along with 13 wins. In the Series, Page won Game Three and again saved the clincher.

In 1961, the screwballing lefty **Luis Arroyo** had a hand in 44 of the Yankees' 109 regular-season victories with 15 relief wins and 29 saves. Arroyo also added a win in the World Series over the Cincinnati Reds.

Bill Nowlin's Response

To begin with, it's kind of a little unfair to put a 6-foot-8 pitcher on the mound. As his long arms come from behind his body and fire the ball toward home plate, his release point may only be 10 or 15 feet from the plate.

Seriously though, those are impressive strikeout stats. I hadn't known. Once Mariano Rivera retired, I thought it was bad enough the Red Sox had to face Robertson, but then to have the New York City–born Betances join the Yankees full-time in 2014, it didn't seem fair. He was so good from the start that he placed third in Rookie of the Year voting that year. And as you point out, he hasn't let up since, a true model of consistency. The best thing I can say about him is that he's 0–3 lifetime against the Red Sox.

Looks like he had truly spectacular seasons in 2014 and 2015, with ERAs of 1.40 and 1.50, and then suddenly had just a good year in 2016 (judged by his 3.08 ERA)—but the last two seasons, in 2017 and 2018, he's brought his ERA back down in each of those years.

Times have changed, though. Relievers are used differently these days. In fact, that's true even just looking back three years, much less thirty years back to Bob Stanley's days. Is the day coming when a starter rarely gets a win, because the ball is handed to a reliever in the first inning? Conventional baseball analytics wisdom is now saying that when batters get a third look at a pitcher in a game, they hit better—so some managers think about pulling the starter after two times through the order.

HEAD-TO-HEAD

David Fischer: Say you're the manager of a team protecting a one-run lead. It's late in the game. Warming up in the bullpen: Bob Stanley and Dellin Betances. Who you gonna call?

Bill Nowlin: Tell you what, let's forget about the discussion here and let's do a deal. I'll trade Bob Stanley for Betances. Of course, Bob Stanley is sixty-four years old and works for another team, but still … .

DF: Stanley in the prime of his career wouldn't get you Betances straight-up. Back to my question, skipper. You signal for Betances, don't you? There's no debating which man is the more intimidating pitcher.

BN: Hey, that's why I was willing to make the trade. I admit, I'd make the trade even when both were in their prime—which Betances still is. Yes, all being equal, I'd signal for Betances.

DF: It's interesting to note how our selections reflect the changing times as it relates to bullpen usage. Today's relievers, for the most part, are one-and-done guys. Pitch the sixth inning, or the seventh, or the eighth, and then hit the showers. So far in his career Betances has averaged 1.067 innings per appearance. By contrast, when Stanley pitched only in relief from 1982 to 1985, he went an average of 2.34 innings per appearance, with a high-water mark of 3.5 innings per appearance in 1982. That's remarkable.

BN: I guess that shows that managers either were willing to entrust Stanley with pitching more innings (or that they leaned on him because they didn't have anyone better and he was a "horse"). Relievers weren't specialists as much in those days—no eighth-inning guy and all that. If the starter ran into trouble, a reliever was called in and he often just went as long as he could. Even the LOOGY was pretty new back then, the Left-Handed One-Out Guy.

DF: In the era when Stanley pitched, he was asked to get outs. Pitching in today's game, Betances is asked to get strikeouts. And boy does he ever!

BN: An out's an out. It was a different era, but—agreed—there's quite a gap from the 65 strikeouts a year that Stanley averaged to the 118 per year that Betances has been averaging for the Yankees.

DF: He has wipeout stuff. Betances allows an average of 5.4 hits per nine innings. That's really stingy. Stanley gave up 9.8 hits per nine. He was a more comfortable at-bat.

BN: And Stanley's 3.64 ERA and 1.364 career WHIP are both significantly above Betances. After five full seasons, the sample size is large enough: I'm throwing in the towel. I'll give the edge to Betances. Kind of pains me to say it, but I'd probably give the edge to Robertson over Stanley, too.

Winner: Dellin Betances

CLOSER

YANKEES CLOSER: MARIANO RIVERA

Career	G	IP	W–L	SV	Awards
1995–2013 (19-year career)	1115	1283 2/3	82–60	652	13x All-Star 2013 All-Star Game MVP 5x Relief Award 2003 ALCS MVP 5x World Series Champ 1999 World Series MVP Hall of Fame Inductee (2019)

Yankees All-Time Rankings:
Games Pitched: 1115 (1st All-Time)
Games Finished: 952 (1st All-Time)
Strikeouts: 1173 (9th All-Time)
Saves: 652 (1st All-Time)
Earned Run Average: 2.21 (2nd All-Time)
Strikeouts Per 9 Innings: 8.224 (7th All-Time)
Hits Per 9 Innings: 6.997 (2nd All-Time)
Walks & Hits Per Inning Pitched (WHIP): 1.000 (1st All-Time)
Strikeout to Walk Ratio: 4.101 (3rd All-Time)

Reason for Decision

If there was one relief pitcher who personifies the word "closer," it is Mariano Rivera. Since taking over the closer's role for the New York Yankees in 1997 until his retirement in 2013, Rivera saved 30 or more games in every full season but one. He is also the all-time career leader in saves with 652. While records are made to be broken, this one should last a while.

In 1996, Rivera was the setup man for John Wetteland, logging a career-high 107 2/3 innings and earning his first World Series ring, while Wetteland captured the World Series MVP Award. After that season,

Rivera became the closer for the Yankees until his retirement, recording 40 or more saves nine times, including a mind-boggling 44 saves at age forty-three in 2013—the year he chose to walk away from the game.

In 11 of Rivera's 19 major-league seasons, he had an ERA below 2.00. His career 2.21 ERA is second best in team history to Rich "Goose" Gossage, and his 1,115 appearances are the most by any Yankees pitcher, more than double Dave Righetti's 522, the next pitcher on the list. In fact, Rivera is the only pitcher in major-league history to appear in 1,000 or more games all for the same team.

More than any other player on the team, it was Rivera that propelled the Yankees to be World Series champions five times, as he was on the mound to record the final out in four clinching Series games in 1998, 1999, 2000, and 2009. Rivera's impact on the team's postseason success is preeminent. Twelve people have walked on the moon, but only 11 have scored an earned run off Rivera in the postseason. His lifetime postseason earned run average of 0.70 in 141 innings is the major-league record. During the Yankees' memorable 1998 season, Rivera did not give up a run in 10 postseason appearances. He did the same again during eight appearances in 1999, when he was the World Series MVP. More astonishing still, his major-league record 42 postseason saves, with 11 of them coming in the World Series, are 24 more than his next closest competitor, Brad Lidge (18), which explains why Rivera is the king of all closers.

With the Yankee Stadium sound system blaring Metallica's "Enter Sandman," fans knew the music meant that Rivera was entering the game and, more times than not, he'd record the three toughest outs in baseball. Five-time All-Star Mike Sweeney has compared Rivera's entrance music to the soundtrack of a horror movie, because "you hear the music and you're scared to death, because you know what's going to happen: Mariano will finish the game and get the save." And Rivera accomplished it all mostly with one devastating pitch: his signature cut fastball. Batters knew the pitch was coming, but they could never solve it. Rivera not only baffled the best major-league hitters with his cutter, he often shattered their bats.

Mariano, known as Mo, was 8–1 in his postseason career, which is astounding yet pedestrian when compared to his other October numbers.

To wit: He surrendered only two home runs in 141 postseason innings and registered a WHIP well under 1.0 (.759). And in 22 of his 32 postseason series, he surrendered no earned runs. His ERA was less than 1.00 at every level of the postseason: 0.32 in 39 Division Series games, 0.92 in 33 Championship Series games, and 0.99 in 24 World Series games.

What may have been Rivera's most memorable performance came in Game Seven of the 2003 ALCS at Yankee Stadium, when he entered a tie game in the ninth inning against a Red Sox team that had led the majors with 961 runs scored. Rivera pitched three shutout innings, his longest outing since his days as Wetteland's setup man in 1996, and the Yankees eventually won on Aaron Boone's unforgettable walk-off home run in the bottom of the 11th. As Boone circled the bases, an emotional and exhausted Rivera ran to the mound and collapsed on the hill in tears of joy. Mo won that game, saved two others, and was named the Series MVP.

In 2019, during his first year of eligibility, he became the first unanimous selection to enter Cooperstown.

Honorable Mention

The Hall of Fame closer **Rich Gossage** possessed a fastball nearly as intimidating as his scowl. Signed as a free agent prior to the 1978 season, he inherited the closer role from the previous year's Cy Young Award winner, Sparky Lyle, prompting third baseman Graig Nettles to tell Lyle he had gone from Cy Young to Sayonara. That year, "Goose" won 10 games and saved 27 more. He pitched 134 innings, fourth most on the staff. Then he surrendered all of one hit in six innings in the World Series victory over the Dodgers. He saved 33 games in 1980 and was at his overpowering best during the strike-shortened 1981 season. Limited to just 32 appearances, Gossage still managed 20 saves and allowed just 22 hits in 47 innings to go with 48 strikeouts. He gave up only four earned runs for a 0.77 ERA. In the 1981 postseason he didn't give up a run in 14 1/3 innings and he saved six games. His six years as the Yankees closer included four All-Star appearances, 150 saves—almost half his career total of 310—a 42–28 record, and a 2.14 ERA. He was also on the mound to finish off the Red Sox in that 1978 playoff game.

Prior to the 1972 season, the Yankees acquired a mustachioed left-handed reliever in exchange for first baseman Danny Cater in yet another lopsided trade with the Boston Red Sox. **Sparky Lyle** emerged from the pinstriped bullpen car, tossed his warm-up jacket aside and, using his wicked slider, went on to thrill Stadium fans en route to saving 141 games in seven seasons with the club from 1972 to 1978. He was 57–40 with a 2.14 ERA in 420 appearances, and helped the team win two World Series titles in 1977 and '78. Sparky led the league in saves twice, with 35 in 1972 and 23 in 1976. His greatest season was in 1977 when he became the first AL reliever to win the Cy Young Award, going 13–5 with 26 saves and a 2.17 ERA in 137 innings over 72 regular-season games. Then he won three straight postseason games, including a win in Game One of the World Series as the Yankees beat the Dodgers in six for their first title in 15 years. In 1979, Lyle authored a book about his experiences with the Yankees titled *The Bronx Zoo*. He often instigated clubhouse antics (a favorite involved sitting on birthday cakes), but on the mound he was a calming presence at the end of tight games.

Dave Righetti set a record (since broken) with 46 saves in 1986 and saved 224 games in seven seasons as the Yankees' closer. He began his career as a starter and won the Rookie of the Year Award in 1981 with an 8–4 record and 2.06 ERA. In his only postseason appearances, he won two games against the Milwaukee Brewers in the Division Series and one against the Oakland Athletics in the League Championship Series. In 1983, he threw a no-hitter against the Boston Red Sox on July 4 at Yankee Stadium, fanning Wade Boggs for the final out. It was the first no-hitter thrown by a Yankees pitcher since Don Larsen's perfect game in the 1956 World Series. Moved to the bullpen the next year to replace Rich Gossage as the team's closer, "Rags" made a smooth transition to relief pitching and went on to average 32 saves over the next seven seasons.

Bill Nowlin's Response

I don't know about you, but I find it interesting that, for two teams that have been competitive enough over the decades (despite the huge Yankees edge in world championships), there are quite a few positions where it's "no contest." The selection one of us makes is clearly superior to anyone the other could possibly come up with.

I'm almost inclined to just stop at this point and say nothing more, bowing down to the great Mariano Rivera. No Red Sox fans I know ever disliked him; they were just upset that he was so good. There were ways in which Sox fans could dislike a Derek Jeter or some other more palatable Yankee. But with Mariano, I never picked that up. Just envy that the Yankees had him. The first unanimous Hall of Famer. As you suggest, it's hard to imagine how anyone could have come up with a reason not to vote for him, other than to maintain the somewhat pointless tradition of no one ever having been a unanimous choice.

You may claim Game Seven of the 2003 ALCS as his most memorable postseason moment. For Sox fans, there was another moment we prefer to recall. Red Sox fans do happily remember his back-to-back blown saves in Games Four and Five of the 2004 ALCS.

There were admittedly two things which can be cited as mitigating that. One was the fact that his ERA in that ALCS was 1.29! And then a fond memory: the next spring, the Fenway home opener was on April 11, 2005, against the Yankees. As the players were introduced and the PA announcer intoned, "Number 42, Mariano Rivera," a huge roar of applause thundered from the stands. Rivera took it in good spirits with a smile and a tip of his cap.

But he did blow both of those games, thank you very much.

RED SOX CLOSER: JONATHAN PAPELBON

Career	G	IP	W–L	SV	Awards
2005–2016 (12-year career)	689	725 2/3	41–36	368	6x All-Star 2007 World Series Champ

Red Sox Career	G	IP	W–L	SV
2005–2011	396	429 1/3	23–19	219

Red Sox All-Time Rankings:
Games Pitched: 396 (3rd All-Time)
Games Finished: 334 (2nd All-Time)
Saves: 219 (1st All-Time)

Reason for Decision

The selection of Jonathan Papelbon is largely based on two things: he's the Red Sox franchise leader in terms of saves by a big margin; and he also saved some big postseason games on the big stage.

First on the number of saves. Papelbon, who played for the Red Sox from 2005 through 2011, is credited with 219 saves. The next two on the list (understanding that it was a different era and the role of closer was not then what it has become today) are Bob Stanley (with 132 saves) and Craig Kimbrel (with 108 regular-season saves). It should be noted that the "save" was only first calculated in 1969, and then adjusted in 1974 and 1975. Thus, Dick Radatz's 104 saves are actually retrospective ones. Papelbon only finished four games in 2005; ignoring that one year he averaged over 36 saves for his six seasons with the Red Sox.

In the postseason, Papelbon pitched in 18 games, finishing 12 of them and earning saves in seven. World championships count for a lot, of course. The 2007 season was Papelbon's big postseason year. He got the win in Game Two of the Division Series against the Angels, and then got a save in Game Seven of the ALCS against the Cleveland Indians. Come the World Series against the red-hot Colorado Rockies, he wasn't needed in Game One since the Red Sox had piled up a 13–1 lead through five innings. Pap did earn saves in Games Two, Three, and Four. Games Two and Four were one-run games, 2–1 and 4–3. He worked a total of 4 2/3 innings in the World Series, walking no one and allowing just two hits and no runs. One of the iconic photographs of the twenty-first century

Red Sox is Papelbon embracing catcher Jason Varitek after striking out the final Rockie to clinch the win.

He picked up three saves and a win in the 2008 postseason, but come Game Seven of the ALCS against Tampa Bay, the Red Sox never established a lead for him to protect.

Honorable Mention

Craig Kimbrel was the Red Sox closer in 2016, 2017, and for the 2018 championship team. He saved more games each year than the year before: 31, 35, and 42 (as well as being an All-Star each year). His won-loss record over those three years was 12–7, with an overall 2.44 earned run average. His accomplishments in 2018 were especially noteworthy because he missed the first half of spring training while his infant daughter Lydia Joy underwent a series of life-saving heart operations at Boston's Children's Hospital. He was 5–0 in 2017 and 5–1 in 2018. Kimbrel slotted into the role in a very precise way—if he came into a true save situation, in a "clean inning," he was lights-out. If he was asked to get four or five outs, or came in with inherited runners, he was unpredictable. By the time the Red Sox reached the postseason, however, fans started talking about needing a lead of three or four runs, a "Kimbrel-proof lead." But over the course of his three years with the Red Sox, he struck out 305 batters in 184 1/3 innings, an average of 1.65 strikeouts per inning.

The role of closer simply hasn't been one which had seen that many standouts for the Red Sox in the few decades there has been such a role. But **Koji Uehara** holds a fond place in recent memory. He was, after all, the closer who saw the Sox through the 2013 campaign. That was the first of his four seasons with Boston, over which he finished 128 games. His record was 14–13 with an excellent 2.19 earned run average, while saving 79 games. In 2013, he had his best season: his 1.09 ERA helped him place seventh in Cy Young Award voting that year.

The right-hander pitched in 15 postseason games for the Red Sox, 13 of them in 2013 (there were only three postseason games in which he did not appear). He lost Game Three of the ALDS, allowing one fatal run, but saved two and balanced the loss with a win in Game Two of the League Championship Series against the Tigers. He went on to save Games Three,

Five, and Six. In the five ALCS games in which he appeared, he worked a total of six innings, giving up four hits but striking out nine and not walking a batter. More importantly, he didn't allow a run. He was named MVP of the ALCS. In the 2013 World Series, Koji pitched in five of the six games. He saved two of them, and once more did not yield even one run.

Keith Foulke was imported after the disastrous 2003 ALCS against the—ahem—Yankees, so that the Red Sox would have a bona fide closer. Pitching for Oakland, he'd led the majors with 67 games finished in 2003 and his 43 saves led the American League. The Red Sox signed the free agent closer in early January, and it immediately paid off. He saved 32 games and finished 61 in all. Come the postseason, he picked up a save in each series, pitching three innings without a run in the Division Series against the Angels, then six innings against the Yankees in the League Championship Series without a run. Then, in the World Series against St. Louis, he threw five innings, giving up just one run in Game Three.

Most memorably, he was on the mound for Game Four of the 2004 World Series. The Red Sox had only been waiting 86 years for a World Series victory, losing four consecutive Game Sevens, losing two single-game playoffs for the pennant, and then losing Game Seven of the ALCS just the year before. October 27, 2004. The Red Sox held a 3–0 lead heading into the bottom of the ninth. Win the game and they win the World Series. What could go wrong? Manager Terry Francona called on Foulke to close the game. He gave up a single to the first batter. A fly ball out and a strikeout brought it all down to two outs in the bottom of the ninth. Again, what could go wrong? Red Sox fans of a certain age could still remember Game Six of the 1986 World Series. On a 1-0 count, Edgar Renteria hit the ball—right back to Foulke.

Joe Castiglione made the call on Red Sox radio: "The 1-0 pitch. Here it is. Swing and a ground ball stabbed by Foulke. He has it. He underhands to first and the Boston Red Sox are the world champions. For the first time in 86 years the Red Sox have won baseball's world championship. Can you believe it!?"

Bob Stanley's career is described at length elsewhere in this book as our selection for right-handed reliever. His 132 saves rank him second in franchise history, but he wasn't so much a closer as a long reliever, so we'll mention him here (and honorably so), but not include him on the list of honorable mentions. Because we have already mentioned Dick Radatz and Ellis Kinder in our consideration of relievers, we won't again include them here.

David Fischer's Response

What is it about Red Sox right-handers that I love to hate? Roger Clemens, Pedro Martinez, Curt Schilling. Can't stand 'em. Never did, even the one who played for my team. But I respected the heck out of 'em. Wanted to beat them—and beat them bad. Because it was an extremely difficult task. No matter the outcome, however, each relished hearing the boos pour out of the Yankee Stadium crowd. Martinez tipped his cap and called the Yankees his Daddy. Schilling famously said of Yankee Stadium karma, "Mystique and aura? Those are dancers at a nightclub." And though Clemens won his 300th game in the Bronx, he won't soon be receiving any invitations from the Yankees to return for a championship team reunion. Good riddance to good rubbish.

So here now you give me another right-handed reason to get all riled up: Jonathan Papelbon. Let's face it, there was a lot to dislike about Papelbon—unless he was on your team—and I can think of at least one teammate who would respectfully disagree. His mound presence was notable for his hard glare and sneer as he looked to get the sign from the catcher. He was combustible and combative. He had a chip on his shoulder. And he always seemed to have an attitude. Sometimes that got him in trouble. Like in Philadelphia in September 2014 when he blew a save, was booed by the fans at Citizens Bank Park, and while walking off the field responded by grabbing his crotch. One imagined his inner self screaming, "I got your blown save right heeeeeere." Pap's despicable action led to an ejection and a seven-game suspension. Despite his success in Philadelphia, that freeze frame became Papelbon's iconic moment as a Phillie. Rather than learn from past mistakes, he kept opening his mouth and making enemies. As a member of the Washington Nationals, he choked teammate Bryce Harper during a dugout scuffle. That added another chapter to Papelbon's history of being one of the game's modern-day antiheroes.

But enough of my Pap smearing. Besides, those incidents occurred when he was a member of other National League teams. Our concern here is Papelbon as a Boston Red Sox closer. The electric arm out of Mississippi State garnered an impressive statline across his 12 years as a pitcher in the major leagues. With 368 career saves, a 2.44 ERA, 10 K/9, and just 2.3 BB/9, he was certainly in the upper echelon of closers. He was even better during his seven seasons closing games for the Red Sox: 2.33 ERA, 10.7 K/9, and 2.4 BB/9.

Papelbon was never better than during the 2007 postseason run during which he allowed just 10 baserunners (five hits and five walks) and no runs in 10 2/3 innings pitched. And by picking off Colorado's Matt Holliday, he ripped the heart out of the Rockies in Game Two of the World Series. But where the 2004 team had "the idiots," the 2007 team had Papelbon dancing his version of an Irish jig while wearing spandex. Despite his ability to throw a high-90s fastball with late life, Papelbon displayed terrible fashion sense (for a time sporting a Mohawk hairstyle) and rotten musical taste, based upon his use of "Wild Thing" as an entrance song at Fenway Park. (He opted for the original Troggs version rather than Joan Jett's—an inexcusable decision.)

Truth be told, with the Red Sox winning the 2018 world championship, I would rather have seen Craig Kimbrel save all four games and win the World Series MVP Award, in the hopes that he would have overtaken Papelbon in your mind. Kimbrel is the more palatable choice for my churning stomach enzymes. Heck, I'd lobby hard for Jeff Reardon, too, if only to refract focus from Papelbon. But you're right, Papelbon is the best choice at this juncture in Kimbrel's career. If that sounds like a backhanded compliment, good.

Showing a mean streak, it is a pleasure to review my favorite of Papelbon's Boston failures. Against the Angels in Game Three of the 2009 AL Division Series, with Boston down two games to none, Papelbon blew the save and Boston was swept. *Papelbon was one strike away from extending the series with three different batters*—he allowed four hits and three runs. All of those runs scored with two outs. He had never allowed a postseason run until that inning. His difficulties continued into the next season. In 2010, he blew eight saves, including one against the Yankees on May 17 when he allowed four earned runs and a walk-off home run for the first time in his career. Alex Rodriguez hit the tying homer off Papelbon in the ninth inning and Marcus Thames connected moments later for a two-run shot of his own, giving the Yankees a wild 11–9 victory over the Sox. The game is must-see-TV when the YES Network runs it as a Yankee Classic.

I've got more. In 2011, Papelbon blew just three saves all season long, but two occurred during the final month of the season—including the final game of the regular season. The Red Sox and Rays were tied in the standings for the AL Wild Card, and Papelbon blew a 3–2 lead against the Baltimore Orioles, allowing them a 4–3 walk-off win. Just moments later, the Rays won their game against the Yankees with a walk-off home run by Evan Longoria to clinch the wild card (you're welcome), capping a nine-game comeback in the standings against Boston and officially eliminating the Red Sox from the playoffs. The team's collapse led to the ouster of manager Terry Francona and ushered in the hilarious one-year reign of skipper Bobby Valentine, a historical footnote which Boston fans would rather skip over.

Following the 2011 regular-season debacle Papelbon became a free agent and signed with the Philadelphia Phillies. He went on to save 123 games for Philly, becoming the all-time saves leader for two franchises. To his credit, Papelbon had great success playing in the pressure cookers of Boston and Philadelphia—two similarly tough fan and media environments. Who knows why? Despite a great deal of success at the very highest level, perhaps it was because Papelbon seemed to thrive on controversy, much of it self-created.

HEAD-TO-HEAD

David Fischer: Admittedly, I'm feeling overconfident that this one goes my way.

Bill Nowlin: I'll put up an argument here for Jonathan Papelbon, but I know I'm not going to win this one. That said, in a short hypothetical series, anything can happen. Unfortunately, I do have to own up to the fact that in his career against the Yankees, Papelbon was 0–6 with a 4.14 ERA. Rivera lost even more games against the Red Sox, though—he lost seven.

DF: When you play against a division rival 18 times a season over a 19-year career, as did Rivera against the Red Sox, there are ample opportunities to blow saves and lose games. The fact that he lost only seven games in 115 appearances against Boston only serves to confirm the greatness of Rivera. For the record, Rivera's 58 saves against the Red Sox are the most against the franchise by any closer; his 13 wins over the Red Sox are his most against any team; and his 16 regular-season blown saves against the Red Sox are his most against any team. As with any great closer, it is the rare failures that are seared in memory.

BN: I do get the impression that you didn't really like Jonathan Papelbon. I'm not sure he wanted to be liked. Many competitors thrive on adversity. It's like a starter putting on their "game face," scowling in a way that makes even their teammates shy away from them before a game. Quite a contrast between the two relievers and our reactions to them. I really liked Rivera. But that's no reason you need to like Pap.

DF: The personality differences between Papelbon and Rivera are striking. Rivera had form as well as substance. He was a star in the grand old Yankee tradition: humble, gracious, and poised. The fact that he's also a spiritual man made him an inspiration to his teammates. At least that's the impression I got while editing a book about him, titled *Facing Mariano Rivera*. Those to whom I spoke lauded Rivera for his sportsmanship, classy comportment, and professional demeanor. To a man, everyone admired him as a human being, respected him as a competitor, and marveled at the high level of performance he sustained for a storied franchise in a pressure-cooker environment.

BN: Maybe Papelbon was spirited, instead of spiritual. I remember once seeing him in the Red Sox clubhouse messing around with a crossbow. I'm not sure what that was all about, but I don't need any more convincing. I never needed any convincing to begin with. It was a hopeless task. Your "overconfidence" was not misplaced. I'm ready to concede.

Winner: Mariano Rivera

THE ALL-TIME SIMULATION MATCH-UP

PRE-SERIES

Bill Nowlin: The all-time Red Sox team is suited up—some in flannels and some in polyester—ready to take on the all-time Yankees team in a best-of-seven series. It's a daunting proposition.

In the current century, the Red Sox have won four world championships (2004, 2007, 2013, and 2018) to the Yankees' one (2009). But we're talking about all-time teams, and so New York would seem to have much more than just an edge.

Through 2018, there have been 114 World Series. The New York Yankees have won 27 of them—almost a quarter of every World Series played. And they've won exactly three times as many as the Red Sox have, those 27 championships to the Red Sox nine.

We're talking about all the great Yankees over all the years of the franchise taking on the best of the Red Sox. Is it even a fair contest?

Well, it is what it is. And almost any given team can win any given game. But when the two teams with the most regular-season wins (the 1906 Cubs and the 2001 Mariners, who each won 116 games) hit the postseason, they both got stopped. The 1906 Cubs lost the World Series in six games. The 2001 Mariners didn't even make it to the World Series (the Yankees beat them, taking four out of five games in the ALCS). Dominating over the length of the regular season is clearly no guarantee of postseason success.

Even winning the first three games of an ALCS doesn't mean your team won't lose the next four. (I don't need to remind anyone when that occurred.)

Some of the individual player records in our lineups present a mixed bag. The Yankees' record in the 12 World Series in which Mickey Mantle played was only 7–5. Babe Ruth played for both teams and was on 10 World Series teams—his teams were 3–0 for the Red Sox and 4–3 for the Yankees. Wade Boggs, on the other hand, was 0–1 for Boston and 1–0 for New York. Looking at the starting lineups as a whole, various Yankees were on 42 Series-winning teams and 19 Series-losing teams (68.8 percent). Various Red Sox were on 14 Series-winning teams and six Series-losing teams for a nearly identical 70 percent.

All that said, in the big picture, the safer bet would seem to be on the Yankees.

But the Red Sox have recently been on a roll, and that counts for something in my mind—maybe not rationally, but since when has fandom been rational? Anyhow, plain and simple, I'm pulling for my team.

David Fischer: The festive red-white-and-blue decorative bunting has been draped from the upper deck of Yankee Stadium and Fenway Park, appropriate trimmings for a grand pageant pitting our all-time teams in a head-to-head best-of-seven series.

New York vs. Boston. The two cities are separated by roughly 200 miles, distinct Northeastern accents, and, at last count, 18 championship banners. Red Sox fans can talk about recent history all they want, but there are 27 reasons Yankees fans are confident their team will be triumphant.

The lineups tell a definitive story. My all-time Yankees team (true to its Bronx Bombers nickname) has out-homered Bill's all-time Red Sox lineup 3,570 to 2,410—a difference of Ruthian proportion in a short series. Yet if history repeats, Boston's heartbreak will come in the form of an unlikely power hitter becoming a folk hero by going deep, sending a bitter Red Sox nation to face a long, cold winter as the Yankees frolic off to another champagne-soaked celebration.

If I have one worry with a computer simulation it's that no matter how realistic and objective the programmer, a computer, after all, cannot feel human emotions like pressure or the will to hit in the clutch. A machine can't comprehend that for much of the twentieth century the Red Sox were a tortured outfit, a sad sack team that not only couldn't win a World Series but had frittered away big moments in tragic and inventive ways. At times it was just a matter of inches. (Had Bill Buckner just kept his mitt down …) Being a storied franchise doesn't necessarily mean it's because of winning. Sometimes, it's the losses that add to the legend. Unfortunately, there's no computer virus known as the Curse of the Bambino.

As to the science of in-game baseball strategy, I wonder if a computer program can account for the vagaries of randomness that camouflage the game's inner forces—the way a dominant pitcher like Whitey Ford got battered occasionally and a pipsqueak named Bucky Dent hit one of the most famous home runs ever.

In any case, the data has been entered, the fans are growing restless, and the public address announcer is about to introduce the starting line-ups. Whether its bragging rights for one week in April or the AL pennant and a trip to the World Series, the New York-Boston rivalry has been boiling for 116 years. The bickering, to borrow reporter Ian O'Connor's quip, make the Hatfield and McCoy hostilities look like Jack and Jill at a Sunday school picnic. Player-hating adds to the fun, especially the heck-ling that goes on during games … you know, the abuse that A-Rod always received at Fenway and the boos that Big Papi always heard at Yankee Stadium. So clear your lungs, ladies and gentlemen. It's going to be a heck of a series.

MANAGERS' PRE-SERIES PRESS CONFERENCE

Bill Nowlin: The Boston Red Sox are ready to go. I'm starting Pedro Martinez to open the series. He told me he doesn't believe in a damn curse. He said, "Wake up the damn Bambino and have me face him. Maybe I'll drill him in the ass, pardon me the word." Well, now he'll have his chance—but I don't want him giving the Babe a free pass and putting him on base. Tek and Pedro know each other well. They're set.

The relievers are all talking trash, laying one-dollar bets on whether they'll ever get used in this series.

Ted Williams, Bobby Doerr, and Joe Cronin are all ready to rock. Each of them only had one shot at a World Series and came up just short. They're "all out" for this one—the All-Time Rivalry Series, or whatever you want to call it. Some might say this is bigger than any World Series, and they're all chomping at the bit.

Yaz feels the same way. He had two shots at a Series win and saw both go down in flames in another couple of Game Sevens.

Hooper, Ortiz, and Speaker are all telling tales of championships of the past. And Boggs has been showing off his Yankees ring, telling them all he wants is one for the Red Sox, too, and then petitioning the Hall of Fame to update his plaque in Cooperstown.

The bench players are all a little subdued, wondering how it's come to pass that they're sitting on the bench for such a big game. Heck, three of them are Hall of Famers. They've read this book, though. And while they might not agree with being passed over, they understand their roles and are duly respectful of the selections made. After all, they just want the opportunity to prove their mettle.

The coaching staff is ready. So's the batboy! Let's get to the anthem and see who's throwing out the ceremonial first pitch.

Play Ball!

David Fischer: The New York Yankees are clean-shaven and loaded for bear. According to reports, in the clubhouse before game time, the players seemed a happy, carefree, almost cocky bunch.

The Babe and the Mick are in the trainer's room regaling one another with stories of the previous night's escapades, while Jeter and Gehrig are front and center at their lockers, answering reporters' questions while never actually saying anything. A-Rod tries to get the reporters' attention, exactly what Lazzeri hopes to avoid. Yogi and Godzilla are deep in a discussion about hitting, but nobody understands what is being said—perhaps not even them. Roy White is looking around, wondering how he got here.

Joe DiMaggio is stewing in the corner, chafed that he's not in the starting lineup, but the Yankee Clipper is eager to be called upon as a pinch-hitter in a clutch situation with runners on the basepaths.

To counteract the seven left-handed batters in the all-time Red Sox lineup, I'm giving the ball to Whitey Ford, no stranger to the occasion. Whitey was New York's World Series Game One pitcher on eight occasions, the only hurler to start four consecutive Series openers, a streak he reached twice. Ford and Berra have an easy rapport. "[Ford] is always around the plate. He's so easy to catch I could do it sitting in a rocking chair," said Yogi.

Teddy Ballgame can hit anybody, so we're going to do our best to neutralize Yaz and Ortiz. For his career, "Captain Carl" hit .283 with 52 homers and 163 RBIs in 329 games against the Yankees. Ortiz did some damage, too, hitting .303 with 53 homers and 171 RBIs in 243 games. I know you guys probably think that our pitchers have been told to pitch around them. I guess you'll all find out.

"The Chairman of the Board" will go as hard as he can for as long as he can, knowing that the underlying strength of this all-time Yankees team is its deep bullpen, with Mariano Rivera, Rich "Goose" Gossage, and Sparky Lyle combining for an even 1,200 saves between them. If the Yankees have the lead by the sixth inning, it should be game over.

Each team is loaded with talent. The prognosticators have said their piece, and now it's game on. Go Yanks!

EDITOR'S NOTE

The following simulation was supplied by Dave Koch and the good people at Action! PC Baseball.

In anticipation for this simulation, we supplied Action! PC Baseball with the following:

- Starting lineups for both all-time teams
- Pitching rotations and bullpens
- Potential bench players (to be used if deemed necessary)
- Team with home-field advantage (Red Sox won via coin toss)
- Stadiums being used[1]

Once that information was supplied, Action! PC Baseball ran a simulation for a seven-game series, which included play-by-play, box scores, and stats for each game. The additional full series stats that appear at the end were compiled internally so that advanced statistics could be supplied.

Once we at Sports Publishing received these simulations, the authors were sent one game at a time to avoid any possible spoilers. Once we received their postgame notes from the first game, they would receive the simulation for the second game, and so on. Aside from putting together the rosters, location, and home-field advantage, everything to follow was left up to the simulation. (In other words, the computer alone managed both teams from the first pitch of Game One through the end of the series.)

---

1 The authors agreed that, rather than using the current stadiums and dimensions, the games be played in 1949. We used the dimensions of Yankee Stadium and Fenway Park as they were in that year.

All-Time Yankees

Starting Lineup
SS: Derek Jeter
CF: Mickey Mantle
RF: Babe Ruth
1B: Lou Gehrig
3B: Alex Rodriguez
C: Yogi Berra
DH: Hideki Matsui
2B: Tony Lazzeri
LF: Roy White

Pitchers
Starting RHP: Red Ruffing
Starting LHP: Whitey Ford
Second RHP: Allie Reynolds
Second LHP: Andy Pettitte
Main Reliever: Dellin Betances
Secondary Reliever: Rich "Goose" Gossage
Secondary Reliever: Sparky Lyle
Closer: Mariano Rivera

Bench
C: Jorge Posada
INF: Robinson Cano
INF: Phil Rizzuto
OF: Joe DiMaggio
OF: Dave Winfield
DH: Don Baylor

All-Time Red Sox

Starting Lineup
3B: Wade Boggs
CF: Tris Speaker
LF: Ted Williams
DH: David Ortiz
1B: Carl Yastrzemski
2B: Bobby Doerr
SS: Joe Cronin
RF: Harry Hooper
C: Jason Varitek

Pitchers
Starting RHP: Pedro Martinez
Starting LHP: Jon Lester
Second RHP: Roger Clemens
Second LHP: Lefty Grove
Main Reliever: Bob Stanley
Secondary Reliever: Mike Timlin
Secondary Reliever: Dick Radatz
Closer: Jonathan Papelbon

Bench
C: Carlton Fisk
INF: Jimmie Foxx
INF: Nomar Garciaparra
OF: Jim Rice
OF: Jackie Jensen
DH: Manny Ramirez

All-Time Boston Red Sox vs. All-Time New York Yankees
Game One, Series Tied, 0–0
Pedro Martinez (219–100, 2.93 ERA) vs. Red Ruffing (273–225, 3.80 ERA)
Time 2:20, 68°, Clear, Threatening, Wind: 11 MPH Right to Left

```
Inn Out B-S  On  NYY-Bos  Result
                          1-New York
1   0   0-2  -   0-0      Jeter grounded to short, 1 out
1   1   2-2  -   0-0      Mantle struck out, 2 out
1   2   0-2  -   0-0      Ruth grounded to third, 3 out
-------------------------------------------------------------------
                          1-Boston
1   0   2-1  -   0-0      Boggs flied to deep center, 1 out
1   1   1-2  -   0-0      Speaker lined a double to right center
1   1   2-1  2   0-0      Williams grounded to third, Speaker to 3rd,
                              2 out
1   2   2-1  3   0-0      Ortiz flied to shallow right, 3 out
-------------------------------------------------------------------
                          2-New York
2   0   1-2  -   0-0      Gehrig singled to right center
2   0   0-2  1   0-0      Rodriguez struck out, 1 out
2   1   1-0  1   0-0      Berra grounded to short, Gehrig to 2nd, 2 out
2   2   2-0  2   0-0      Matsui flied deep down the right field line,
                              3 out
-------------------------------------------------------------------
                          2-Boston
2   0   0-1  -   0-0      Yastrzemski flied to shallow left center,
                              1 out
2   1   0-0  -   0-0      Doerr flied to deep right center, 2 out
2   2   0-2  -   0-0      Cronin grounded to third, 3 out
-------------------------------------------------------------------
                          3-New York
3   0   1-1  -   0-0      Lazzeri flied deep down the left field line,
                              1 out
3   1   0-2  -   0-0      White doubled to left center
3   1   1-2  2   0-0      Jeter struck out, 2 out
3   2   1-2  2   0-0      Mantle struck out, 3 out
-------------------------------------------------------------------
                          3-Boston
3   0   0-1  -   0-0      Hooper hit a solo homer to right center,
                              Boston 1 New York 0
3   0   1-2  -   0-1      Varitek grounded to third, 1 out
3   1   0-2  -   0-1      Boggs singled on the infield
3   1   1-1  1   0-1      Speaker lined a single between first
                              and second, Boggs to 2nd
3   1   2-0  12  0-1      Williams singled up the middle, Boggs to 3rd,
                              Speaker to 2nd
3   1   2-1  123 0-1      Ortiz flied deep down the right field line,
                              sacrifice, Boggs scored, 2 out,
                              Boston 2 New York 0
3   2   2-1  12  0-2      Yastrzemski popped to second, 3 out
-------------------------------------------------------------------
                          4-New York
4   0   0-2  -   0-2      Ruth struck out, 1 out
4   1   1-2  -   0-2      Gehrig lined a double down the
                              right field line
4   1   2-2  2   0-2      Rodriguez struck out, 2 out
4   2   0-1  2   0-2      Berra singled between third and short,
                              Gehrig scored, Boston 2 New York 1
4   2   2-0  1   1-2      Matsui flied to deep left center, 3 out
-------------------------------------------------------------------
```

```
Inn Out B-S  On  NYY-Bos  Result
                           4-Boston
 4   0  0-1  -    1-2      Doerr grounded to second, 1 out
 4   1  1-1  -    1-2      Cronin flied to deep left, 2 out
 4   2  1-2  -    1-2      Hooper singled on the infield
 4   2  0-0  1    1-2      Varitek grounded to third, forcing Hooper
                             at second, 3 out
-------------------------------------------------------------------
                           5-New York
 5   0  3-2  -    1-2      Lazzeri struck out, 1 out
 5   1  2-2  -    1-2      White grounded to short, 2 out
 5   2  3-2  -    1-2      Jeter grounded to second, 3 out
-------------------------------------------------------------------
                           5-Boston
 5   0  2-0  -    1-2      Boggs grounded a single between third
                             and short
 5   0  0-2  1    1-2      Speaker struck out, 1 out
 5   1  1-2  1    1-2      Williams doubled off the wall down the
                             right field line, Boggs out at home,
                             Williams to 3rd, 2 out
 5   2  3-1  3    1-2      Ortiz intentionally walked
 5   2  0-0  13   1-2      Yastrzemski doubled to left center,
                             Williams scored, Ortiz to 3rd,
                             Boston 3 New York 1
 5   2  2-0  23   1-3      Doerr flied deep down the left field line,
                             3 out
-------------------------------------------------------------------
                           6-New York
 6   0  1-0  -    1-3      Mantle doubled down the right field line
 6   0  0-0  2    1-3      Mantle caught stealing 3rd, 1 out
 6   1  3-0  -    1-3      Ruth walked
 6   1  1-2  1    1-3      Gehrig struck out, 2 out
 6   2  1-0  1    1-3      Rodriguez flied to right center, 3 out
-------------------------------------------------------------------
                           6-Boston
 6   0  2-0  -    1-3      Cronin lined to short, 1 out
 6   1  1-0  -    1-3      Hooper flied to deep left center, 2 out
 6   2  1-1  -    1-3      Varitek grounded to second, 3 out
-------------------------------------------------------------------
                           7-New York
 7   0  0-0  -    1-3      Berra lined to third, 1 out
 7   1  1-2  -    1-3      Matsui hit a solo homer down the
                             right field line, Boston 3 New York 2
 7   1  2-1  -    2-3      Lazzeri grounded to short, 2 out
 7   2  3-2  -    2-3      White grounded to first, 3 out
-------------------------------------------------------------------
```

```
Inn Out B-S  On  NYY-Bos  Result
                          7-Boston
7   0   2-1  -   2-3      Boggs lined a single to right center
7   0   2-0  1   2-3      Speaker doubled off the wall in right center,
                              Boggs to 3rd
7   0   1-0  23  2-3      Williams grounded to first, 1 out
7   1   1-2  23  2-3      Ortiz struck out, 2 out
7   2   3-2  23  2-3      Yastrzemski intentionally walked
7   2   0-2  123 2-3      Doerr lined a single between third and short,
                              Boggs scored, Speaker scored,
                              Yastrzemski to 2nd, Boston 5 New York 2
7   2   1-1  12  2-5      Cronin grounded to third, 3 out
-----------------------------------------------------------------------
                          8-New York
8   0   1-1  -   2-5      Jeter grounded to second, 1 out
                          >Timlin pitching
8   1   0-0  -   2-5      Mantle doubled off the wall down the
                              right field line
8   1   1-2  2   2-5      Ruth lined a double to left center,
                              Mantle scored, Boston 5 New York 3
8   1   0-1  2   3-5      Gehrig flied to deep center, Ruth to 3rd,
                              2 out
                          >Radatz pitching
8   2   2-1  3   3-5      Rodriguez flied to shallow right center,
                              3 out
-----------------------------------------------------------------------
                          8-Boston
8   0   0-0  -   3-5      Hooper bunted to the catcher, 1 out
8   1   1-1  -   3-5      Varitek flied to shallow right center, 2 out
8   2   0-2  -   3-5      Boggs grounded to first, 3 out
-----------------------------------------------------------------------
                          9-New York
                          >Papelbon pitching
9   0   0-1  -   3-5      Berra flied to shallow right center, 1 out
9   1   3-1  -   3-5      Matsui walked
9   1   0-2  1   3-5      Lazzeri flied to left center, 2 out
9   2   2-0  1   3-5      White grounded to second, 3 out
```

Game One	1	2	3	4	5	6	7	8	9	R	H	E
All-Time New York Yankees	0	0	0	1	0	0	1	1	0	3	8	0
All-Time Boston Red Sox	0	0	2	0	1	0	2	0	-	5	12	0

New York	AB	R	H	RBI	BB	K	LOB	PO	A	E
Jeter, SS	4	0	0	0	0	1	0	1	0	0
Mantle, CF	4	1	2	0	0	2	0	5	0	0
Ruth, RF	3	0	1	1	1	1	1	2	1	0
Gehrig, 1B	4	1	2	0	0	1	0	8	0	0
Rodriguez, 3B	1	0	0	0	0	2	2	0	5	0
Berra, C	4	0	1	1	0	0	0	3	1	0
Matsui, DH	3	1	1	1	1	0	2	0	0	0
Lazzeri, 2B	4	0	0	0	0	1	0	3	3	0
White, LF	4	0	1	0	0	0	1	2	0	0
	34	3	8	3	2	8	6	24	10	0

New York		IP	H	R	ER	HR	BB	K	Pit	S	B	ERA	BF
Ruffing	L(0-1)	8.0	12	5	5	1	2	2	126	84	42	5.63	37
		8.0	12	5	5	1	2	2	126	84	42	5.63	37

Boston	AB	R	H	RBI	BB	K	LOB	PO	A	E
Boggs, 3B	5	2	3	0	0	0	0	2	1	0
Speaker, CF	4	1	3	0	0	1	0	5	0	0
Williams, LF	4	1	2	0	0	0	0	1	0	0
Ortiz, DH	3	0	0	1	1	1	1	0	0	0
Yastrzemski, 1B	3	0	1	1	1	0	2	9	0	0
Doerr, 2B	4	0	1	2	0	0	2	0	3	0
Cronin, SS	4	0	0	0	0	0	2	0	4	0
Hooper, RF	4	1	2	1	0	0	0	2	0	0
Varitek, C	4	0	0	0	0	0	1	8	1	0
	35	5	12	5	2	2	8	27	9	0

Boston		IP	H	R	ER	HR	BB	K	Pit	S	B	ERA	BF
Martinez	W(1-0)	7.1	6	2	2	1	1	8	114	80	34	2.45	28
Timlin		0.1	2	1	1	0	0	0	7	6	1	27.00	3
Radatz		0.1	0	0	0	0	0	0	4	2	2	0.00	1
Papelbon	S(1)	1.0	0	0	0	0	1	0	13	7	6	0.00	4
		9.0	8	3	3	1	2	8	138	95	43	3.00	36

GAME ONE POSTGAME COMMENTS

Red Sox Manager

Pedro at Fenway Park—a good, solid job. He's talked about drilling the Bambino in the ass, but got Ruth on a grounder the first time up and then struck him out in the top of the fourth. Ruth worked a walk in the sixth. I was worried about giving him a fourth shot at Ruth in the eighth, so after Pedro got Jeter to ground out and already at 114 pitches, I was glad the computer simulation brought in Timlin.

Ruffing got roughed up; it's not often a team gets 12 hits off the man. I was happy when Hooper put the first run on the board with a home run in the bottom of the third. When The Kid singled, we had the bases loaded with just one out. They got lucky; Ortiz just missed a grand slam. Still, 2–0 looked good.

Berra got one for the Yanks, but then Ted and Yaz put together a pair of doubles for another run. We needed it; Matsui homered in the seventh, making it a one-run game again. A single and double but then Ruffing buckled down and got both Ted and Papi. Praise be to Yaz for a big two-run seventh, the hit that made the difference.

Timlin will be available if we need him tomorrow, as he only threw seven pitches. A double by Mantle and then Ruth got a little revenge with a double of his own, and another run. I don't mind saying my heart skipped a beat when Gehrig flied out deep, and glad the computers brought in the Monster. Radatz got A-Rod, and then Pap closed out the ninth.

Yankees Manager

I was expecting Whitey Ford to start the opener, but if you told me Red Ruffing would pitch a complete game in Fenway Park, I'd have been feeling pretty good about our chances to win Game One. Alas, an eight-inning complete game is never good news for the visiting team. Chalk it up to bad luck. I lost each of the coin flips to determine the home team for both series. The adage "tails never fails" proved fallible. But this all-time simulation is being played in our respective ballparks as they stood in 1949, which was a pretty good year to be a Yankees fan—and a heart-breaking season for Red Sox devotees. So, let's hope history repeats. Besides, one game does not make a series.

Several situations jump out as to why the Yankees lost the series opener. Ruffing struggled through two innings—the third and the seventh—in which he faced seven batters and allowed two runs in each frame. That seemed to gas him. The three batters at the top of the Red Sox lineup—Wade Boggs, Tris Speaker, and Ted Williams—combined to collect eight hits in 13 at-bats and score four of Boston's five runs. My team will need to do a better job containing these table setters if this series is going to be competitive. The other run was a Harry Hooper solo homer that, according to the computer, traveled over 400 feet. Welcome to the era of the live ball, Harry.

Another factor contributing to the loss was a boneheaded mistake by Mickey Mantle in the top of the sixth with the Yanks trailing, 3–1. The Mick led off with a double but was immediately thrown out attempting to steal third base with Babe Ruth batting, to be followed by Lou Gehrig and Alex Rodriguez. It was a heinous mental mistake by Mantle to make the first out at third, especially with his team down by two runs and with over 1,900 career home runs coming to bat.

On the bright side, Hideki Matsui still owns Pedro Martinez, no matter the year, no matter the uniform. Matsui homered off Pedro in the seventh and nearly hit another earlier in the game when he flew out to deep left-center with a man aboard in the fourth. Perhaps Pedro should start calling Godzilla "*his* daddy."

My team is going to shake off this loss and come back tomorrow to seek their revenge.

All-Time Boston Red Sox vs. All-Time New York Yankees
Game Two, Boston Leads, 1–0
Jon Lester (177–98, 3.50 ERA) vs. Whitey Ford (236–106, 2.75 ERA)
Time 3:03, 65°, Wind: 8 MPH Out to LF

```
Inn Out B-S  On   NYY-Bos  Result
                           1-New York
 1   0  3-2  -    0-0      Jeter grounded to second, 1 out
 1   1  2-0  -    0-0      Mantle flied to very deep center, 2 out
 1   2  1-1  -    0-0      Ruth lined a single over short
 1   2  1-2  1    0-0      Gehrig lined a double to right center,
                              Ruth to 3rd
 1   2  3-2  23   0-0      Rodriguez walked
 1   2  1-1  123  0-0      Berra flied to right center, 3 out
---------------------------------------------------------------
                           1-Boston
 1   0  0-1  -    0-0      Boggs flied to deep left center, 1 out
 1   1  2-2  -    0-0      Speaker grounded a single up the middle
 1   1  1-1  1    0-0      Williams flied to deep right center, 2 out
 1   2  0-0  1    0-0      Ortiz flied to shallow right, 3 out
---------------------------------------------------------------
                           2-New York
 2   0  2-2  -    0-0      Matsui singled to right
 2   0  1-2  1    0-0      Lazzeri struck out, 1 out
 2   1  0-2  1    0-0      White flied to deep right center, 2 out
 2   2  0-1  1    0-0      Jeter flied to shallow left center, 3 out
---------------------------------------------------------------
                           2-Boston
 2   0  0-0  -    0-0      Yastrzemski tripled to right center
 2   0  3-2  3    0-0      Doerr walked
 2   0  2-2  13   0-0      **Cronin doubled off the wall down the
                              third base line, Yastrzemski scored,
                              Doerr to 3rd, Boston 1 New York 0**
 2   0  0-0  23   0-1      **Hooper flied to deep right center, sacrifice,
                              Doerr scored, Cronin to 3rd, 1 out,
                              Boston 2 New York 0**
 2   1  0-2  3    0-2      **Varitek hit a two run homer to left center,
                              Boston 4 New York 0**
 2   1  0-0  -    0-4      Boggs grounded to the pitcher, 2 out
 2   2  1-0  -    0-4      Speaker singled to right
 2   2  1-1  1    0-4      Williams lined a single up the middle,
                              Speaker to 3rd
 2   2  1-1  13   0-4      Ortiz flied to right, 3 out
---------------------------------------------------------------
                           3-New York
 3   0  3-0  -    0-4      Mantle grounded to short, 1 out
 3   1  0-2  -    0-4      Ruth lined to second, 2 out
 3   2  0-2  -    0-4      Gehrig popped to first, 3 out
---------------------------------------------------------------
                           3-Boston
 3   0  0-1  -    0-4      Yastrzemski flied to deep right center, 1 out
 3   1  3-2  -    0-4      Doerr struck out, 2 out
 3   2  2-2  -    0-4      Cronin doubled off the wall down the
                              right field line
 3   2  1-2  2    0-4      Hooper flied to deep center, 3 out
---------------------------------------------------------------
```

```
Inn Out B-S  On  NYY-Bos  Result
                          4-New York
 4   0  2-0  -    0-4     Rodriguez grounded to the pitcher, 1 out
 4   1  0-2  -    0-4     Berra hit a solo homer down the
                            right field line, Boston 4 New York 1
 4   1  1-2  -    1-4     Matsui lined a single to center
 4   1  3-1  1    1-4     Lazzeri flied to deep center, 2 out
 4   2  1-1  1    1-4     White doubled to left center, Matsui to 3rd
 4   2  1-1  23   1-4     Jeter lined to short, 3 out
---------------------------------------------------------------------
                          4-Boston
 4   0  1-0  -    1-4     Varitek grounded to short, 1 out
 4   1  2-0  -    1-4     Boggs grounded to the pitcher, 2 out
 4   2  3-2  -    1-4     Speaker walked
 4   2  3-2  1    1-4     Williams walked, Speaker to 2nd
 4   2  0-1  12   1-4     Ortiz popped to first, 3 out
---------------------------------------------------------------------
                          5-New York
 5   0  3-2  -    1-4     Mantle walked
 5   0  0-1  1    1-4     Ruth hit a two run homer to right center,
                            Boston 4 New York 3
 5   0  0-2  -    3-4     Gehrig struck out, out at 1st, 1 out
 5   1  2-2  -    3-4     Rodriguez struck out, 2 out
 5   2  3-2  -    3-4     Berra grounded a single up the middle
 5   2  1-2  1    3-4     Matsui grounded a single between third
                            and short, Berra to 3rd
 5   2  2-0  13   3-4     Lazzeri lined to right, 3 out
---------------------------------------------------------------------
                          5-Boston
 5   0  1-1  -    3-4     Yastrzemski flied to deep left center, 1 out
 5   1  2-0  -    3-4     Doerr doubled to left center
 5   1  0-1  2    3-4     Cronin grounded to second, Doerr to 3rd,
                            2 out
 5   2  2-0  3    3-4     Hooper flied to deep center, 3 out
---------------------------------------------------------------------
                          6-New York
                          >Stanley pitching
 6   0  2-2  -    3-4     White lined to right, 1 out
 6   1  1-0  -    3-4     Jeter lined a single up the middle
 6   1  0-0  1    3-4     Jeter caught stealing 2nd, 2 out
 6   2  0-1  -    3-4     Mantle singled to right center
 6   2  0-2  1    3-4     Ruth hit a two run homer down the
                            right field line, New York 5 Boston 4
 6   2  1-2  -    5-4     Gehrig flied to deep right center, 3 out
---------------------------------------------------------------------
                          6-Boston
 6   0  0-0  -    5-4     Varitek doubled to right center
 6   0  1-2  2    5-4     Boggs lined a single between third and short,
                            Varitek scored, New York 5 Boston 5
 6   0  0-1  1    5-5     Speaker bunted out to first, Boggs to 2nd,
                            sacrifice, 1 out
 6   1  0-2  2    5-5     Williams doubled to right center,
                            Boggs scored, Boston 6 New York 5
 6   1  2-2  2    5-6     Ortiz struck out, 2 out
 6   2  0-2  2    5-6     Yastrzemski flied to very deep right center,
                            3 out
---------------------------------------------------------------------
```

```
Inn Out B-S  On  NYY-Bos  Result
                          7-New York
  7   0  0-2  -    5-6    Rodriguez lined to third, 1 out
  7   1  3-1  -    5-6    Berra grounded a single between third
                            and short
  7   1  2-2  1    5-6    Matsui flied down the left field line, 2 out
  7   2  3-2  1    5-6    Lazzeri lined to second, 3 out
---------------------------------------------------------------------
                          7-Boston
  7   0  3-2  -    5-6    Doerr doubled down the left field line
  7   0  0-1  2    5-6    Cronin grounded to third, 1 out
  7   1  0-0  2    5-6    Hooper flied to very deep left center,
                            Doerr to 3rd, 2 out
  7   2  1-2  3    5-6    Varitek singled on the infield, Doerr scored,
                            Boston 7 New York 5
                          >Betances pitching
  7   2  0-2  1    5-7    Boggs grounded to second, 3 out
---------------------------------------------------------------------
                          8-New York
                          >Radatz pitching
  8   0  0-2  -    5-7    White hit by pitch
  8   0  1-0  1    5-7    Jeter struck out, 1 out
  8   1  2-2  1    5-7    Mantle flied to deep right, 2 out
                          >Timlin pitching
  8   2  3-2  1    5-7    Ruth walked, White to 2nd
                          >Papelbon pitching
  8   2  0-2  12   5-7    Gehrig lined to short, 3 out
---------------------------------------------------------------------
                          8-Boston
  8   0  2-1  -    5-7    Speaker flied to deep right, 1 out
  8   1  2-2  -    5-7    Williams struck out, 2 out
  8   2  0-2  -    5-7    Ortiz struck out, 3 out
---------------------------------------------------------------------
                          9-New York
  9   0  0-0  -    5-7    Rodriguez lined to left, 1 out
  9   1  1-2  -    5-7    Berra doubled off the wall down the
                            third base line
  9   1  3-2  2    5-7    Matsui struck out, 2 out
  9   2  2-1  2    5-7    Lazzeri flied deep down the right field line,
                            3 out
```

Game Two	1	2	3	4	5	6	7	8	9	R	H	E
All-Time New York Yankees	0	0	0	1	2	2	0	0	0	5	14	0
All-Time Boston Red Sox	0	4	0	0	0	2	1	0	-	7	13	0

New York	AB	R	H	RBI	BB	K	LOB	PO	A	E
Jeter, SS	5	0	1	0	0	1	3	0	1	0
Mantle, CF	4	2	1	0	1	0	0	7	0	0
Ruth, RF	4	2	3	4	1	0	0	5	0	0
Gehrig, 1B	5	0	1	0	0	1	2	7	1	0
Rodriguez, 3B	4	0	0	0	1	1	0	0	1	0
Berra, C	5	1	4	1	0	0	3	4	0	0
Matsui, DH	5	0	3	0	0	1	0	0	0	0
Lazzeri, 2B	5	0	0	0	0	1	5	1	2	0
White, LF	3	0	1	0	0	0	0	0	0	0
	40	5	14	5	3	5	13	24	7	0

New York		IP	H	R	ER	HR	BB	K	Pit	S	B	ERA	BF
Ford	L(0-1)	6.2	13	7	7	1	3	2	126	85	41	9.45	36
Betances		1.1	0	0	0	0	0	2	19	15	4	0.00	4
		8.0	13	7	7	1	3	4	145	100	45	6.75	40

Boston	AB	R	H	RBI	BB	K	LOB	PO	A	E
Boggs, 3B	5	1	1	1	0	0	1	1	0	0
Speaker, CF	3	0	2	0	1	0	0	4	0	0
Williams, LF	4	0	2	1	1	1	0	3	0	0
Ortiz, DH	5	0	0	0	0	2	5	0	0	0
Yastrzemski, 1B	4	1	1	0	0	0	1	5	0	0
Doerr, 2B	3	2	2	0	1	1	0	2	1	0
Cronin, SS	4	1	2	1	0	0	0	3	1	0
Hooper, RF	4	0	0	1	0	0	3	5	0	0
Varitek, C	4	2	3	3	0	0	0	4	2	0
	36	7	13	7	3	4	10	27	5	0

Boston		IP	H	R	ER	HR	BB	K	Pit	S	B	ERA	BF
Lester		5.0	9	3	3	2	2	3	110	72	38	5.40	26
Stanley	W(1-0)	2.0	4	2	2	1	0	0	41	29	12	9.00	9
Radatz		0.2	0	0	0	0	0	1	14	11	3	0.00	3
Timlin		0.0	0	0	0	0	1	0	7	3	4	27.00	1
Papelbon	S(2)	1.1	1	0	0	0	0	1	24	18	6	0.00	5
		9.0	14	5	5	3	3	5	196	133	63	4.00	44

GAME TWO POSTGAME COMMENTS

Red Sox Manager

This was a battle between two determined and time-tested teams; it could well have gone either way. Frankly, it was a shock to see Whitey get hit so hard. Only once in his illustrious career—I had our stats guy look it up just now, and it was back in '63—did he ever get hammered for more earned runs in a ballgame.

How about 'Tek? Before the game, Cronin and Doerr were talking with Speaker and Hooper, reminding them there had never been seats on the left-field wall in their day, either. Nor in Yaz's day—and then Tek puts one up in the Monster seats in the second inning. Cronin had already doubled in Yaz—that was *some* triple, wasn't it?

Big Papi still hasn't found his stroke. He's struggling, but he's going to put in some extra time on video and maybe a little extra BP.

Them Yankees know how to work the count. They got Lester up over 100 pitches in just five innings. He got a second wind there, though, after Ruth took him deep. Striking out Gehrig and A-Rod back-to-back—how often are you ever going to see a pitcher do that? I was so glad to see Hooper corral that ball that Lazzeri hit to right for the game's last out. That could have been the ballgame if it had gotten into the corner there.

Good to see Boggsie single in Varitek in the sixth, and then Speaker laid down a perfect bunt, setting things up for Ted to come through.

The Babe got to Steamer, just like he had Lester, but the back of the bullpen came through fine. See you in the City.

Yankees Manager

This game was decided in favor of the Red Sox because they were the team to capitalize on their early scoring opportunities. The Yankees loaded the bases in the first but failed to score, and an inning later they were facing a nearly insurmountable four-run deficit. I did say "nearly." A home run by Berra and a pair of two-run shots by the Babe put the Yanks back in front, 5–4, entering the bottom of the sixth. At this point, Whitey Ford should have been given the hook, and had Casey Stengel been orchestrating the simulation instead of a computer, I can guarantee that Ford would be hitting the showers as the pitcher of record on the winning side of the ledger. As it turned out, the push-button manager indeed did stay too long with Ford, and my team's ace spit the bit by allowing three more runs for a total of seven—all earned. Ford was hit hard; he gave up 13 hits, with eight going for extra bases.

Ford wasn't the only disappointment of the series. Lazzeri and A-Rod are also performing miserably. In the first two games at Fenway, the two have combined for zero hits in 17 at-bats. Their ineptitude has spiked many a potential rally, and has rendered the hot hitting of Matsui and Berra (nine hits in 17 at-bats) to be an almost meaningless afterthought.

I'm worried, yet hopeful and optimistic my team can turn things around once play begins inside the Stadium of mystique and aura. But it'll be a tough row to hoe. My team will need to win four out of five. We better have Bucky Dent on hand to throw out the ceremonial first pitch for Game Three in the Bronx.

All-Time Boston Red Sox @ All-Time New York Yankees
Game Three, Boston Leads, 2–0
Roger Clemens (354–184, 3.12 ERA) vs.
Allie Reynolds (182–107, 3.30 ERA)
Time 4:14, 65°, Wind: 17 MPH Right to Left

Inn	Out	B-S	On	Bos-NYY	Result
					1-Boston
1	0	0-2	-	0-0	Boggs doubled to right center
1	0	0-2	2	0-0	Speaker lined a single up the middle, Boggs to 3rd
1	0	3-2	13	0-0	Williams walked, Speaker to 2nd
1	0	0-1	123	0-0	**Ortiz lined to right, sacrifice, Boggs scored, 1 out, Boston 1 New York 0**
1	1	0-1	12	1-0	**Yastrzemski lined a single to left, Speaker scored, Williams to 3rd, Boston 2 New York 0**
1	1	1-1	13	2-0	**Doerr singled to center, Williams scored, Yastrzemski to 2nd, Boston 3 New York 0**
1	1	0-1	12	3-0	Cronin flied to right center, 2 out
1	2	3-2	12	3-0	Hooper flied to deep center, 3 out
					1-New York
1	0	0-2	-	3-0	**Jeter hit a solo homer to left, Boston 3 New York 1**
1	0	2-2	-	3-1	Mantle struck out, 1 out
1	1	3-1	-	3-1	Ruth walked
1	1	2-2	1	3-1	**Gehrig doubled off the wall in right, Ruth scored, Boston 3 New York 2**
1	1	3-2	2	3-2	Rodriguez walked
1	1	0-0	12	3-2	Berra lined to second, 2 out
1	2	2-2	12	3-2	Matsui singled on the infield, Gehrig to 3rd, Rodriguez to 2nd
1	2	3-2	123	3-2	Lazzeri struck out, 3 out
					2-Boston
2	0	3-1	-	3-2	Varitek walked
2	0	1-0	1	3-2	Varitek stole 2nd, to third on error
2	0	2-0	3	3-2	**Boggs flied to right, sacrifice, Varitek scored, 1 out, Boston 4 New York 2**
2	1	0-0	-	4-2	Speaker grounded to second, 2 out
2	2	0-1	-	4-2	Williams flied to left center, 3 out
					2-New York
2	0	2-0	-	4-2	White flied to shallow right center, 1 out
2	1	0-2	-	4-2	Jeter flied to shallow left, safe at 2nd on an error, Jeter to 2nd
2	1	0-2	2	4-2	Mantle struck out, 2 out
2	2	2-2	2	4-2	Ruth struck out, 3 out
					3-Boston
3	0	1-2	-	4-2	Ortiz struck out, 1 out
3	1	1-2	-	4-2	Yastrzemski struck out, 2 out
3	2	1-1	-	4-2	Doerr grounded a single up the middle
3	2	0-1	1	4-2	Cronin popped to short, 3 out

```
Inn Out B-S  On  NYY-Bos  Result
                          3-New York
 3   0  2-1  -    4-2     Gehrig hit a solo homer to right center,
                              Boston 4 New York 3
 3   0  1-0  -    4-3     Rodriguez popped to short, 1 out
 3   1  2-0  -    4-3     Berra flied down the right field line, 2 out
 3   2  1-2  -    4-3     Matsui struck out, 3 out
---------------------------------------------------------------------
                          4-Boston
 4   0  0-0  -    4-3     Hooper grounded to second, 1 out
 4   1  3-1  -    4-3     Varitek walked
 4   1  1-1  1    4-3     Boggs lined a single between first
                              and second, Varitek to 2nd
 4   1  0-1  12   4-3     Speaker bunted out to the catcher,
                              Varitek to 3rd, Boggs to 2nd,
                              sacrifice, 2 out
 4   2  1-2  23   4-3     Williams flied deep down the
                              right field line, 3 out
---------------------------------------------------------------------
                          4-New York
 4   0  0-1  -    4-3     Lazzeri flied to very deep left, 1 out
 4   1  0-1  -    4-3     White bunted for a single
 4   1  2-0  1    4-3     Jeter lined a single to right, White to 3rd
 4   1  1-2  13   4-3     Mantle flied deep down the right field line,
                              sacrifice, White scored, 2 out,
                              Boston 4 New York 4
 4   2  2-1  1    4-4     Ruth flied to very deep right center, 3 out
---------------------------------------------------------------------
                          5-Boston
 5   0  2-2  -    4-4     Ortiz struck out, 1 out
 5   1  2-0  -    4-4     Yastrzemski flied to deep right center, 2 out
 5   2  0-2  -    4-4     Doerr struck out, 3 out
---------------------------------------------------------------------
                          5-New York
 5   0  3-1  -    4-4     Gehrig walked
 5   0  1-1  1    4-4     Rodriguez hit a two run homer down the
                              left field line, New York 6 Boston 4
 5   0  1-1  -    4-6     Berra grounded a single between first
                              and second
 5   0  3-2  1    4-6     Matsui struck out, 1 out
 5   1  1-2  1    4-6     Lazzeri lined to second, 2 out
 5   2  3-2  1    4-6     White flied to deep left center, 3 out
---------------------------------------------------------------------
```

```
Inn Out B-S   On  NYY-Bos  Result
                           6-Boston
 6   0  1-2   -    4-6     Cronin grounded a single between third
                             and short
 6   0  1-0   1    4-6     Hooper grounded a single between third
                             and short, Cronin to 3rd
 6   0  3-2   13   4-6     Varitek struck out, 1 out
 6   1  2-1   13   4-6     Boggs flied to very deep right center,
                             sacrifice, Cronin scored, 2 out,
                             New York 6 Boston 5
 6   2  1-0   1    5-6     Speaker hit a two run homer down the
                             right field line, Boston 7 New York 6
 6   2  0-2   -    7-6     Williams grounded a single between first
                             and second
 6   2  0-2   1    7-6     Ortiz flied to deep right center, 3 out
---------------------------------------------------------------------
                           6-New York
 6   0  2-1   -    7-6     Jeter grounded to short, 1 out
                           >Stanley pitching
 6   1  0-1   -    7-6     Mantle doubled to right center
 6   1  3-0   2    7-6     Ruth walked
 6   1  3-2   12   7-6     Gehrig grounded to third, safe on
                             throwing error, Ruth to 3rd, 2 out
 6   2  1-2   13   7-6     Rodriguez flied to deep left center, 3 out
---------------------------------------------------------------------
                           7-Boston
 7   0  1-1   -    7-6     Yastrzemski lined a single up the middle
 7   0  0-0   1    7-6     Doerr bunted out to first, Yastrzemski
                             to 2nd, sacrifice, 1 out
 7   1  1-2   2    7-6     Cronin struck out, 2 out
 7   2  1-1   2    7-6     Hooper intentionally walked
 7   2  1-0   12   7-6     Varitek lined a single to right center,
                             Yastrzemski scored, Hooper to 3rd,
                             Boston 8 New York 6
                           >Betances pitching
 7   2  2-2   13   8-6     Wild pitch, Hooper scored, Varitek to 2nd,
                             Boston 9 New York 6
 7   2  3-2   2    9-6     Boggs walked
 7   2  1-2   12   9-6     Speaker flied deep down the right field line,
                             3 out
---------------------------------------------------------------------
                           7-New York
 7   0  1-2   -    9-6     Berra hit a solo homer down the
                             right field line, Boston 9 New York 7
 7   0  2-0   -    9-7     Matsui grounded to first, 1 out
 7   1  0-1   -    9-7     Lazzeri flied to deep right, 2 out
 7   2  3-2   -    9-7     White grounded to short, 3 out
---------------------------------------------------------------------
                           8-Boston
 8   0  0-0   -    9-7     Williams grounded to second, 1 out
 8   1  1-2   -    9-7     Ortiz lined to right, 2 out
 8   2  1-2   -    9-7     Yastrzemski struck out, 3 out
---------------------------------------------------------------------
```

```
Inn Out B-S  On  NYY-Bos  Result
                          8-New York
                          >Radatz pitching
 8   0  0-1  -      9-7   Jeter flied to deep right, 1 out
 8   1  2-1  -      9-7   Mantle flied to shallow right center, 2 out
                          >Timlin pitching
 8   2  1-1  -      9-7   Ruth hit a solo homer to left,
                             Boston 9 New York 8
                          >Papelbon pitching
 8   2  2-1  -      9-8   Gehrig doubled off the wall in right
 8   2  2-2  2      9-8   Rodriguez flied deep down the
                             left field line, 3 out
----------------------------------------------------------------------
                          9-Boston
 9   0  1-1  -      9-8   Doerr lined to center, 1 out
 9   1  2-2  -      9-8   Cronin struck out, 2 out
 9   2  3-2  -      9-8   Hooper flied to deep center, 3 out
----------------------------------------------------------------------
                          9-New York
 9   0  1-2  -      9-8   Berra hit a solo homer to left,
                             Boston 9 New York 9
 9   0  2-2  -      9-9   Matsui grounded a single up the middle
 9   0  0-1  1      9-9   Lazzeri bunted out to the catcher,
                             Matsui to 2nd, sacrifice, 1 out
 9   1  0-2  2      9-9   White struck out, 2 out
 9   2  1-2  2      9-9   Jeter flied to deep center, 3 out
----------------------------------------------------------------------
                          10-Boston
                          >Lyle pitching
10   0  1-0  -      9-9   Varitek lined a single to left
10   0  3-1  1      9-9   Boggs walked, Varitek to 2nd
10   0  3-1  12     9-9   Speaker grounded to first, Varitek to 3rd,
                             Boggs to 2nd, 1 out
10   1  3-1  23     9-9   Williams walked
10   1  2-0  123    9-9   Ortiz flied to shallow center, 2 out
10   2  2-2  123    9-9   Yastrzemski flied to shallow left center,
                             3 out
----------------------------------------------------------------------
                          10-New York
10   0  1-2  -      9-9   Mantle flied to left center, 1 out
10   1  0-2  -      9-9   Ruth doubled off the wall down the
                             right field line
10   1  1-1  2      9-9   Gehrig intentionally walked
10   1  1-2  12     9-9   Rodriguez struck out, 2 out
10   2  0-2  12     9-9   Berra popped to short, 3 out
----------------------------------------------------------------------
                          11-Boston
11   0  2-1  -      9-9   Doerr flied to deep left center, 1 out
11   1  3-2  -      9-9   Cronin walked
11   1  2-0  1      9-9   Hooper flied deep down the right field line,
                             2 out
11   2  2-2  1      9-9   Varitek struck out, 3 out
----------------------------------------------------------------------
```

```
Inn Out B-S  On  NYY-Bos  Result
                          11-New York
11   0   1-1  -     9-9   Matsui flied to very deep right center, 1 out
11   1   2-2  -     9-9   Lazzeri struck out, 2 out
11   2   3-1  -     9-9   White flied to deep right center, 3 out
-------------------------------------------------------------------
                          12-Boston
12   0   3-0  -     9-9   Boggs walked
12   0   0-0  1     9-9   Speaker bunted out to the catcher,
                              Boggs to 2nd, sacrifice, 1 out
12   1   3-2  2     9-9   Williams lined a single to right,
                              Boggs to 3rd
12   1   1-1  13    9-9   Ortiz grounded to second, Williams to 2nd,
                              2 out
                          >Rivera pitching
12   2   2-2  23    9-9   Yastrzemski intentionally walked
12   2   1-1  123   9-9   Doerr flied deep down the right field line,
                              3 out
-------------------------------------------------------------------
                          12-New York
12   0   0-1  -     9-9   Jeter grounded a single up the middle
12   0   1-2  1     9-9   Mantle grounded a single between first
                              and second, Jeter to 2nd
12   0   3-1  12    9-9   Ruth grounded a single up the middle,
                              Jeter scored, Mantle to 2nd,
                              New York 10 Boston 9
```

Game Three	1	2	3	4	5	6	7	8	9	10	11	12	R	H	E
All-Time Boston Red Sox	3	1	0	0	0	3	2	0	0	0	0	0	9	14	1
All-Time New York Yankees	2	0	1	1	2	0	1	1	1	0	0	1	10	18	1

Boston	AB	R	H	RBI	BB	K	LOB	PO	A	E
Boggs, 3B	4	1	2	2	3	0	0	1	0	0
Speaker, CF	5	2	2	2	0	0	2	5	0	0
Williams, LF	5	1	2	0	2	0	0	3	0	1
Ortiz, DH	7	0	0	1	0	2	3	0	0	0
Yastrzemski, 1B	6	1	2	1	1	2	3	3	0	0
Doerr, 2B	6	0	2	1	0	1	3	3	0	0
Cronin, SS	5	1	1	0	1	2	1	2	2	0
Hooper, RF	5	2	1	0	1	0	2	7	0	0
Varitek, C	4	1	2	1	2	2	1	9	1	0
	47	9	14	8	10	9	15	33	3	1

Boston		IP	H	R	ER	HR	W	K	Pit	S	B	ERA	BF
Clemens		5.1	8	6	6	3	3	6	125	78	47	10.13	28
Stanley		1.2	2	1	1	1	1	0	35	21	14	7.36	8
Radatz		0.2	0	0	0	0	0	0	6	4	2	0.00	2
Timlin		0.0	1	1	1	1	0	0	3	2	1	54.00	1
Papelbon	L(0-1)	3.1	7	2	2	1	1	3	76	52	24	3.18	18
		11.0	18	10	10	6	5	9	245	157	88	5.59	57

New York	AB	R	H	RBI	BB	K	LOB	PO	A	E
Jeter, SS	7	2	3	1	0	0	1	1	0	0
Mantle, CF	7	0	2	1	0	2	0	7	0	0
Ruth, RF	5	2	3	2	2	1	2	10	0	0
Gehrig, 1B	4	2	3	2	2	0	0	4	1	0
Rodriguez, 3B	5	1	1	2	1	1	3	0	0	0
Berra, C	6	2	3	2	0	0	2	9	2	1
Matsui, DH	6	0	2	0	0	2	0	0	0	0
Lazzeri, 2B	5	0	0	0	0	2	3	3	4	0
White, LF	6	1	1	0	0	1	1	1	0	0
	51	10	18	10	5	9	12	36	7	1

New York		IP	H	R	ER	HR	W	K	Pit	S	B	ERA	BF
Reynolds		6.2	12	9	8	1	4	6	130	90	40	10.80	36
Betances		2.1	0	0	0	0	1	2	40	27	13	0.00	8
Lyle		2.2	2	0	0	0	4	1	61	27	34	0.00	14
Rivera	W(1-0)	0.1	0	0	0	0	1	0	12	7	5	0.00	2
		12.0	14	9	8	1	10	9	243	151	92	6.43	60

GAME THREE POSTGAME COMMENTS

Yankees Manager

The series shifts to Yankee Stadium and, despite facing a two-game deficit, I had plenty of confidence with Allie Reynolds on the mound. He has a superb 7–2 record with four saves and a 2.79 ERA in 15 career World Series games. He led New York to the World Series six times during his eight seasons wearing pinstripes and was there for all of the record five straight World Series titles, cementing his spot in Monument Park.

Sadly, on this day, he didn't have his best stuff. In fact, he got tattooed. The Red Sox built up a 9–7 lead and ended Reynolds's day in the seventh. Terrific catches by Ruth in the first and sixth with runners aboard kept the Sox from padding their lead. Yes, matters could have been worse.

I've got to hand it to my team; these players will not be denied. Jeter, Gehrig, Ruth, and A-Rod stroked home runs. Berra blasted two. His second—a game-tying, opposite-field shot off Papelbon in the ninth—saved our bacon and sent the game to extra innings. The roly-poly catcher (his body resembles the number eight on the back of his jersey) is an amazing bad-ball hitter. Yogi is skilled at reaching for balls out of the strike zone and hitting them out of the park. He's one of the great clutch hitters of his day, "the toughest man in baseball in the last three innings" is how Baltimore manager Paul Richards describes his uncanny ability to come through in the clutch.

I admit to sweating bullets. The game remained knotted until the bottom of the 12th inning when Ruth sent the fans home happy with a game-ending single to score Jeter. The Babe now has seven RBIs in the first three games. Without this victory, the Yanks would have trailed the BoSox three games to none, leaving them no margin for error while having to win games started by all-time greats Lefty Grove, Pedro Martinez, Jon Lester, and Roger Clemens—in that order—over the remainder of the series.

For the Yankees, the unsung heroes of the game were Betances and Lyle, who combined to pitch five scoreless innings of relief against Boston's most dangerous hitters. Due to their yeoman efforts, my closer, the great Rivera, needed just 12 pitches to earn the win. The Red Sox went for the jugular, sticking with Papelbon for 3 1/3 innings and letting him throw 76 pitches! The strategy backfired, and now Boston might be without its closer for the foreseeable future.

The worm has turned.

Red Sox Manager

The Yankees manager likens his team to a worm? I'd better not comment on that.

This was a tough loss. We jumped to a quick lead, saw it diminish, and then saw them tie it up—and go ahead. We grabbed the lead again in the sixth, when Speaker hit his homer—he led the league in homers back in 1912. When we added a couple of insurance runs in the seventh—loved that wild pitch by Betances—I thought things were going our way.

Yogi Berra. What can I say? That guy never stops fighting. Ten World Series rings to his credit! One for every finger on both hands—even his thumbs. Deceptive, but he's a proven winner. They spread it around, though. Each one of the top six guys in the lineup drove in one or more runs.

I'm afraid the computer drove Papelbon too hard. He's not going to be available tomorrow night. But we've got a good staff. We'll be OK.

We scored nine runs but needed more. I've got every faith in Big Papi coming through big time. Talk about a proven winner! He's always been a monster in the postseason, but is 0-for-15 through the first three games of this series. I'm not afraid of jinxing him by saying that. Bases loaded in the 10th, two men on in the 12th. He's not the kind of guy who gets down, or who you can get down on. Mark my words: we'll be hearing from him … and hopefully soon.

All-Time Boston Red Sox @ All-Time New York Yankees
Game Four, Boston Leads, 2–1
Lefty Grove (300–141, 3.06 ERA) vs. Andy Pettitte (256–153, 3.85 ERA)
Time 3:01, 66°, Wind: 6 MPH In from RCF

```
Inn Out B-S  On  Bos-NYY  Result
                          1-Boston
 1   0  0-0  -    0-0     Boggs grounded to second, 1 out
 1   1  1-2  -    0-0     Speaker grounded a single between first
                            and second
 1   1  1-1  1    0-0     Williams grounded to second, Speaker to 2nd,
                            2 out
 1   2  2-2  2    0-0     Ortiz struck out, 3 out
----------------------------------------------------------------
                          1-New York
 1   0  1-0  -    0-0     Jeter grounded a single between third
                            and short
 1   0  1-1  1    0-0     Mantle popped to third, 1 out
 1   1  2-0  1    0-0     Ruth singled on the infield, Jeter to 2nd
 1   1  3-2  12   0-0     Gehrig struck out, 2 out
 1   2  0-1  12   0-0     Rodriguez flied to deep left center, 3 out
----------------------------------------------------------------
                          2-Boston
 2   0  2-1  -    0-0     Yastrzemski grounded to the pitcher, 1 out
 2   1  1-2  -    0-0     Doerr flied to very deep left, 2 out
 2   2  1-2  -    0-0     Cronin struck out, 3 out
----------------------------------------------------------------
                          2-New York
 2   0  3-2  -    0-0     Berra flied to deep left center, 1 out
 2   1  0-1  -    0-0     Matsui grounded to short, 2 out
 2   2  1-2  -    0-0     Lazzeri struck out, 3 out
----------------------------------------------------------------
                          3-Boston
 3   0  1-2  -    0-0     Hooper flied shallow down right field line,
                            1 out
 3   1  2-0  -    0-0     Varitek grounded to first, 2 out
 3   2  1-0  -    0-0     Boggs grounded to first, 3 out
----------------------------------------------------------------
                          3-New York
 3   0  2-1  -    0-0     White lined a single to right center
 3   0  2-2  1    0-0     Jeter singled to right, White to 2nd
 3   0  2-2  12   0-0     Mantle struck out, 1 out
 3   1  2-2  12   0-0     Ruth struck out, 2 out
 3   2  1-0  12   0-0     Gehrig hit a three run homer down the
                            right field line, New York 3 Boston 0
 3   2  1-2  -    0-3     Rodriguez struck out, 3 out
----------------------------------------------------------------
                          4-Boston
 4   0  0-0  -    0-3     Speaker flied to deep left center, 1 out
 4   1  0-1  -    0-3     Williams grounded to first, 2 out
 4   2  1-1  -    0-3     Ortiz lined a single to right
 4   2  2-0  1    0-3     Yastrzemski flied to left center, 3 out
----------------------------------------------------------------
```

Inn	Out	B-S	On	NYY-Bos	Result
					4-New York
4	0	3-1	-	0-3	Berra walked
4	0	2-2	1	0-3	Matsui lined to third, 1 out
4	1	3-1	1	0-3	Lazzeri walked, Berra to 2nd
4	1	3-2	12	0-3	White grounded to first, safe on an error, Berra to 3rd, Lazzeri to 2nd
4	1	0-2	123	0-3	**Jeter grounded to short, forcing White at second, Berra scored, Lazzeri to 3rd, 2 out, New York 4 Boston 0**
4	2	1-1	13	0-4	**Mantle hit a three run homer down the left field line, New York 7 Boston 0**
4	2	3-1	-	0-7	Ruth walked
4	2	3-2	1	0-7	**Gehrig hit a two run homer to right center, New York 9 Boston 0**
4	2	2-1	-	0-9	Rodriguez flied to shallow center, 3 out
					5-Boston
5	0	1-0	-	0-9	Doerr lined a single to right
5	0	3-1	1	0-9	Cronin walked, Doerr to 2nd
5	0	2-1	12	0-9	Hooper flied to very deep left, Doerr to 3rd, 1 out
5	1	1-2	13	0-9	**Varitek grounded a single between third and short, Doerr scored, Cronin to 2nd, New York 9 Boston 1**
5	1	3-1	12	1-9	Boggs walked, Cronin to 3rd, Varitek to 2nd
5	1	2-0	123	1-9	**Speaker flied to deep right, sacrifice, Cronin scored, Varitek to 3rd, 2 out, New York 9 Boston 2**
5	2	0-1	13	2-9	Williams flied to shallow right center, 3 out
					5-New York
5	0	3-2	-	2-9	Berra struck out, 1 out
5	1	2-2	-	2-9	Matsui grounded a single up the middle
5	1	1-2	1	2-9	Lazzeri struck out, 2 out
5	2	1-0	1	2-9	White grounded a single between third and short, Matsui to 2nd
5	2	3-0	12	2-9	Jeter walked, Matsui to 3rd, White to 2nd
5	2	2-2	123	2-9	Mantle struck out, 3 out
					6-Boston
6	0	0-0	-	2-9	Ortiz grounded to second, 1 out
6	1	0-1	-	2-9	Yastrzemski lined to first, 2 out
6	2	3-0	-	2-9	Doerr walked
6	2	0-1	1	2-9	Cronin flied deep down the left field line, 3 out

```
Inn Out B-S  On  NYY-Bos  Result
                          6-New York
 6   0  1-1   -    2-9    Ruth hit a solo homer to right center,
                              New York 10 Boston 2
 6   0  2-2   -    2-10   Gehrig lined a single to center
 6   0  2-2   1    2-10   Rodriguez struck out, 1 out
 6   1  1-2   1    2-10   Berra hit a two run homer down the
                              right field line, New York 12 Boston 2
                          >Timlin pitching
 6   1  3-2   -    2-12   Matsui struck out, 2 out
 6   2  2-0   -    2-12   Lazzeri flied to deep center, 3 out
----------------------------------------------------------------------
                          7-Boston
 7   0  2-1   -    2-12   Hooper popped to the catcher, 1 out
 7   1  0-2   -    2-12   Varitek struck out, 2 out
 7   2  0-2   -    2-12   Boggs struck out, 3 out
----------------------------------------------------------------------
                          7-New York
 7   0  3-1   -    2-12   White flied to deep left center, 1 out
 7   1  0-1   -    2-12   Jeter lined a single to right
 7   1  0-1   1    2-12   Mantle lined a single to right center,
                              Jeter to 3rd
 7   1  3-2  13    2-12   Ruth walked, Mantle to 2nd
 7   1  0-2 123    2-12   Gehrig struck out, 2 out
 7   2  3-0 123    2-12   Rodriguez walked, Jeter scored,
                              Mantle to 3rd, Ruth to 2nd,
                              New York 13 Boston 2
                          >Stanley pitching
 7   2  1-0 123    2-13   Berra flied to shallow right center, 3 out
----------------------------------------------------------------------
                          8-Boston
 8   0  1-0   -    2-13   Speaker grounded to second, 1 out
 8   1  0-2   -    2-13   Williams hit a solo homer down the
                              right field line, New York 13 Boston 3
 8   1  1-2   -    3-13   Ortiz grounded to first, 2 out
 8   2  3-2   -    3-13   Yastrzemski lined to left, 3 out
----------------------------------------------------------------------
                          8-New York
 8   0  1-1   -    3-13   Matsui grounded to third, 1 out
 8   1  1-2   -    3-13   Lazzeri struck out, 2 out
 8   2  0-2   -    3-13   White doubled off the wall down the
                              right field line
 8   2  1-1   2    3-13   Jeter grounded to second, 3 out
----------------------------------------------------------------------
                          9-Boston
 9   0  3-1   -    3-13   Doerr walked
                          >Gossage pitching
 9   0  1-2   1    3-13   Cronin struck out, 1 out
 9   1  2-2   1    3-13   Hooper doubled to right center, Doerr to 3rd
 9   1  0-2  23    3-13   Varitek flied to left, 2 out
 9   2  2-2  23    3-13   Boggs flied to shallow left center, 3 out
```

Game Four	1	2	3	4	5	6	7	8	9	R	H	E
All-Time Boston Red Sox	0	0	0	0	2	0	0	1	0	3	6	1
All-Time New York Yankees	0	0	3	6	0	3	1	0	-	13	15	0

Boston	AB	R	H	RBI	BB	K	LOB	PO	A	E
Boggs, 3B	4	0	0	0	1	1	2	2	1	0
Speaker, CF	4	0	1	1	0	0	0	5	0	0
Williams, LF	4	1	1	1	0	0	2	1	0	0
Ortiz, DH	4	0	1	0	0	1	1	0	0	0
Yastrzemski, 1B	4	0	0	0	0	0	0	3	0	1
Doerr, 2B	2	1	1	0	2	0	1	1	1	0
Cronin, SS	3	1	0	0	1	2	1	0	2	0
Hooper, RF	4	0	1	0	0	0	0	0	0	0
Varitek, C	4	0	1	1	0	1	0	12	0	0
	33	3	6	3	4	5	7	24	4	1

Boston		IP	H	R	ER	HR	W	K	Pit	S	B	ERA	BF
Grove	L(0-1)	5.1	12	12	6	5	4	9	160	97	63	10.13	33
Timlin		1.1	2	1	1	0	2	2	32	16	16	16.20	8
Stanley		1.1	1	0	0	0	0	1	16	12	4	5.40	5
		8.0	15	13	7	5	6	12	208	125	83	6.08	46

New York	AB	R	H	RBI	BB	K	LOB	PO	A	E
Jeter, SS	5	3	3	1	1	0	1	0	0	0
Mantle, CF	5	1	2	3	0	2	3	1	0	0
Ruth, RF	3	2	2	1	2	1	0	3	0	0
Gehrig, 1B	5	3	3	5	0	2	0	10	0	0
Rodriguez, 3B	4	0	0	1	1	2	0	0	0	0
Berra, C	4	2	1	2	1	1	5	6	0	0
Matsui, DH	5	0	1	0	0	1	0	0	0	0
Lazzeri, 2B	4	1	0	0	1	3	0	0	4	0
White, LF	5	1	3	0	0	0	0	7	0	0
	40	13	15	13	6	12	9	27	5	0

New York		IP	H	R	ER	HR	W	K	Pit	S	B	ERA	BF
Pettitte	W(1-0)	8.0	5	3	3	1	4	4	117	73	44	3.38	33
Gossage		1.0	1	0	0	0	0	1	22	17	5	0.00	4
		9.0	6	3	3	1	4	5	139	90	49	5.59	37

GAME FOUR POSTGAME COMMENTS

Yankees Manager

The pitching matchup seemed well scripted for a duel, with left-handers Grove and Pettitte facing off in a game the Yankees desperately needed to win. Thankfully, it turned out to be a laugher.

It's no mean feat when your team jumps ahead to a 9–0 lead in the fourth inning against the great Lefty Grove. He was pounded for 12 hits and got knocked out early, having thrown a total of 160 pitches.

This Yankees squad is a slugging team with a new Murderers' Row: Mantle, Ruth, Gehrig, and Berra. Here they combined to hit five home runs and drive in 11 runs. Larrupin' Lou led the way, mashing two taters and plating five. Babe and Yogi continue to rip the cover off the ball, with each now having homered in three straight games.

For his part, Pettitte sure wasn't intimidated. The big Texan pitched eight strong and proved his mettle in a pressure-packed game. Then the Goose put a bow on it. He was snarly, dude!

Red Sox Manager

That was a little unfair, taking advantage of a 118-year old pitcher like Mose. He got hammered worse than any time in his whole career. Before this he'd pitched in 616 big-league ballgames but only once gave up as many as 10 runs, and that was way back in 1935—and only two of those were earned, though after a point runs are runs. So Yaz flubbed a grounder. Grove's a grown-up. He knows that the home runs were on him.

We got skunked. No two ways about it. We've got to start keeping the ball in the ballpark. Six home runs in Game Three and now we give up five more in Game Four. I'm sorry, but our pitchers are just not that bad.

The Series has evened up. It's a best-of-three from this point forward.

All-Time Boston Red Sox @ All-Time New York Yankees
Game Five, Series Tied, 2–2
Pedro Martinez (219–100, 2.93 ERA) vs. Red Ruffing (273–225, 3.80 ERA)
Time 1:53, 64°, Wind: 7 MPH In from RCF

```
Inn Out B-S  On  Bos-NYY  Result
                          1-Boston
 1   0  0-1  -    0-0     Boggs grounded to the pitcher, 1 out
 1   1  1-1  -    0-0     Speaker singled to right center
 1   1  2-0  1    0-0     Williams grounded to second,
                              forcing Speaker at second, 2 out
 1   2  0-0  1    0-0     Ortiz popped to second, 3 out
 -------------------------------------------------------------
                          1-New York
 1   0  1-0  -    0-0     Jeter grounded a single between first
                              and second
 1   0  0-2  1    0-0     Mantle hit a two run homer down the
                              right field line, New York 2 Boston 0
 1   0  2-2  -    0-2     Ruth struck out, 1 out
 1   1  0-2  -    0-2     Gehrig struck out, 2 out
 1   2  2-1  -    0-2     Rodriguez hit by pitch
 1   2  0-0  1    0-2     Rodriguez stole 2nd
 1   2  0-1  2    0-2     Berra lined a single to center,
                              Rodriguez scored, New York 3 Boston 0
 1   2  1-2  1    0-3     Matsui struck out, 3 out
 -------------------------------------------------------------
                          2-Boston
 2   0  3-1  -    0-3     Yastrzemski flied to deep left center, 1 out
 2   1  3-2  -    0-3     Doerr walked
 2   1  0-1  1    0-3     Cronin grounded to short, second to first
                              double play, 3 out
 -------------------------------------------------------------
                          2-New York
 2   0  3-2  -    0-3     Lazzeri struck out, 1 out
 2   1  2-1  -    0-3     White grounded to short, 2 out
 2   2  1-2  -    0-3     Jeter tripled to left
 2   2  2-2  3    0-3     Mantle struck out, 3 out
 -------------------------------------------------------------
                          3-Boston
 3   0  2-1  -    0-3     Hooper flied to deep right center, 1 out
 3   1  0-2  -    0-3     Varitek flied to deep right center, 2 out
 3   2  3-1  -    0-3     Boggs walked
 3   2  1-2  1    0-3     Speaker popped to the catcher, 3 out
 -------------------------------------------------------------
                          3-New York
 3   0  1-2  -    0-3     Ruth hit a solo homer down the
                              right field line, New York 4 Boston 0
 3   0  0-2  -    0-4     Gehrig grounded to second, 1 out
 3   1  1-2  -    0-4     Rodriguez struck out, 2 out
 3   2  0-2  -    0-4     Berra struck out, 3 out
 -------------------------------------------------------------
                          4-Boston
 4   0  1-1  -    0-4     Williams flied to center, 1 out
 4   1  0-1  -    0-4     Ortiz flied down the right field line, 2 out
 4   2  0-2  -    0-4     Yastrzemski lined a single to center
 4   2  1-0  1    0-4     Doerr lined to third, 3 out
 -------------------------------------------------------------
```

```
Inn Out B-S  On  NYY-Bos  Result
                           4-New York
 4   0   0-0  -    0-4     Matsui doubled off the wall in right center
 4   0   2-2  2    0-4     Lazzeri struck out, 1 out
 4   1   1-1  2    0-4     White grounded to second, Matsui to 3rd,
                             2 out
 4   2   3-0  3    0-4     Jeter walked
 4   2   0-0  13   0-4     Mantle grounded to first, 3 out
---------------------------------------------------------------------
                           5-Boston
 5   0   0-2  -    0-4     Cronin struck out, 1 out
 5   1   2-2  -    0-4     Hooper popped to first, 2 out
 5   2   1-2  -    0-4     Varitek flied to right, 3 out
---------------------------------------------------------------------
                           5-New York
 5   0   2-2  -    0-4     Ruth struck out, 1 out
 5   1   3-0  -    0-4     Gehrig singled on the infield
 5   1   0-2  1    0-4     Rodriguez struck out, 2 out
 5   2   0-0  1    0-4     Gehrig stole 2nd
 5   2   1-0  2    0-4     Berra flied to deep center, 3 out
---------------------------------------------------------------------
                           6-Boston
 6   0   1-2  -    0-4     Boggs grounded to third, 1 out
 6   1   0-1  -    0-4     Speaker popped to second, 2 out
 6   2   2-0  -    0-4     Williams flied to deep right center, 3 out
---------------------------------------------------------------------
                           6-New York
 6   0   0-2  -    0-4     Matsui flied to deep right, 1 out
 6   1   0-2  -    0-4     Lazzeri popped to second, 2 out
 6   2   2-2  -    0-4     White grounded to short, 3 out
---------------------------------------------------------------------
                           7-Boston
 7   0   0-0  -    0-4     Ortiz lined a single up the middle
 7   0   2-1  1    0-4     Yastrzemski flied to very deep right center,
                             1 out
 7   1   0-0  1    0-4     Doerr flied down the right field line, 2 out
 7   2   0-1  1    0-4     Cronin grounded to second, forcing Ortiz
                             at second, 3 out
---------------------------------------------------------------------
                           7-New York
 7   0   2-0  -    0-4     Jeter flied to left, 1 out
 7   1   1-2  -    0-4     Mantle struck out, 2 out
 7   2   2-2  -    0-4     Ruth struck out, 3 out
---------------------------------------------------------------------
                           8-Boston
 8   0   0-2  -    0-4     Hooper grounded to first, 1 out
 8   1   2-2  -    0-4     Varitek struck out, out at 1st, 2 out
 8   2   0-0  -    0-4     Boggs popped to second, 3 out
---------------------------------------------------------------------
                           8-New York
 8   0   0-1  -    0-4     Gehrig flied to very deep right center, 1 out
                           >Timlin pitching
 8   1   2-2  -    0-4     Rodriguez grounded to third, 2 out
 8   2   3-1  -    0-4     Berra walked
 8   2   1-2  1    0-4     Matsui struck out, 3 out
---------------------------------------------------------------------
Inn Out B-S  On  NYY-Bos  Result
                           9-Boston
 9   0   0-2  -    0-4     Speaker flied to deep left center, 1 out
 9   1   1-0  -    0-4     Williams grounded to second, 2 out
 9   2   0-2  -    0-4     Ortiz struck out, 3 out
```

Game Five	1	2	3	4	5	6	7	8	9	R	H	E
All-Time Boston Red Sox	0	0	0	0	0	0	0	0	0	0	3	0
All-Time New York Yankees	3	0	1	0	0	0	0	0	-	4	7	0

Boston	AB	R	H	RBI	BB	K	LOB	PO	A	E
Boggs, 3B	3	0	0	0	1	0	0	0	1	0
Speaker, CF	4	0	1	0	0	0	0	2	0	0
Williams, LF	4	0	0	0	0	0	1	1	0	0
Ortiz, DH	4	0	1	0	0	1	1	0	0	0
Yastrzemski, 1B	3	0	1	0	0	0	0	6	0	0
Doerr, 2B	2	0	0	0	1	0	1	1	2	0
Cronin, SS	3	0	0	0	0	1	2	0	2	0
Hooper, RF	3	0	0	0	0	0	0	1	0	0
Varitek, C	3	0	0	0	0	1	0	13	0	0
	29	0	3	0	2	3	5	24	5	0

Boston		IP	H	R	ER	HR	W	K	Pit	S	B	ERA	BF
Martinez	L(1-1)	7.1	7	4	4	2	1	12	124	87	37	3.68	31
Timlin		0.2	0	0	0	0	1	1	16	9	7	11.57	3
		8.0	7	4	4	2	2	13	140	96	44	5.80	34

New York	AB	R	H	RBI	BB	K	LOB	PO	A	E
Jeter, SS	3	1	2	0	1	0	0	1	2	0
Mantle, CF	4	1	1	2	0	2	3	6	0	0
Ruth, RF	4	1	1	1	0	3	0	4	0	0
Gehrig, 1B	4	0	1	0	0	1	0	6	1	0
Rodriguez, 3B	3	1	0	0	0	2	0	1	1	0
Berra, C	3	0	1	1	1	1	1	3	1	0
Matsui, DH	4	0	1	0	0	2	2	0	0	0
Lazzeri, 2B	3	0	0	0	0	2	0	5	2	0
White, LF	3	0	0	0	0	0	0	0	0	0
	31	4	7	4	2	13	6	27	8	0

New York		IP	H	R	ER	HR	W	K	Pit	S	B	ERA	BF
Ruffing	W(1-1)	9.0	3	0	0	0	2	3	108	78	30	2.65	31
		9.0	3	0	0	0	2	3	108	78	30	2.65	31

GAME FIVE POSTGAME COMMENTS

Yankees Manager

In the first game of the series, Ruffing pitched like he did back in the days when he was a member of the Red Sox—horribly. This time he was the dominant pitcher the Yankees had come to know and rely on.

Red made it look easy against a lineup comprised of seven current Hall of Famers and one surefire bet to make it (when the time comes). In nine innings he allowed only five batters to reach base safely. He scattered three hits—in the first, fourth, and seventh—and issued two walks—in the second and third. No Red Sox runner ever got past first base. In fact, Boston never put two men on base in the same inning! Red finished the job in less than two hours. Maybe he had an early dinner reservation.

Pedro was good but, on this day, a good performance was not enough. My guys jumped on him early, taking a 2–0 lead just two batters into the game thanks to Mantle's two-run homer. After Pedro struck out Ruth and Gehrig, with two outs and nobody on, he then beaned A-Rod—probably on purpose. A-Rod promptly swiped second and scored when Yogi whistled a liner through the box, giving my team a quick 3–0 lead. That was more than enough cushion for Ruffing, though for good measure Ruth did add a solo homer in the fourth. The Babe now leads all batters in the series with five homers and nine RBIs. Pedro finished with 12 Ks, but the early damage did him in.

Each team is taking care of business in its home ballpark. Boston won the first two at Fenway and my boys won all three in the Bronx. Even though the Red Sox won the first two games at home, I still had faith in my team. "I'll pay you when we return," I told the visiting clubhouse man in Boston, meaning that I expected to be back for a Game Six.

Red Sox Manager

Pedro doesn't often give up two home runs in a game. I take affront, though, at the notion he would bean A-Rod on purpose. Remember, at one time the two of them were almost teammates, when the Red Sox were courting A-Rod and thought they had him. Anyone who can strike out Ruth and Gehrig back-to-back has to be feeling pretty good about his stuff—even if he had just given up a two-run homer to Mantle.

The Yankees skipper is right—we took the first two, and wanted at least one at the Stadium, but feel good about playing at Fenway. You can be sure we're not going to get shut out again, not at home. We got 22 runs in the first three games of this set and only three runs in the last two. The balance is due to tip again.

I'm still looking for my two big guns—Big Papi and The Kid—to come through strong, and anyone who remembers how Yaz poured it on the last week or so of the 1967 season knows he's a clutch performer.

A trip back home, a day of rest, we'll see what happens.

All-Time Boston Red Sox vs. All-Time New York Yankees
Game Six, New York Leads, 3–2
Jon Lester (177–98, 3.50 ERA) vs. Whitey Ford (236–106, 2.75 ERA)
Time 3:10, 63°, Wind: 16 MPH Right to Left

```
Inn Out B-S  On  NYY-Bos  Result
                          1-New York
 1   0  2-0  -    0-0     Jeter doubled off the wall in left center
 1   0  2-1  2    0-0     Mantle flied to deep left center,
                             Jeter to 3rd, 1 out
 1   1  2-1  3    0-0     Ruth doubled off the wall in right center,
                             Jeter scored, New York 1 Boston 0
 1   1  1-2  2    1-0     Gehrig hit a two run homer to right center,
                             New York 3 Boston 0
 1   1  3-2  -    3-0     Rodriguez walked
 1   1  3-0  1    3-0     Berra walked, Rodriguez to 2nd
 1   1  1-2  12   3-0     Matsui flied to deep right center,
                             Rodriguez to 3rd, 2 out
 1   2  1-2  13   3-0     Lazzeri grounded to second, 3 out
-----------------------------------------------------------------
                          1-Boston
 1   0  3-2  -    3-0     Boggs walked
 1   0  0-1  1    3-0     Speaker grounded to short, forcing Boggs
                             at second, 1 out
 1   1  0-2  1    3-0     Williams lined a single to right center,
                             Speaker to 2nd
 1   1  2-0  12   3-0     Ortiz doubled off the wall down the
                             right field line, Speaker scored,
                             Williams scored, New York 3 Boston 2
 1   1  1-2  2    3-2     Yastrzemski lined to first, Ortiz caught
                             off 2nd, 3 out
-----------------------------------------------------------------
                          2-New York
 2   0  0-0  -    3-2     White popped to third, 1 out
 2   1  1-2  -    3-2     Jeter struck out, 2 out
 2   2  1-2  -    3-2     Mantle struck out, 3 out
-----------------------------------------------------------------
                          2-Boston
 2   0  2-1  -    3-2     Doerr grounded to short, 1 out
 2   1  1-2  -    3-2     Cronin grounded to third, 2 out
 2   2  0-2  -    3-2     Hooper flied to deep right center, 3 out
-----------------------------------------------------------------
                          3-New York
 3   0  2-2  -    3-2     Ruth grounded to second, 1 out
 3   1  3-2  -    3-2     Gehrig walked
 3   1  0-2  1    3-2     Rodriguez popped to short, 2 out
 3   2  2-2  1    3-2     Berra flied to deep center, Berra safe at 1st
                             on an error, Gehrig to 3rd
 3   2  0-2  13   3-2     Matsui grounded a single up the middle,
                             Gehrig scored, Berra to 2nd,
                             New York 4 Boston 2
 3   2  1-1  12   4-2     Lazzeri lined a single to center,
                             Berra scored, Matsui to 3rd,
                             New York 5 Boston 2
 3   2  2-0  13   5-2     White flied to left, 3 out
-----------------------------------------------------------------
                          3-Boston
 3   0  0-1  -    5-2     Varitek flied to left, 1 out
 3   1  0-2  -    5-2     Boggs flied to shallow right center, 2 out
 3   2  2-1  -    5-2     Speaker flied to deep right, 3 out
-----------------------------------------------------------------
```

```
Inn Out B-S  On  NYY-Bos  Result
                          4-New York
 4   0  3-2   -    5-2    Jeter walked
 4   0  1-2   1    5-2    Mantle grounded to third, second to first
                              double play, 2 out
 4   2  1-2   -    5-2    Ruth hit a solo homer down the
                              right field line, New York 6 Boston 2
                          >Stanley pitching
 4   2  0-0   -    6-2    Gehrig grounded a single between first
                              and second
 4   2  0-1   1    6-2    Rodriguez lined to short, 3 out
-----------------------------------------------------------------------
                          4-Boston
 4   0  3-2   -    6-2    Williams flied to shallow right, 1 out
 4   1  1-2   -    6-2    Ortiz grounded to second, 2 out
 4   2  0-2   -    6-2    Yastrzemski flied to left center, 3 out
-----------------------------------------------------------------------
                          5-New York
 5   0  1-0   -    6-2    Berra flied to deep right center, 1 out
 5   1  0-2   -    6-2    Matsui doubled off the wall down the
                              right field line
 5   1  1-2   2    6-2    Lazzeri struck out, 2 out
 5   2  1-2   2    6-2    White grounded to short, 3 out
-----------------------------------------------------------------------
                          5-Boston
 5   0  3-1   -    6-2    Doerr walked
 5   0  2-0   1    6-2    Cronin grounded a single between first
                              and second, Doerr to 2nd
 5   0  0-0  12    6-2    Hooper flied to shallow center, 1 out
 5   1  1-0  12    6-2    Varitek flied to deep left center,
                              Doerr to 3rd, 2 out
 5   2  0-2  13    6-2    Boggs grounded to first, safe on an error,
                              Doerr scored, Cronin to 2nd,
                              New York 6 Boston 3
 5   2  0-0  12    6-3    Speaker grounded to second, 3 out
-----------------------------------------------------------------------
                          6-New York
 6   0  2-0   -    6-3    Jeter hit a solo homer down the
                              left field line, New York 7 Boston 3
 6   0  3-1   -    7-3    Mantle walked
 6   0  1-0   1    7-3    Ruth flied very deep down the
                              right field line, Mantle to 2nd, 1 out
 6   1  3-1   2    7-3    Gehrig walked
 6   1  0-0  12    7-3    Rodriguez doubled off the wall in
                              right center, Mantle scored,
                              Gehrig to 3rd, New York 8 Boston 3
 6   1  3-0  23    8-3    Berra walked
 6   1  1-1  123   8-3    Matsui flied to left center, sacrifice,
                              Gehrig scored, 2 out, New York 9 Boston 3
                          >Timlin pitching
 6   2  0-2  12    9-3    Lazzeri struck out, 3 out
-----------------------------------------------------------------------
```

```
Inn Out B-S   On   NYY-Bos  Result
                             6-Boston
 6   0  3-2   -      9-3     Williams grounded to first, 1 out
 6   1  0-0   -      9-3     Ortiz grounded a single between first
                               and second
 6   1  0-0   1      9-3     Yastrzemski lined a single between third
                               and short, Ortiz to 2nd
 6   1  0-0   12     9-3     Doerr grounded to second, Ortiz to 3rd,
                               Yastrzemski to 2nd, 2 out
 6   2  3-0   23     9-3     Cronin walked
 6   2  1-1   123    9-3     Hooper grounded to second, forcing Cronin
                               at second, 3 out
-----------------------------------------------------------------------
                             7-New York
 7   0  0-0   -      9-3     White flied to deep center, 1 out
 7   1  1-1   -      9-3     Jeter grounded to the pitcher, 2 out
 7   2  0-2   -      9-3     Mantle hit a solo homer down the
                               right field line, New York 10 Boston 3
 7   2  2-1   -     10-3     Ruth singled between first and second
 7   2  0-1   1     10-3     Gehrig lined to short, 3 out
-----------------------------------------------------------------------
                             7-Boston
 7   0  3-0   -     10-3     Varitek walked
 7   0  3-2   1     10-3     Boggs walked, Varitek to 2nd
 7   0  2-0   12    10-3     Speaker grounded to short, second to first
                               double play, Varitek to 3rd, 2 out
 7   2  3-0   3     10-3     Williams walked
 7   2  0-2   13    10-3     Ortiz hit a three run homer down the
                               right field line, New York 10 Boston 6
 7   2  0-0   -     10-6     Yastrzemski grounded to short, 3 out
-----------------------------------------------------------------------
                             8-New York
 8   0  2-1   -     10-6     Rodriguez flied to very deep right center,
                               1 out
 8   1  1-1   -     10-6     Berra flied to left center, 2 out
 8   2  2-0   -     10-6     Matsui flied to deep right center, 3 out
-----------------------------------------------------------------------
                             8-Boston
 8   0  1-1   -     10-6     Doerr lined a single to right center
 8   0  0-0   1     10-6     Cronin flied to left center, 1 out
 8   1  1-2   1     10-6     Hooper grounded to short, Doerr to 2nd, 2 out
 8   2  3-1   2     10-6     Varitek walked
 8   2  0-2   12    10-6     Boggs singled to left center, Doerr scored,
                               Varitek to 3rd, New York 10 Boston 7
                             >Lyle pitching
 8   2  0-0   13    10-7     Speaker grounded to third, forcing Boggs
                               at second, 3 out
-----------------------------------------------------------------------
```

```
Inn Out B-S  On  NYY-Bos  Result
                          9-New York
                          >Papelbon pitching
9   0   1-2  -   10-7     Lazzeri struck out, 1 out
9   1   1-1  -   10-7     White singled on the infield
9   1   2-2  1   10-7     Jeter flied to center, 2 out
9   2   1-2  1   10-7     Mantle hit a two run homer down the
                             right field line, New York 12 Boston 7
9   2   0-1  -   12-7     Ruth doubled off the wall in left center
9   2   0-1  2   12-7     Gehrig lined a single to right center,
                             Ruth scored, New York 13 Boston 7
9   2   0-2  1   13-7     Rodriguez flied to deep left, 3 out
--------------------------------------------------------------------
                          9-Boston
9   0   3-0  -   13-7     Williams walked
9   0   0-1  1   13-7     Ortiz grounded a single between first
                             and second, Williams to 2nd
9   0   3-2  12  13-7     Yastrzemski walked, Williams to 3rd,
                             Ortiz to 2nd
9   0   0-2  123 13-7     Doerr struck out, 1 out
9   1   0-0  123 13-7     Cronin flied to deep center, sacrifice,
                             Williams scored, 2 out,
                             New York 13 Boston 8
9   2   3-1  12  13-8     Hooper walked, Ortiz to 3rd,
                             Yastrzemski to 2nd
9   2   1-2  123 13-8     Varitek grounded to third,
                             forcing Yastrzemski at third, 3 out
```

Game Six	1	2	3	4	5	6	7	8	9	R	H	E
All-Time New York Yankees	3	0	2	1	0	3	1	0	3	13	16	1
All-Time Boston Red Sox	2	0	0	0	1	0	3	1	1	8	9	1

New York	AB	R	H	RBI	BB	K	LOB	PO	A	E
Jeter, SS	5	2	2	1	1	1	0	2	6	0
Mantle, CF	5	3	2	3	1	1	0	5	0	0
Ruth, RF	6	3	4	2	0	0	0	2	0	0
Gehrig, 1B	4	3	3	3	2	0	1	10	1	1
Rodriguez, 3B	5	0	1	1	1	0	2	1	2	0
Berra, C	3	1	0	0	2	0	0	1	0	0
Matsui, DH	5	0	2	2	0	0	0	0	0	0
Lazzeri, 2B	5	0	1	1	0	3	4	3	4	0
White, LF	5	1	1	0	0	0	3	3	0	0
	43	13	16	13	7	5	10	27	13	1

New York (A)		IP	H	R	ER	HR	BB	K	Pit	S	B	ERA	BF
Ford	W(1-1)	7.2	8	7	6	1	7	0	133	82	51	8.16	37
Lyle	S(1)	1.1	1	1	1	0	3	1	29	16	13	2.25	8
		9.0	9	8	7	1	10	1	162	98	64	4.91	45

Boston	AB	R	H	RBI	BB	K	LOB	PO	A	E
Boggs, 3B	3	0	1	1	2	0	0	1	2	0
Speaker, CF	5	1	0	0	0	0	4	6	0	1
Williams, LF	3	3	1	0	2	0	0	3	0	0
Ortiz, DH	5	1	4	5	0	0	0	0	0	0
Yastrzemski, 1B	4	0	1	0	1	0	1	5	0	0
Doerr, 2B	4	2	1	0	1	1	0	1	2	0
Cronin, SS	4	0	1	1	1	0	0	3	1	0
Hooper, RF	4	0	0	0	1	0	3	3	0	0
Varitek, C	3	1	0	0	2	0	3	5	0	0
	35	8	9	7	10	1	11	27	6	1

Boston		IP	H	R	ER	HR	BB	K	Pit	S	B	ERA	BF
Lester	L(0-1)	3.2	6	6	4	2	4	2	103	70	33	7.27	21
Stanley		2.0	4	3	3	1	3	1	42	23	19	7.71	13
Timlin		2.1	2	1	1	1	0	1	26	18	8	7.71	9
Papelbon		1.0	4	3	3	1	0	1	26	21	5	6.75	7
		9.0	16	13	11	5	7	5	197	132	65	6.67	50

GAME SIX POSTGAME COMMENTS

Yankees Manager

This game wasn't a thing of beauty, but we're proud to win the series. Hats off to those Boston players. They made us scratch, claw, and fight for everything. We knew it was going to be a tough series, and losing the first two games made it that much tougher. But this team is a resilient bunch. They know how to win. I never lost confidence, even down, 0–2. But had you asked me if either team could win four straight games against the other, I'd have said you were crazy. Yet that's exactly what my guys accomplished. They're amazing!

Ford didn't have his best stuff; he got by on guile alone. He nibbled too much, not challenging the Red Sox batters. He walked seven, which is un-Ford like. The coaching staff anticipated pulling him after six, but when the lead extended to 10–3, sending Whitey back out for the seventh seemed like the right move. Then walks got him into more trouble in the seventh. With two outs, we liked the lefty-lefty match-up against Ortiz and left him in. It didn't work out. Big Papi went deep. We've seen that too many times before.

The bats bailed us out. Every player in the lineup had at least one hit, except Yogi, who walked twice. Even Lazzeri finally got on the board, which was nice to see. The top of the lineup was simply unstoppable in this game. Jeter, Mantle, Ruth, and Gehrig combined for 11 hits in 20 at-bats, with five homers, 11 RBIs, and nine runs scored. That's a one through four that stacks up to any all-time team.

It'll be an uproarious ride back home—the Babe will see to that. We'll enjoy this win for one day, and then prepare to share the victory with all New Yorkers at a ticker tape parade through the Canyon of Heroes, which runs along Broadway from the Battery to City Hall. All Yankees fans know the route well.

Red Sox Manager

That was very definitely not a thing of beauty. I guess facing Lou Gehrig and Babe Ruth was a little too much for Lester the second time around. Ruth had his number back in Game Two and this game wasn't any different. A couple of tough customers—about as tough as they come. Three runs before our guys even got up to bat.

We got two back. A two-run double by David. I knew it was a matter of time before he was going to come up big. He did in today's game—two runs in the first and then that three-run homer in the bottom of the seventh. Five runs by one batter off the Chairman of the Board—how often does that happen? But one batter alone can't do it against Murderers's Row and Company—the company being another 80 or 90 years' worth of Yankees greats. We got eight runs, but it wasn't enough. After we took the first two games, I almost couldn't believe it but I thought we had a shot at winning the series. At the end of the day, their hitting just over-matched our pitching.

MANAGERS' POST-SERIES PRESS CONFERENCE

Yankees Manager

The Bronx Bombers put on their hitting shoes for this series, swatting 22 home runs in six games, while the feeble Boston batters only managed to put five balls over the fence. New York's ability to hit for power is the story of the series. Total bases: Yankees 164, Red Sox 87.

We put a hurtin' on the Boston starting pitchers to the tune of 33 runs scored and 48 hits—including 15 homers—in 34 innings. And we rudely greeted their relievers, as the Boston bullpen got lit up for 15 runs and 30 hits—including seven homers—in 20 innings. By contrast, the Yankees boasted a shutdown bullpen: nine innings, four hits, one run. In the pre-series press conference, I stated that the underlying strength of this all-time Yankees team is its deep bullpen, and if they had the lead by the sixth inning it should be game over. Call me prescient!

The match-up turned in favor of the Yankees with dominant pitching performances in Games Four and Five by Andy Pettitte and Red Ruffing, who combined to limit the Red Sox to eight hits and three runs over 17 innings. The Yankees won both games and took a stranglehold on the series. Overall, New York's starting pitchers allowed 31 runs in 46 innings, which is admirable when you consider how poorly Whitey Ford performed. Although he won the clinching Game Six thanks to a multitude of run support, Ford was rocked in both his starting assignments:

he allowed 14 runs (13 earned), 21 hits, and 10 walks in 14 innings. And Whitey wasn't fooling anybody—he struck out just two batters in the series.

The familiar four-man wrecking crew led the Yankees offense: Ruth (2.085 OPS), Gehrig (1.746), Mantle (1.248), and Berra (1.458), along with the usual supporting cast that included a bevy of capable hitters such as Jeter (1.137 OPS) and Matsui (.935). It was particularly gratifying to watch Roy White hold his own, finishing with a respectable .280 batting average. He proved the doubters wrong and showed he belongs on the same field as the legends who are honored in Monument Park.

On the flip side, Alex Rodriguez and Tony Lazzeri were huge disappointments. They combined for only three hits in 51 at-bats, with 20 strikeouts. Lazzeri struck out 12 times and didn't get a hit until the final game of the series. In hindsight, Robinson Cano would have been a better selection at second base. As for A-Rod, his critics often focus on his postseason ineptitude (the lone exception being 2009), and during this series a bevy of boobirds were singing a familiar tune. Poor Alex; for all his natural talent he once again was exposed to be the hollow man.

As for the Red Sox all-time team, Tris Speaker was most impressive. He led Boston's all-timers in batting average (no surprise) and slugging percentage (big surprise). Wade Boggs did as expected at the top of the order by reaching base 13 times, but scored only three runs in six games. That's due mainly to my pitchers' ability to hold Ted Williams and Carl Yastrzemski in check, as the two combined to drive in a measly four runs. Finally, we got the best of Big Papi, who was a non-factor until Game Six. And although he led his team with seven RBIs, he did very little damage with six hits and a .231 batting average.[1] Also practically non-existent were Harry Hooper (.174 average, two RBIs) and Joe Cronin (.182, two RBIs). You convinced me that Hooper was a better choice in right than Dwight Evans, but you should have heeded my advice and selected Nomar Garciaparra for shortstop. That said, it's only fair to admit your decision to select Varitek over Fisk paid off handsomely. Tek was MVP of Game Two, and his six RBIs ranked second on your team.

History, as often happens, repeats itself. And baseball is a game

---

[1] Aside from his monstrous Game Six, in which he went 4-for-5 with a home run and five RBIs, he went 2-for-21 the rest of the series.

steeped in tradition. So the all-time Yankees team *has to* defeat the all-time Red Sox team, right? *La forza del destino*, meaning "the power of destiny." Both franchises are represented by many of the greatest players to ever lace up spikes. But for whatever reason—be it 27 world championships, the Curse of the Bambino, Bucky Dent, Aaron Boone, mystique and aura—in the long run the Yankees always seem to come out on top against the Red Sox, their most hated rivals.

And when that happens, all is right in the world.

Red Sox Manager

When this series was scheduled, I wasn't sure how well we'd fare. I knew we had a team populated with truly great ballplayers, but also was aware of two big numbers: 9 and 27. And by 9, I don't mean Ted Williams. Starting with the first World Series in 1903 through the 2018 World Series, the Red Sox have won nine of them. The Yankees have won 27. That's three times as many. All things being otherwise equal, the historical weight of performance was stacked in favor of the Yankees.

It would have taken an incredible accumulation of … well, runs … to beat the Bombers. And they lived up that moniker—out-homering our guys, 22 to 5.

We got off to a great start. I almost couldn't believe how well the first two games played out, with the Red Sox winning, 5–3 and then 7–5. And we had a one-run lead going into the ninth inning in Game Three as well. We were up by three with nine outs to go. But then the long ball killed us—three solo home runs: Berra off Bob Stanley in the seventh, Ruth off Timlin in the eighth, and then Berra hitting another one off Papelbon in the ninth. If we'd kept the ball in the ballpark, we might have been up three games to none.

Ruth and Gehrig both batted over .500 for the series, with 21 runs batted in between them. Unbelievable. Leaves me a little wistful for David Ortiz batting .688 in the 2013 World Series. He drove in one more run in this series than he did in 2013, but—save for Tek—no one else … well, Boggs did OK from the leadoff spot, but there was definitely a power shortage in Games Four and Five. Only six hits in Game Four and three in Game Five. That Ruffing—the way he pitched in Game Five, I wish we'd never let him go the Yankees. Ruth, that goes without saying.

I'm a little disappointed our sluggers didn't match up as well. I was hoping that Ted Williams, free from the wrist injury that hampered him in the '46 Series, would come through big. He did better, but not by much and not by enough. Yaz was always such a battler. He practically single-handedly *willed* us to the pennant in 1967, but had a tough series.

I'm still wondering about one thing: where was Joe DiMaggio? Sitting on the bench for six games?

The pitching was probably the most surprising overall—for both teams. Whitey was hit hard, but so was Lefty Grove … and Clemens in his Red Sox uniform. The only two of our pitchers who did well were Pedro and Radatz, and Radatz only faced six batters. If only he'd been left in against Ruth in the third game, perhaps the series may have turned out differently.

I can't really fault any one player in particular. We got beat fair and square. We got off to a great start, but couldn't maintain it. I guess Game Three might have taken some of the fight out of the guys. Even then I certainly never thought we'd get swept in the last four games. I thought we'd at least push it to Game Seven. But it was probably preordained. Like I said, 9 and 27.

PARTING SHOTS

David Fischer: I'm glad my team prevailed, but was disappointed the simulation didn't make better use of the extraordinary bench players from both teams. Had I known the great DiMaggio would ride the pine for all six games, I would have approached our early planning meetings for this book differently. I would have lobbied to allow any player to serve in the DH role. Then I could have put Mantle in the DH slot and used DiMaggio in center. Matsui hit well, but he's no Joe D. At the very least, I figured the Clipper would see plenty of action as a pinch-hitter for Roy White, or in crucial spots for the slumping Tony Lazzeri—but the simulation did not take into account much in-game strategy at all.

Bill Nowlin: I agree. "Baseball's Greatest Living Ballplayer" (Joe D.—of course, all of these ballplayers were living for the purpose of this simulation, so there might be more argument about that designation) never saw a single at-bat? Then again, in what proved to be a six-game series that looked early on that it was going in Boston's direction, there was no attempt to use Posada, Cano, Rizzuto, Winfield, or Don Baylor. And as the Red Sox saw our All-Time Greats falter, as things started slipping away, there was no one on the Boston bench who was deemed useful for anything? You questioned my choice of Cronin over Nomar. Well, Nomar was right there on the bench, ready and waiting. Whatever else he did, Manny Ramirez was one of the greatest right-handed hitters of all-time. Not even a pinch-hit appearance? Not in a 12-inning game? Not in a game the Red Sox lost, 13–3? We had Jensen ready, too. Even playing for poor Red Sox teams, he led the American League in RBIs three times, and drove in over 100 runs five times. And I had two Hall of Famers stuck on the bench for the whole series—Jimmie Foxx and Jim Rice. Foxx was a three-time league MVP and Triple Crown winner while also leading the league in on-base percentage three times. In Game Five, the Red Sox mustered only three base hits. Foxx had 2,646 of them in his career. Bizarre. These were the best players in both teams' histories, and yet not one bench player for either team did anything other than ride the pine.

DF: Another cause for head scratching was the bullpen usage for my team. It's downright odd that the Yankees could win an important six-game series with Mariano Rivera pitching to just two batters. Sure, he earned the victory in Game Three, but had the game not gone 12 innings it's possible the greatest closer in history would have been relegated to mere spectator.

BN: You never would have won that game without Clemens giving up six runs. He does have seven Cy Young Awards, though, so I guess it was anomalous. Tell you what, I'll trade you Clemens for Babe Ruth. I think Ruth would look really good in a Red Sox uniform. And maybe Clemens could pitch for the 1999 Yankees.

DF: That trade would have to be a three-way deal with the Blue Jays, a team that didn't exist during Ruth's playing days. No matter. I was pleased my team nicked Clemens for three homers—by Jeter (on an 0-2 pitch, no less), Gehrig, and A-Rod (his first hit of the series)—to ground the Rocket in the sixth inning. There's no better sight than a Boston pitcher being removed from the game and then having to make the walk of shame from the mound to the visitors' dugout.

BN: I've certainly seen that happen often enough. But I've seen Pedro at his peak, seen Clemens's first 20-K game, seen [Dave] Morehead and [Derek] Lowe and Lester all throw no-hitters. I've seen a lot of other great moments at Fenway Park, too. The Fisk home run …

In recent years—like the current century—the Red Sox have won more world championships than any other team in baseball. They lost against the Yankees' All-Time Greats, as one might have anticipated (and as we both probably predicted). I wonder if we were to revisit this book in another 25 years, how the results might turn out.

For that matter, we both had some gripes about the computer. I wonder how this series, and the one pitting the 1998 Yankees against the 2018 Red Sox, might have turned out if the simulation company had done one of those things where they ran the simulation 100 times, or 1,000 times.

DF: I've been a witness to history, too. I've seen Tom Seaver win career game 300, seen [David] Wells and [David] Cone throw perfect games, cheered Bernie's walk-off homer against Boston's Rod Beck in the 10th inning of Game One of the 1999 ALCS, and felt Yankee Stadium shake from Jeter's Game Four–winning home run in the 2001 World Series.

If we were to revisit this book in another 25 years, and run 1,000 simulations, I imagine the results would be the same: the Yankees All-Time Greats would dominate the Red Sox All-Time Near-Greats. As for the 1998 Yankees against the 2018 Red Sox? I'm sure that my team would fare better over the long haul, assuming we can reset the computer model to use the postseason roster and engineer a batting order that is based on reality.

BN: If I were to call in my experts to reset the computer, the Red Sox might win 1,000 times, or at least three out of every four. As for now, I'll take my lumps. It wasn't as though I didn't expect it to turn out this way. It was fun winning those first couple of games, though!

ATG Boston Red Sox Hitting

Pos	Name	G	PA	AB	R	H	1B	2B	3B	HR	RBI	BB	SO	SB	CS	BA	OBP	SLG	TB	HBP	SAC	ROE	GDP
3B	Boggs	6	31	21	3	7	6	1	0	0	4	6	1	0	0	.333	.448	.381	8	0	2	1	0
CF	Speaker	6	29	24	4	10	6	2	0	1	3	1	1	0	0	.417	.379	.583	14	0	4	0	1
LF	Williams	6	29	24	6	8	5	2	0	1	2	5	1	0	0	.333	.448	.542	13	0	0	0	0
DH	Ortiz	6	29	26	1	6	4	1	0	1	7	1	7	0	0	.231	.241	.385	10	0	2	0	0
1B	Yastrzemski	6	27	24	2	6	4	1	1	0	2	3	2	0	0	.250	.333	.375	9	0	0	0	1
2B	Doerr	6	27	21	5	7	5	2	0	0	3	5	3	0	0	.333	.444	.429	9	0	1	0	0
SS	Cronin	6	26	22	3	4	2	2	0	0	2	3	5	0	0	.182	.269	.273	6	0	1	0	1
RF	Hooper	6	26	23	3	4	2	1	0	1	2	2	0	0	0	.174	.231	.348	8	0	1	0	0
C	Varitek	6	26	22	4	6	4	1	0	1	6	3	4	1	0	.273	.360	.455	10	0	0	0	0

ATG Boston Red Sox Pitching

Pos	Name	W	L	ERA	G	GS	GF	CG	SHO	SV	R	ER	IP	H	HR	BB	SO	BF	H9	HR9	BB9	SO9	SO/W
SP	Martinez	1	1	3.68	2	2	0	0	0	0	6	6	14.2	13	3	2	20	59	7.98	1.84	1.23	12.28	10.00
SP	Lester	0	1	7.27	2	2	0	0	0	0	9	7	8.2	15	4	6	5	47	15.59	4.16	6.24	5.20	0.83
SP	Clemens	0	0	10.13	1	1	0	0	0	0	6	6	5.1	8	3	3	6	28	13.51	5.07	5.07	10.13	2.00
SP	Grove	0	1	10.13	1	1	0	0	0	0	12	6	5.1	12	5	4	9	33	20.26	8.44	6.75	15.20	2.25
RP	Stanley	1	0	7.71	4	0	1	0	0	0	6	6	7.0	11	3	4	2	35	14.14	3.86	5.14	2.57	0.50
RP	Papelbon	0	1	6.76	4	0	4	0	0	2	5	5	6.2	12	2	1	5	34	16.22	2.70	1.35	6.76	5.00
RP	Timlin	0	0	7.73	6	0	1	0	0	0	4	4	4.2	7	2	4	4	25	13.52	3.86	7.73	7.73	1.00
RP	Radatz	0	0	0.00	3	0	0	0	0	0	0	0	1.2	0	0	0	1	6	0.00	0.00	0.00	5.42	0.00

ATG New York Yankees Hitting

Pos	Name	G	PA	AB	R	H	1B	2B	3B	HR	RBI	BB	SO	SB	CS	BA	OBP	SLG	TB	HBP	SAC	ROE	GDP
SS	Jeter	6	32	27	8	10	6	1	1	2	3	3	3	0	1	.370	.433	.704	19	0	0	1	0
CF	Mantle	6	31	28	8	9	3	3	0	4	9	2	9	0	1	.321	.355	.893	25	0	1	0	1
RF	Ruth	6	31	25	10	14	4	4	0	6	11	6	6	0	0	.560	.645	1.440	36	0	0	0	0
1B	Gehrig	6	30	25	9	13	5	4	0	4	10	4	5	1	0	.520	.586	1.160	29	0	0	1	0
3B	Rodriguez	6	30	25	2	2	0	1	0	1	4	4	8	1	0	.080	.233	.240	6	1	0	0	0
CF	Berra	6	29	24	6	10	5	1	0	4	7	4	2	0	0	.417	.500	.958	23	0	0	1	0
DH	Matsui	6	29	27	1	10	7	2	0	1	3	1	6	0	0	.370	.379	.556	15	0	1	0	0
2B	Lazzeri	6	28	26	1	1	1	0	0	0	1	1	12	0	0	.038	.071	.038	1	0	1	0	0
LF	White	6	27	25	3	7	4	3	0	0	0	0	1	0	0	.280	.308	.400	10	1	0	1	0

ATG New York Yankees Pitching

Pos	Name	W	L	ERA	G	GS	GF	CG	SHO	SV	R	ER	IP	H	HR	BB	SO	BF	H9	HR9	BB9	SO9	SO/W
SP	Ruffing	1	1	2.65	2	2	2	2	1	0	5	5	17.0	15	1	4	5	68	7.94	0.53	2.12	2.65	1.25
SP	Ford	1	1	8.36	2	2	0	0	0	0	14	13	14.0	21	2	10	2	73	13.50	1.29	6.43	1.29	0.20
SP	Reynolds	0	0	10.81	1	1	0	0	0	0	9	8	6.2	12	1	4	6	36	16.22	1.35	5.41	8.11	1.50
SP	Pettitte	1	0	3.38	1	1	0	0	0	0	3	3	8.0	5	1	4	4	33	5.63	1.13	4.50	4.50	1.00
RP	Betances	0	0	0.00	2	0	1	0	0	0	0	0	3.2	0	0	1	4	12	0.00	0.00	2.46	9.84	4.00
RP	Lyle	0	0	2.25	2	0	1	0	0	1	1	1	4.0	3	0	7	2	22	6.75	0.00	15.75	4.50	0.29
RP	Gossage	0	0	0.00	1	0	1	0	0	0	0	0	1.0	1	0	0	1	4	9.00	0.00	0.00	9.00	0.00
CL	Rivera	1	0	0.00	1	0	1	0	0	0	0	0	0.1	0	0	1	0	2	0.00	0.00	27.27	0.00	0.00

ALL-TIME BEST YANKEES TEAM: 1998 YANKEES

Record: 114–48 (Best Record in MLB)

Batting Stats

Hits	RBIs	Runs	BA	OBP
1625 (2nd in AL, 3rd in ML)	907 (1st in ML)	965 (1st in ML)	.288 (2nd in AL, 3rd in ML)	.364 (1st in ML)

Pitching Stats

Hits Allowed	Walks Allowed	ERA
1357 (1st in AL, 3rd in ML)	466 (2nd in AL, 3rd in ML)	3.82 (1st in AL, 6th in ML)

Awards

Won 1998 World Series (Playoff Record: 11–2)
All-Stars: 5 (Brosius, Jeter, O'Neill, Wells, Williams)
Manager of the Year: Joe Torre
Batting Champion: Bernie Williams (.339/.422/.575)
Gold Gloves: 1 (Bernie Williams, OF)
HOFers: Tim Raines and Mariano Rivera

Reason for Decision

In terms of Hall of Fame star power, the **1998 Yankees** were no match for the '27 "Murderers' Row" Yankees of Babe Ruth, Lou Gehrig, Tony Lazzeri, and Earle Combs; or the '36 Yankees of Gehrig, Joe DiMaggio, Bill Dickey, Lefty Gomez, and Red Ruffing. Indeed, the 1998 Yankees were not the most talented team ever, but they were the most complete team in franchise history. Each member of the 25-man roster had a role to play, and each man executed that role to near perfection. Manager Joe Torre's squad possessed a winning combination of youth and experience, power and speed, to go along with a trustworthy defense that ably supported a stingy pitching staff that was equally represented with right-handed and left-handed hurlers.

These Yankees won an impressive 114 regular-season games, second-most all-time behind the 1906 Chicago Cubs (who lost in the World Series to the White Sox) and the 2001 Seattle Mariners (who lost to the Yankees in the ALCS). The team opened the season losing four of their first five games, and then reeled off a stunning 64–16 run—the most dominant 80-game stretch in franchise history. They finished the regular season with a 114–48 record (a .704 winning percentage), 22 games ahead of the second-place Red Sox, barely visible in their rearview mirror.

In a season of steroid-induced excess, when Mark McGwire and Sammy Sosa both toppled Roger Maris's single-season home-run record with 70 and 66, respectively, no one on the '98 Yanks hit more than 28 home runs (Tino Martinez), but the team still managed to lead the majors in runs scored with 965 (5.96 per game), and outscored opponents by 309 runs, nearly two per game. The defense allowed only 37 unearned runs the entire season, one of the lowest totals in recent history. The hitters accumulated 187 walks more than the pitchers allowed.

Table-setters at the top of the batting order were second baseman Chuck Knoblauch, who led the team in steals (31) and walks (76), and shortstop Derek Jeter, the team leader in hits (203) and runs scored (127). They were followed by right fielder Paul O'Neill, with a team-best 40 doubles, center fielder Bernie Williams, the AL batting leader with a .339 average and team-high .997 OPS, and the aforementioned slugging first baseman Martinez, who also led the team with 123 RBIs. Rounding out the lineup was Jorge Posada, an emerging switch-hitting catcher with pop, third baseman Scott Brosius—with 98 RBIs hitting out of the nine-hole—and designated hitter Darryl Strawberry, who hit 24 homers in 295 at-bats. A late-season call-up, Shane Spencer, blasted 10 homers in 27 September games for good measure.

Though the Yankees were seventh in the majors with 207 homers, theirs was a balanced attack, with 10 players hitting at least 10 homers. All eight of the everyday position players had an on-base percentage of at least .350. The team's .364 on-base percentage and .825 OPS both led the majors, while their .288 batting average ranked third and their .460 slugging percentage fifth. Adding depth to an already talented pool of players, the bench was comprised of former everyday players who will-ingly accepted their limited role—guys such as Tim Raines (a Hall of Famer), Chili Davis, Luis Sojo, and Joe Girardi.

These Yankees were much more than just an offensive machine. The pitching staff was top-shelf and sported the lowest ERA in the league, 3.82. David Cone, David Wells (who pitched a perfect game), Andy Pettitte, Orlando "El Duque" Hernandez, and Hideki Irabu combined for a 79–35 record. The bullpen of Mariano Rivera, Jeff Nelson, Mike Stanton, Graeme Lloyd, and Ramiro Mendoza was lights out, going 25–6. Rivera, the anchor, had 36 saves with a 1.91 ERA, and was such a force at the end of games that opposing teams knew if they didn't have the lead after seven innings, the game was over.

The Yanks breezed through the 1998 postseason, winning 11 of 13 games and outscoring their opponents, 62–34, in the three rounds of the postseason, which culminated in a World Series sweep over the San Diego Padres. That gave the '98 Yankees a total of 125 wins for the season, which is an MLB record that should stand for a very long time. In fact, the championship ring is engraved with their incredible 125–50 record above the words "Best Ever"—an assessment that holds up to the scrutiny of even the most biased of BoSox fans.

Honorable Mention

The **1927 Yankees** bludgeoned their opponents, winning 110 regular-sea-son games (while losing just 44), capturing the AL pennant by 19 games over the second-place A's (the Red Sox finished in the cellar—59 games back), and then whipping the Pittsburgh Pirates to win the World Series in a four-game sweep.

Manager Miller Huggins's squad held first place every day of the sea-son. Babe Ruth hit 60 home runs, one more than the record 59 he had hit in 1921. Lou Gehrig hit 47 homers and set a record for RBIs with 175. There was strength in the middle with centerfielder Earle Combs (who batted .356 and led the league in hits with 213) and the young keystone combination of shortstop Mark Koenig and second baseman Tony Lazzeri, the latter of which was third in the league in homers with 18. Ruth, Gehrig, Lazzeri, Combs, and Bob Meusel (.337 average) were dubbed "Murderers' Row"; of the five, only Combs did not reach 100 RBIs.

The offense was frighteningly good. The team's batting average was .307 and there wasn't a regular player who batted under .269. The team's slugging percentage was a whopping .488. Their run differential was a staggering 376. The offense was held scoreless only once all season, and that was by Philadelphia's Lefty Grove. After New York defeated Washington during a July 4 doubleheader by a combined score of 33–2, Senators first baseman Joe Judge remarked, "Those fellows not only beat you, but they tear your heart out."

It was pitching, though, that made this team all but unbeatable. Waite Hoyt led the league with 22 wins and had a 2.63 ERA. Herb Pennock was 19–8, Urban Shocker was 18–6, and Wilcy Moore went 19–7 with a league-leading 13 saves.

With Babe Ruth gone, manager Joe McCarthy set about the task of assembling a new Yankees dynasty. He would ultimately manage his way into the Hall of Fame, and his **1936 Yankees** included five players—Lou Gehrig, Bill Dickey, Lefty Gomez, Red Ruffing, and Joe DiMaggio—who would join him in Cooperstown.

The '36 team dazzled and demoralized opponents. The club scored more than 1,000 runs and outscored the competition by a whopping 334 runs. Seven regulars hit 10 or more homers, with five knocking in over 100 runs each. Gehrig hit a career-high 49 homers and drove in 152 runs while batting .354; he was a shoo-in as the league's MVP. Dickey hit a lifetime high of .362 with 22 home runs and 107 RBIs. The rookie DiMaggio hit .323 with 29 HRs and 125 RBIs. Lazzeri drove in 107 and scored 82. Even weak-hitting shortstop Frankie Crosetti came up with a .288 average.

The pitching was deep and effective, with six hurlers winning 12 games or more, anchored by Red Ruffing (20–12, 3.85 ERA), Monte Pearson (19–7, 3.71 ERA), and Lefty Gomez (13–7, 4.39 ERA). A first glance at the pitching staff's 4.17 ERA for the season might suggest that this was a team that lived by its bats—but 4.17 led the AL in '36.

These Yankees won 102 regular-season games and finished the season 19 1/2 games ahead of the Detroit Tigers, assuring themselves the pennant on September 9, the earliest clinching date in AL history. When they beat the New York Giants in six games to win the World Series, it would be the first of four consecutive world championships.

The **1953 Yankees** had it all—dominant pitching, timely hitting, solid defense—and there were plenty of heroes to go around among the squad's six Hall of Famers: Yogi Berra, Phil Rizzuto, Johnny Mize, Whitey Ford, Mickey Mantle, and manager Casey Stengel. This 99-win team got out of the gate at a blistering 41–11 pace—which included an 18-game winning streak—and glided to the finish, spending an incredible 162 days in first place.

The regular starters provided a balanced attack. Berra (who hit .296) and Mantle (who batted .295) combined for 200 RBIs, and Gene Woodling (.306 with a league-best .429 on-base percentage) and Hank Bauer (.304) led the lineup in batting average. Billy Martin, setting career highs with 15 homers and 75 RBIs, became a rock in his second year starting at second base. In all, seven position players hit 10 or more homers, 20 or more doubles, and drove in 50 or more runs.

The major strength of the team was its pitching, which led the league in ERA, shutouts, and saves. Ford returned from the service to join the Big Three of Allie Reynolds, Vic Raschi, and Eddie Lopat, forming a Big Four starting rotation.

No one will ever claim that this Yankees team was the greatest of all time, but it remains the only in baseball's long history to win five straight World Series. In the four major professional sports, only the Montreal Canadiens in hockey and the Boston Celtics in basketball have ever won five or more consecutive world championships.

For fence-busting power, one would be hard-pressed to top the **1961 Yankees**: the team hit 240 homers to set a mark that would stand for 35 years. First-year manager Ralph Houk's team was dominant, finishing with a 109–53 record and were nearly unbeatable in Yankee Stadium, playing over .800 ball in the Bronx.

The '61 team will always be remembered for the long-ball heroics of Roger Maris and Mickey Mantle, the M & M Boys, and their chase of Babe Ruth's single-season home run record. Maris, of course, achieved the magic 61, while Mantle, slowed with a late-season injury, checked in with a mere 54. They remain the only teammates in history to hit 50-plus homers in the same season.

The Yankees' power didn't stop at Maris and Mantle. Behind them in the lineup were four other players who belted 20 or more home runs: first baseman Moose Skowron (28), left fielder Yogi Berra (22), and catchers Elston Howard and Johnny Blanchard (21 apiece).

While the team pounded opponents with the long ball, they could also win games with pitching and defense. The infield consisted of the acrobatic Clete Boyer at third, Gold Glovers Bobby Richardson and Tony Kubek at second and short, respectively, and Skowron at first. The pitching staff was led by Whitey Ford, who went 25–4 and won the Cy Young Award, as well as the screwballing Luis Arroyo who was 15–5 with a league-leading 29 saves and a 2.19 ERA in 119 innings out of the bullpen. Ford went on to pitch 14 scoreless innings in two World Series wins and take home the MVP honors as the Yankees defeated the Cincinnati Reds in five games.

The **1978 Yankees** were no strangers to comebacks. In July, the defending world champions were in fourth place, 14 games behind the division-leading Red Sox, but they battled back to eventually overtake Boston in a one-game playoff. (You might remember that game.) The Bombers then went on to defeat the Royals for the third straight year in the ALCS, this time in four games. Then they met the Dodgers in the World Series once again, overcame a two-games-to-none deficit, and won four straight for the title. No team in Series history ever did that before.

The '78 team rallied with the media spotlight lessened because the city's major newspapers didn't publish during a summer labor strike. The team also underwent an upheaval in late July when turbulent manager Billy Martin was canned and replaced by the easygoing Bob Lemon. Under Lemon, the Yanks went 48–20 and, in early September, swept the Red Sox in what would become known as the "Boston Massacre," outscoring them, 42–9.

The lineup featured Chris Chambliss, Willie Randolph, Bucky Dent, Graig Nettles, Lou Piniella, Mickey Rivers, Reggie Jackson, and Thurman

Munson. Chambliss and Nettles won Gold Glove Awards. Randolph led the team with 36 stolen bases. Longtime favorite Roy White was still with the club as well. On the mound, Ron Guidry finished 25–3 with a 1.74 ERA, winning the Cy Young Award unanimously. The southpaw also finished second in the MVP voting behind Boston's Jim Rice. In addition to Guidry, the Yanks had Rich Gossage on the mound, who won the Relief Award with 27 saves, and righty starter Ed Figueroa, who won 20 games and remains the only pitcher born in Puerto Rico to accomplish that feat.

Bill Nowlin's Response

I wish you'd forgotten to include the 1978 Yankees. That team gave me nightmares for years. I was there at Fenway Park for Game 163. I had seen the Red Sox with a nine-game lead over everyone in the AL East on July 19 (and a 14-game lead over the Yankees). I saw that lead frittered away. They had a nine-game lead over the Yankees as late as August 13. A month later, they were out of first place. They had to win their last eight games of the 162-game schedule just to force the single-game playoff. And then I saw Bucky Dent hit his fifth home run of the year, and then Munson and Reggie Jackson each add runs to ensure the win.

Then I had to, more or less, relive the whole nightmare 25 years later in 2003. But enough about me and the scars to my psyche. The very next year—2004—the healing began.

Somehow—probably because my head was buried deep in the sand for the last three years of the twentieth century—I have to admit I would have never summoned up the 1998 Yankees. I was thinking 1927, just because of that team's iconic status. But I totally buy into your choice. The Yankees won three straight World Series to close out the century— and they won each year with ease, sweeping in 1998 and 1999, and only having one hiccup in 2000, taking 12 out of 13 World Series games.

That stretch started with the 1998 team, though. They set the pace, and the next two teams kind of continued on cruise control.

It's not like I'm telling Yankees fans anything they don't already know. Most Yankees fans have no feeling for what it's like to just *assume* your team is going to lose, one way or another. Maybe Red Sox fans didn't

notice how good some of the other teams were, because we were wallow-
ing in well-earned self-pity.

The Red Sox finished 22 games behind the Yankees in 1998. No surprise that I tuned out early. Sure, the Red Sox were in second place in the
division—but ... 22 games!

The Red Sox got closer—just four games behind in 1999—and finished only 2 1/2 behind in 2000. The '99 team actually got to play the
Yankees in the 1999 ALCS and had that one game they clobbered the
Yankees, 13–1 (Pedro vs. Roger), but that was the only game they could
win, though both Games One and Two were one-run games.

The 1998 Yankees were impressive—*very* impressive. You had 27
world championship teams to choose from (cough cough). I think you
made the right choice.

ALL-TIME BEST RED SOX TEAM: 2018 RED SOX

Record: 108–54 (Best Record in MLB)

Batting Stats

Hits	RBIs	Runs	BA	OBP
1509 (1st in ML)	829 (1st in ML)	876 (1st in ML)	.268 (1st in ML)	.792 (1st in ML)

Pitching Stats

Hits Allowed	Strikeouts	ERA
1305 (4th in AL, 7th in ML)	1558 (3rd in AL, 4th in ML)	.375 (3rd in AL, 8th in ML)

Awards

Won 2018 World Series (Playoff Record: 11–3)
All-Stars: 5 (Betts. Kimbrel, Martinez, Moreland, Sale)
Batting Champion: Mookie Betts (.346/.438/.640)
Silver Slugger: Betts, Martinez (2)
MVP: Mookie Betts
Gold Gloves: 3 (Kinsler*, 2B; Bradley Jr., OF; Betts, OF) *Split time between Angels and Red Sox
Hank Aaron Award: J. D. Martinez (DH)

Reason for Decision

Until the last month or so of the 2018 season, I would have selected the 2004 Red Sox. Many Sox fans still would. Partly to tweak Yankees fans but, really, because that's the way most Sox fans have felt since then. You finally overcome 86 years of seeming futility. Call it a "curse" or whatever, the Red Sox could never win it all. The honorable mentions here will include 1912, 1946, 1967, 1975, 1986—a win in 1912, and then four years in which they came very close, each time taking it all the way to Game Seven of the World Series. I probably could have included the 2003 Red

Sox, too. My honorable mentions now include 2004. But we'll get into that below.

The 2018 Red Sox were an incredible team, winning a franchise-best 108 games in the regular season—and then the requisite 11 more games necessary to win a world championship, the ninth in team history and the fourth already in the young twenty-first century. They only lost one game in each round of the postseason, losing to the Yankees in the Division Series, one to the reigning world champion Astros in the League Championship Series, and one to the Dodgers in the World Series (in 18 innings). Every one of the clinching games was won on the road. There was never a need to clean up the champagne in the Fenway clubhouse. They could dirty up someone else's park.

The team had stars aplenty. Mookie Betts (.346) was the American League Most Valuable Player and the league batting champion; he actually led all of major-league baseball. J. D. Martinez (.330) came in second in the batting race and placed fourth in MVP voting. The same two finished 1-2 in league slugging percentage. Betts tied for the major-league lead in runs scored, too, and his 10.9 wins above replacement led all of baseball in WAR and stands as the highest mark for any position player since Barry Bonds in 2002. Martinez drove in 130 runs, seven more than anyone else in the majors. He also led in total bases (358).

The three B's—Betts, Bradley Jr., and Benintendi—were perhaps the best defensive outfield in all of baseball. Every member of the Red Sox outfield was a nominee for a Gold Glove. Both Betts and Bradley Jr. (and Ian Kinsler) won Gold Gloves. Betts and Martinez both won Silver Sluggers, with J. D. being the first player in history to be awarded two Silver Sluggers in the same season. He had enough plate appearances as an outfielder and as a DH to qualify him in both positions.

But perhaps the most remarkable thing about the 2018 Red Sox was the way the role players contributed—including players who weren't even with the team when the season began. Among them was World Series MVP Steve Pearce, who arrived at the end of June, and RHP Nathan Eovaldi, who arrived on July 26. Eovaldi started Game Three of the ALDS and won it. He started Game Three of the ALCS and won that, too. He worked scoreless relief innings in both World Series wins in Game One and Game Two, and then threw a heroic six innings in relief in the

18-inning game that was Game Three. It was a 3–2 loss to the Dodgers, but Eovaldi reportedly got a standing ovation in the clubhouse after the game for his herculean effort.

The MVPs of the postseason were players one might never have expected—Jackie Bradley Jr. of the ALCS and (as noted) Steve Pearce of the World Series. JBJ drove in nine of the team's 27 total runs in the ALCS. Pearce tied Game Four with a homer and then blasted it open with a three-run double in the top of the ninth. In the deciding Game Five, his two-run first-inning homer off Clayton Kershaw was the game-winner.

It was offense that led the team, despite having something of a black hole in the bottom third of the order. Catchers Sandy Leon (.177) and Christian Vasquez (.207) were clearly there for their skills handling pitchers more than the bat, though magically they each contributed a few key base hits. JBJ was batting just .219 as late as August 21, but he has often shown bursts of streaky offense—and this year he came through particularly big in the postseason.

Pitching was a strength, too, of course, but with huge help from the bullpen. It didn't start out well; the Red Sox lost Opening Day on a blown save. (They then went on to win nine games in a row.) Pitchers who were expected to contribute a lot more than they did included Drew Pomeranz, Carson Smith, Tyler Thornburg, and Steven Wright. In fact, of all the Sox starting pitchers, only two threw enough innings to qualify for any form of pitching award: David Price and Rick Porcello. Chris Sale struck out 237 batters in 158 innings, but that's not enough innings to qualify. (Sale was on the DL twice, and it seemed apparent that he never fully recovered.) Yet there he was on the mound, in relief, gutting it out by throwing the eighth inning of the ALDS Game Four win over the Yankees, and was on the mound again for the final pitches of the World Series, striking out the final three Dodgers. It's a rare feat for one pitcher to record both the first and last out of a World Series.

Craig Kimbrel put up a lot of strikeouts again in 2018 and was the ace closer for almost the full season, but he became a heart-attack threat several times near the end of the season. He gave up seven earned runs in 10 2/3 innings during the playoffs. Joe Kelly, on the other hand, was either all or nothing, pitching brilliantly early on (Opening Day excepted) but execrably at times in midseason, only to recover and pitch extremely well at the end, including pitching 10 1/3 innings in the playoffs, striking out 13 and walking none while giving up just one earned run. In Game Five of the World Series, he struck out the side in the eighth—combined with Sale, the last six Dodgers to face Red Sox relievers all went down with a K, five of the six striking out swinging.

The middle relievers really came through, often, in a season that saw starters around baseball work less than ever before. Hector Velasquez never stood out, but look at his season stats: 7–2 (3.18) in 85 innings. Brandon Workman, left off the World Series roster, was 6–1 (3.27). Ryan Brasier—not even in the majors since 2013—joined the team in midseason and worked in 34 games (2–0, 1.60, with 29 strikeouts and only seven walks.)

First-year manager Alex Cora proved to be a very strong communicator with the team; he seemed to blend analytics and instincts to perfection. He didn't let sentiment stand in the way, several times pulling starters with 4 2/3 innings under their belt and the lead. He had to deal with a team that, as with pitching, didn't have some of the expected starters come through. An injured Dustin Pedroia was only able to play in three games and had just one base hit. An underperforming Hanley Ramirez was hitting only .254 when he was cut loose on May 24, with the Sox eating most of a salary that exceeded $22 million. (They even paid $18 million for Pablo Sandoval, who didn't play a game.)

Cora somehow seemed to have the Midas touch. He made moves that seemed unorthodox, either from an analytics standpoint or a more traditional baseball view. But they worked so often that it was a wonder to see.

And it was appreciated. On the morning of World Series Game Five, in Los Angeles, the team held a breakfast for players and their families. As Tim Keown of ESPN noted: "One by one, perhaps sensing it was their last chance, the parents approached Cora, the fathers' hands extended, the mothers angling in for a hug. They came bearing some version of the same message: 'Thank you for the way you've treated our son.'" Absolutely remarkable. He had fostered a clubhouse culture that built bonds among players to such a degree that even the parents had realized it. Analytics are one thing; chemistry is another. Cora seemed to know how to blend the two.

Whether it was his leadership or not, this was also a gritty, determined team that fought through injuries. Chris Sale aside, in the playoffs alone one saw at least three players suffer what appeared to be serious ankle injuries—J. D. Martinez, Xander Bogaerts, and Eduardo Nunez, who also dove headfirst into the Dodger Stadium stands and probably deserved the World Series Purple Heart.

The 2018 Red Sox won two-thirds of their games. They won the AL East by a full eight games over the second-place Yankees. They were expected to face a harder row to hoe in the postseason than it seems they did.

In retrospect:

- They beat a 100-win Yankees team, taking three out of four in the Division Series.
- They beat the 103-win reigning world champion Houston Astros, taking four out of five in the League Championship Series.
- They beat the National League pennant-winning Los Angeles Dodgers in a World Series that also only lasted five games (despite the top of the order hardly doing a thing on offense).

Interesting side note from a "rivalry" perspective: Dan Shaughnessy reported that, as the Yankees were dispatching the Oakland A's in the wild-card Game on October 3, fans at the Stadium were chanting "We want Boston! We want Boston!" The Yankees did win Game Two of the ALDS and Aaron Judge reportedly lingered outside the Red Sox club-house with a boombox loudly playing a taunting "New York, New York." The next game, Boston won, 16–1. Game Four saw one of the weirder endings of any playoff game, with the Yankees almost tying or winning it. There was a replay review on the last play of the game, and Eduardo Nunez seemed to injure himself in celebration before the replay was requested, but afterward it was the Red Sox playing the Yankees' long-time victory song while dousing themselves in champagne.

They basically breezed through the playoffs, losing only one game in each round. The Red Sox bullpen struck out 63 batters in 63 innings of work during the playoffs, with a 2.71 ERA.

It was an 11–3 postseason. There were two games that stood out from the rest. Even if Yankees/Red Sox weren't the theme of this book, one couldn't ignore Game Three of the ALDS. After the Yankees had the temerity to win Game Two at Fenway Park, rendering David Price 0-for-9 in postseason starts, the Red Sox struck back in the Stadium, slaughtering the New Yorkers, 16–1 (with Brock Holt hitting for the cycle!). And in the World Series, there was the seven-hour, 20-minute Game Three of the World Series. It was tied, 1–1, after nine. The Sox scored once in the top of the 13th, but then the Dodgers scored one, too. It finally ended at 3:29 in the morning, Eastern time. The Red Sox lost, but then came back and won the next two. David Price won one game in the ALCS and was 2–0 in the World Series.

Winning the World Series in five games, the Red Sox have been— beginning with 2004—16–3 against National League opponents, outscoring them by 56 runs.

Honorable Mention

Now to those teams that earn an honorable mention. First among them are the **2004 Red Sox**. They were the "Idiots"—a team that will rest in my heart forever, and in the hearts of Red Sox fans everywhere. It's not that I remember the 1946 Red Sox, as I was only one year old during their run. But that's part of the point. In 2004, I was 59 years old. Unlike Dave Fischer, who had already seen the Yankees win 142 world championships (well, OK, "only" six), I had never seen one. The Patriots winning was nice, but I've always been a baseball guy. I was aware that the Celtics put up a swath of banners during my lifetime, but I didn't care as much. I'd never been to a Celtics game at that time, and still have only been to maybe three.

And the way they did it—the 2004 Red Sox—it was like it had a storybook ending that would have been laughed out of Hollywood had Ben Affleck or Stephen King approached the studio with such a screenplay.

The Red Sox, as many will painfully recall, had lost to the Yankees just the year before, in 2003, thanks to Grady Little but also current Yankees manager Aaron Boone. They were ready to give it another slog in 2004 and, wouldn't you know it, it was the Yankees who stood in the way once again in the ALCS. The Yanks won Games One and Two, and slaughtered the Red Sox in Game Three, 19–8. I wrote a whole book about what happened from that point on, working with Allan Wood on *Don't Let Us Win Tonight!* Well, the Red Sox *did* win that night, after Dave Roberts stole second, Mariano Rivera blew a save for the first time in recorded history, and then, in the bottom of the 12th, David Ortiz hit a home run to win the game and stave off the sweep.

Less than 24 hours later, on the same calendar day, after another blown save by Mariano, the Red Sox won again, once more thanks to Big Papi, this time following a pair of walks (and a pair of strikeouts) with a run-scoring single in the bottom of the 14th.

Then it was back to Yankee Stadium where Mark Bellhorn's three-run homer (drama on its own) gave Boston a 4–2 edge in Game Six, and then finally the 10–3 finale in Game Seven when Boston scored early and often to beat a demoralized New York team. After that, it was anticlimactic that they rolled over the Cardinals in four straight to win their first World Series since 1918. How could any team top that one? It wasn't the easiest of calls. The drama, the improbability, the angst of "the rivalry"— none of that was really around in 2018. But the reasons for my choice were detailed above.

The **1912 Red Sox** kicked off a decade of dynasty for the BoSox. Opening the season in brand-new Fenway Park, the 1912 team won 105 games and only lost 47. They finished a full 14 games ahead of the second-place Washington Senators. (The Yankees, then known as the Highlanders, were 55 games behind, in last place, making them one of my favorite Yankees teams of all time.) The 105 wins gave them a .691 winning percentage, better than the .667 they achieved in 2018 (believe me, I was calculating winning percentage all through September 2018). This was a truly great team, though when it came to the World Series, John McGraw's New York Giants gave them such a battle that it took *eight* games for the Red Sox to win the best-of-seven Series. (Game Two was a 6–6 tie.) Four of the seven games that counted were won by one run, including the final one, in which Smoky Joe Wood beat Christy Mathewson, 3–2, in 10 innings.

The **1946 Red Sox** had such a strong start that, after the game on May 10, they were 21–3. They were not to be denied. A full eight members of the team made the AL All-Star team (held, as it happens, in Fenway Park that year): Ted Williams (who homered twice in the game), Johnny Pesky, Bobby Doerr, Rudy York, Boo Ferriss, Mickey Harris, Hal Wagner—and the DiMaggio in the game was Dominic, not Joe. They finished 104–50 (.675, again a winning percentage better than 2018) and 12 games ahead of any other team. But when it came to the World Series, they couldn't seal the deal. They alternated wins and losses until Game Seven in St. Louis, when a little bloop hit scored a double which prompted Enos Slaughter to make a mad dash, scoring all the way from first base on a ball that dropped in front of the center fielder, scoring the go-ahead run in the bottom of the eighth.

Not sealing the deal is a big thing. It's why the **1967 "Impossible Dream" Red Sox** aren't the top team. That they made it to the World Series at all was a feat, coming from a group that had been in the doldrums for a decade and a half and had finished only a half-game out of last place in 1966 (the Yankees, I will note, were the team in the '66 cellar). The heroics of Carl Yastrzemski got them the pennant. As it says in his SABR biography, "In the final 12 games of the season—crunch time—Carl Yastrzemski had 23 hits in 44 at-bats, driving in 16 runs and scoring 14. He hit 10 homers in his final 100 at-bats of 1967. He had 10 hits in his last 13 at-bats, and when it came to the last two games with the Twins, with the Sox needing to win both games to help avert a tie for the pennant, Yaz went 7-for-8 and drove in six runs." Come the World Series, though, manager Dick Williams had to go to the well one too many times with Jim Lonborg. The Sox lost it in seven—again to St. Louis.

Save for Jim Rice having his hand broken by a Vern Ruhle pitch on September 21, the **1975 Red Sox** might have coasted to a World Series win—even against the "Big Red Machine" Cincinnati Reds. But Rice was unable to play. Even though Bernie Carbo had one of the biggest pinch-hits in World Series history (bottom of the eighth three-run homer in an elimination Game Six) to tie the score 6–6, and even though Carlton Fisk won it in the bottom of the 12th with a majestic home run that just stayed fair—perhaps the most-often replayed TV highlight in baseball history—the hometown Red Sox, despite taking an early 3–0 lead in Game Seven, couldn't hold on to victory and lost, 4–3, when the Reds broke through to break a tie.

Was the ball hit to Bill Buckner of the **1986 World Series** the second-most-often replayed TV moment? It's not a team a lot of Sox fans like to remember, because they truly had victory in their grasp—until they didn't. The Shea Stadium scoreboard operator had even prematurely flashed congratulations to them as World Champions … but they weren't. We won't dwell on that here. There are many reasons the Sox lost that Game Six, and once again they blew an early 3–0 lead in Game Seven.

Now that enough time has passed, it's easy to remember some of those teams without the mental scars being ripped open again. Winning it all in 2004, 2007, and 2013 helped a lot. There were only eight days in which the **2007 Red Sox** were not in first place, and from April 18 on they held the lead all by themselves. They swept Oakland in the Division Series, but then had to overcome a three-games-to-one deficit in the ALCS to make their way past the Cleveland Indians. They won the final three games, though, and then swept the Rockies in the World Series.

The **2013 Red Sox** "band of bearded brothers" were a very likable team. Surprisingly, it was the Tampa Bay Rays who placed second in the AL East, then beating the Indians in the wild-card game. They won a well-fought Game Three in the Division Series, but Boston won three of the four games. The biggest challenge the Red Sox faced was in the ALCS, against a very strong Detroit Tigers team. David Ortiz hit a grand slam in the bottom of the eighth in Game Two, tying the score and putting the Sox in a position to win. And Shane Victorino's Game Five grand slam made all the difference in that game. It took Boston six games to defeat Detroit, but all the games were so close that the ALCS MVP was closer Koji Uehara, who won one game and earned saves in the three other victories. When it came to the World Series, the Sox faced St. Louis again and finally balanced the tables (1946 and 1967 as Cardinals wins, and 2004 and 2013 as Red Sox wins), taking it in six games—and winning the final game at home in Fenway Park for the first time since 1918.

It's a team that Sox fans will always remember. But for the team that was the franchise team of all time, I'm sticking with the 2018 Red Sox. And hoping that another team comes along soon that one-ups them!

David Fischer's Response

It will be debated throughout New England which Red Sox championship team was the best in franchise history, but only two teams in baseball history ever won more than the Red Sox's 119 victories in 2018, and few teams were ever more respected and beloved. "We are one of the greatest teams in history," Red Sox reliever Joe Kelly said, "and now we will have that bond forever." He gets no argument here.

Only the vaunted 1998 Yankees with 125 victories and the 2001 Mariners with 120 victories collected more regular-season and postseason wins combined than the 2018 Red Sox, and let it be noted that the M's that year bowed out against the Yanks in the ALCS. Okay, so the Red Sox are "merely" tied for ninth when it comes to most regular season wins, but just four teams—the aforementioned '98 Yankees, the 1909 Pirates, the 1927 Yankees, and 1961 Yankees—won more games in the regular season than the 2018 Red Sox did while also winning the World Series. So often, the best team in the regular season doesn't wind up hoisting the trophy, and that's in part why the 2018 Sox are in such rarefied air and why you get no argument from me for selecting the squad as your best Red Sox team ever.

For all the Yankees' success in 2018, they took a backseat to the Red Sox. Only twice can I cite examples of the Yankees winning 100 or more games and ending the campaign with such an empty feeling. In 1954, when they won 103 games but fell short to the Indians, winners of 111 games that season, and in 1980, when they won 103 games only to suffer an ignominious sweep at the hands of the Royals in the ALCS. Plain and simple, the Bombers never could solve the BoSox in 2018. The year started with Joe Kelly burying a 98-mph fastball in Tyler Austin's ribs in early April. It ended in late September after Giancarlo Stanton blasted a home run over the top of Fenway Park's infamous Green Monster, and a Red Sox fan grabbed the ball and whipped it back onto the field in protest, hitting Stanton in the arm on a hop as he rounded second base. That's symbolic of how the season went for these two rivals.

Perhaps we should've seen this coming. Boston began the 2018 season winning 17 of its first 19 games. That last happened more than 30 years ago and only four times in the last century. Two of those teams, the 1984 Detroit Tigers and 1955 Brooklyn Dodgers, won the World Series.

But they didn't need to conquer three rounds of playoffs like the Red Sox did. A team that won 108 games during the regular season and were the only team in 2018 not to lose four games in a row, stormed through the postseason, taking down everyone who dared stand in their way. The Yankees, Astros, and Dodgers won a combined 295 games during the regular season. The Red Sox ran that postseason gauntlet while losing just three times in 14 games. Boston earned its 119–57 record while facing the toughest playoff opponents ever. By any sensible measure, that makes them one of the greatest teams in baseball history. "They never stopped coming at you," Houston manager A. J. Hinch said of the Red Sox lineup. "They're a relentless group."

The Red Sox hitters certainly were "grinders," an affectionate baseball term for annoying and infuriating and, finally, devastating at-bats. None more so than in July, when Mookie Betts wore down pitcher J. A. Happ during a 13-pitch at-bat that resulted in a grand slam for Boston's 10th straight victory, the team's longest winning streak of the season. The battle lasted seven minutes and 20 seconds and personified the gritty at-bats taken by Red Sox batters with runners in scoring position, foreshadowing a postseason performance for the ages—especially with two out.

In a final act of desperation, Yankees fans were hoping for an omen from the baseball gods; any sign would do. Boston had not yet clinched the division title when a banner marking the accomplishment was accidentally unveiled. Three Boston-area friends found the banner on a road after it apparently fell off a vendor's delivery truck in Somerville, Massachusetts. In the end, however, nothing could stop these Red Sox— not even bad karma.

Perhaps it *was* destiny. After all, a favorite Yankees punching bag, David Price, who entered the postseason with the stigma of never winning when it counted in October, proved his tenacity in the World Series and forever changed the narrative by starting and winning Game Two, pitching in relief in Game Three, warming up during Game Four, and starting and winning Game Five with a three-hitter through seven innings. Price earned his sweet revenge, and the 2018 Red Sox earned their rightful place in history.

HEAD-TO-HEAD

David Fischer: Since 125 and 119 are a slew of wins, it sparks a natural debate about which of the two teams, separated by exactly two decades, was better. On record alone, the '98 Yankees hold the edge as they went 114–48 in the regular season then 11–2 in the postseason. The '18 Red Sox had a 108–54 record in the regular season then were 11–3 in the play-offs. Case closed!

Bill Nowlin Don't get too carried away. Wins aren't everything. Not in sheer quantity, anyhow. Look at the competition. The closest anyone came to the 1998 Yankees was the Red Sox, 22 games behind. The Jays were 26 behind, the O's 35, and the then-Devil Rays 51. That's a total of 134 games behind.

Now, with that said, the 2018 Orioles were 61 games back, but the Yankees were only eight behind and the Rays were 18. The Sox won six fewer games, but against stiffer competition.

DF: Point taken. Your Red Sox also forged a more difficult path in the postseason. My 100-win Yankees submitted in four games in the ALDS, the 103-win Astros were eliminated in five games in the ALCS—the same number of games it took the Sox to polish off the 92-win Dodgers in the Series. Meanwhile, my '98 Yankees "only" swept the 88-win Rangers three straight, took down the 89-win Indians in six, and then demolished the 98-win Padres in a four-game sweep. The 212 combined wins for the Yankees and Padres is the most ever in a postseason series. You play the team on your schedule.

BN: That's the thing. You leapt ahead and stole some of my thunder. For the Red Sox to win the World Series, they had to do something no team had ever done before—they beat a 100-win team in the Division Series (that would be the Yankees) and then beat a 100-win team in the League Championship Series (the 103-win reigning World Champion Houston Astros) on the way to the pennant. And then they beat the battle-tested Dodgers in the World Series, rather handily. In the final two rounds of the playoffs, the Red Sox beat both teams which had contended in the 2017 World Series.

I can't help but toss in a last-minute barb here aimed at Mr. Bucky Dent. He threw out the first pitch before Game Seven of the 2004 ALCS, and the first pitch before Game Four of the 2018 ALCS. In both cases, the Yankees were eliminated by the Red Sox, in Yankee Stadium. That balances Dent's 1978 home run.

The Yankees manager in 2018 was, of course, Aaron Boone, whose home run in Game Seven of the 2003 ALCS won it all for New York, beating the Red Sox. More than one curse has been reversed.

DF: Let's look at how the team's match up against each other. Offensively, the '98 Yankees had a .288 batting average, .364 on-base percentage, and .460 slugging percentage, while the '18 Red Sox posted a slash line of .268/.339/.453—lower in every important measure. The Yankees also scored 5.96 runs a game, more than half-a-run better than the Red Sox' 5.41 runs a game. The teams hit nearly the identical number of home runs (Red Sox 208 and Yankees 207), but the Yankees stole 153 bases compared to the Sox swiping 125. I'm beginning to like my chances.

BN: These are two great teams—no doubt about it. Those kind of stats don't do a thing for me, though. The Yankees had a larger run differential, too. But if the Red Sox had a .199 batting average and stole a total of four bases all year long, it wouldn't impress me as much as the sheer fact that the 2018 Red Sox were the first team which had to beat TWO teams, each with 100 or more wins, to *just* get to the World Series. They were, as mentioned (this came from the Elias Sports Bureau), the first team which beat both of the prior year's World Series contenders. And (this comes from Jayson Stark) the Red Sox had to face the two teams (Astros and Dodgers) that led each league in ERA on their way to the World Series.

DF: Impressive feats, though purely coincidental. And besides, if the Red Sox hit under the Mendoza line during the regular season, there wouldn't be a postseason berth at all. I know you're not impressed, but from a pitching standpoint the 1998 Yankees ranked better than the 2018 Red

Sox. New York was sixth in the majors with a 3.82 ERA and Boston was ninth with a 3.75 mark. New York's pitchers had a 2.32 strikeout/walk ratio while Boston was at 3.04. Granted, there isn't a whole lot of difference between the two teams taking into account the era in which they played. Boston's offensive output is more prominent in the context of playing during a time when the hitting environment was more difficult. Meanwhile, New York's pitching prowess is more impressive when one factors in the offensive explosion of a steroids-charged era.

BN: I'm not sure where we're going with this. I'm prepared to argue that the 2018 Red Sox are the best team of all time, not just the best Red Sox team. You're making a strong case for the 1998 Yankees. I think we can both agree that they were both exceptional teams. Maybe neither has a clear edge over the other. Fresh in both our minds is Game Three of the 2018 World Series—the game that went on forever and ever. Tied after nine, then both the Red Sox and Dodgers score one run in the 13th inning and it went on and on until Nathan Eovaldi threw one bad pitch and lost it in the 18th—after seven hours and 20 minutes (the one game taking longer to play than all four games of the 1939 World Series combined). That game was starting to get to the point—each team having used nine pitchers—that I thought they were going to have to start rotating in position players. We could probably each pump out a few thousand more words about our respective choices. I'm not sure either of us is prepared to budge. We need one of those computer programs that can run a simulation between the two teams 10,000 times and see if either team comes out on top.

Winner: Tie between 2018 Red Sox and 1998 Yankees

THE BEST TEAM
SIMULATION MATCH-UP

PRE-SERIES

David Fischer: The 1998 Yankees team has morphed through a time warp and is ready to take on the 2018 Red Sox team in a best-of-seven series. It's sure to be a nail-biting affair. In such close contests, New York in 1998 went 21–10 in one-run games (.677 winning percentage) and 9–2 in extra-inning games (.818), while the 2018 Red Sox went 25–14 (.641) and 8–5 (.615), indicating those '98 Yankees often came up just a little bigger in clutch situations. That's a good omen for me.

The Yankees of 1998 won 125 total games, the most in major-league history, including 114 regular-season games. The Red Sox of 2018 won (yawn) just 108 regular-season games; that's merely *tied* for ninth in major-league history. Four other teams have had a better regular-season record than the 2018 Boston Red Sox and have gone on to win the World Series: the 1909 Pittsburgh Pirates, the 1927 New York Yankees, the 1961 Yankees, and the best team ever: the '98 Yanks (three out of four ain't bad).

The '98 Yankees dominated with great team chemistry. They played with supreme confidence and had smart players who knew how to win ballgames. Oakland GM Billy Beane liked to say the Yankees were such a complete team and so thoroughly and successfully completed the job that "it's almost as if they beat you wearing tuxedoes." So, fancy this: The Yankees finished the 1998 season with a combined record of 125–50—a whopping 75 games over .500. The Red Sox ended 2018 just 62 games over for a 13-game discrepancy, or the equivalent of two weeks of regular-season victories in favor of my pinstriped heroes.

For straight-up comparison, I know that much will be made of the Red Sox' success in postseason play, and we acknowledge they dispatched two 100-win AL teams (including the Yankees) and the NL defending champions with relative ease, going 11–3 en route to the championship. But that doesn't obscure the fact that Boston took advantage of a historic competitive imbalance during the regular season, particularly within the AL East. The Red Sox went 16–3 against the 115-loss Orioles, and 15–4 against a Blue Jays team that finished 16 games under .500. Boston also won 19 of 23 match-ups against the Marlins, Rangers, Royals, and Tigers—teams that all lost at least 95 games (and went a combined 250–397). Of course, a team is supposed to beat its inferior competition but, by contrast, the Yanks in '98 played only three teams with 95 or more losses, taking care of business to the tune of 22–4. There's no denying that the 2018 Red Sox played many more games against putrid competition than did the '98 Yankees, and yet the only team to post a winning record against the '98 Bronx Bombers was the Angels with a 6–5 record, while the 2018 Sawx dropped their season series to the Athletics, Astros, Indians, and White Sox. Pretty shabby, don't you think?

Okay, I admit it, both teams are formidable foes, but the '98 Yankees get the edge here based not only on their higher regular-season win total, but their higher level of dominance from wire to wire against a better crop of opponents. I'll bet you can't prove me wrong.

Bill Nowlin: One thing that's good for the Red Sox prospects is playing the 1998 Yankees in the early days of 2019 (as this simulation is taking place) is that Mariano Rivera is forty-eight years old, with the average age on the Yankees staff being just a shade over 50. Oh, right, you're taking advantage of that time warp.

So the Yankees won 114 games back in 1998. It's one of those years where trauma seems to have been kind to the injured and erased some of my memories of that year.

Good idea to look at all the one-run games in each year. I guess that means the 2018 Red Sox need to strive for bigger margins of victory, not leaving everything to the vagaries of one-run games. OK, Sox, here's my prescription: win big! In the 2018 Division Series (against the Yankees, I will remind you), the Red Sox won both one-run games but also (ahem) a 16–1 game.

You've assembled a persuasive array of data. What's my comeback? What can I cite? Hmm, let's see. The run differential for the 1998 Yankees was 965 to 656 (309 runs) while the Red Sox in 2018 was 876–647 (229). Maybe that's not the answer, either. Do I have a rational basis for my belief that Boston has a good shot?

Rely on luck? Timing? Underdoggery? Not an unfamiliar place for a Red Sox fan to be. Heck, who would have ever thought a team could be down 0–3 in a possible seven-game series, losing Game Three, 19–8, and then go on to sweep the last four games? It's been done. I remember it well. You may, too.

Prove you wrong? I get the feeling that I might not be able to come up with a convincing argument. We'll have to let the games play out. I have to agree, your figures regarding competitive imbalance during the 2018 regular season are, in a way, pretty shocking. Maybe my best plan is to simply hide from the facts and . . . hope. After all, what good is it being a fan if you can't take refuge in a degree of denial?

It's not like I'm giving up or conceding. No chance. Whoever they played, the 2018 Red Sox won the games they needed to win. They were a team with chemistry, too. They were the best team in baseball.

When it came to the postseason, both teams dominated. The 1998 Yankees swept the Rangers and Padres. In between, they lost a couple of games to the Indians but wrapped it up in six. The 2018 Red Sox granted one loss in each round of the postseason, but saw no series ever reach its final game.

I'll grant the '98 Yankees appear to have the edge going into this match-up, but it's not an unfamiliar place for a Red Sox fan to be.

MANAGERS' PRE-SERIES PRESS CONFERENCE

David Fischer: The Boss, Mr. Steinbrenner, wants me to guarantee victory. I told him there's no sure thing in sports, but I can guarantee that we won't lose this series. Boston is going to have to win it.

Both squads captured the biggest trophy of them all—the Commissioner's Trophy—and both teams possessed that season's American League batting champion (Bernie Williams for the Yanks and Mookie Betts for the Sox). However, the Red Sox in 2018 dominated in the individual hardware department, most prominently winning the Most Valuable Player Award (Betts), Hank Aaron Award (J. D. Martinez), three Silver Sluggers (Betts and two by Martinez), and three Gold Gloves (Betts, Bradley Jr., and Kinsler) to just one major award captured by a player on the '98 Yankees: a Gold Glove for Williams. But baseball is a team game, and that's what makes this Yankees group so special. The power of the players' teamwork; how they've pulled together throughout the grind of a long season is a key element.

Much credit is to be shared with the coaching staff; particularly third-base coach Willie Randolph, pitching coach Mel Stottlemyre, and bench coach Don Zimmer. Zim helped alleviate much of the media burden and also diffused tension on the bench, mocking Paul O'Neill for his outrageous outbursts after a frustrating at-bat and allowing Derek Jeter to stroke his bald head for good luck. Derek began to show what it takes to become captain of this team, and was named so in 2003.

As important as it is to have good coaches, the players pretty much policed themselves. Joe Girardi is one of two players on the team who will become a big-league manager. The other is Dale Sveum, who was released midseason but liked his teammates so much that he decided to hang around as a bullpen catcher and throw batting practice for the rest of the season rather than go home.

As you can tell, this team is a close-knit bunch. In May against Baltimore, two days after David Wells pitched a perfect game, O's closer Armando Benitez served up a go-ahead three-run home run to Bernie Williams in the eighth. On the next pitch, Benitez drilled Tino Martinez in the back, inciting an ugly bench-clearing brawl that lasted more than 10 minutes, spilled into the visitors' dugout, and led to five suspensions. Darryl Strawberry and Graeme Lloyd threw vicious haymakers that are forever preserved on YouTube. The narrative promoted by many in the media that the brawl brought the team together makes for a provocative headline, but the fact of the matter is they kept winning because they were a very good team—I'd say the best of all-time. Nothing could stop them. Not a 500-pound concrete-and-steel beam falling in April, shutting down Yankee Stadium for a week and forcing them to play "home" games at Shea Stadium. Not when the players got rocked by medical scares: Darryl Strawberry's late-season colon cancer diagnosis, the same cancer ravaging the body of Scott Brosius's dad; and Pettitte's dad, Tom, who underwent open-heart surgery just days before his son's World Series start. Then Andy went out and threw 7 1/3 innings of scoreless ball in the clincher. The kid's got heart—and plenty of guts. That's why he has more postseason victories than any other pitcher.

Pitching is what sets this group apart. They'll rely on the duo of Davids—Wells and Cone—Pettitte and El Duque as the starters. All four are expected to pitch deep into games. The formidable lefty-righty bullpen combination of Mike Stanton and Jeff Nelson will serve as the bridge to closer Mariano Rivera. Mo is well rested for the occasion, having appeared in 54 games with 61 1/3 innings pitched in 1998. He saved 36 games, but had so few save opportunities (41) because his teammates consistently blew out their opponents. He did spend a few weeks on the disabled list, yet that doesn't fully account for his low workload. This does: the '98 Yankees won 42 games by five runs or more. A manager's delight, if ever there was one.

So here we go: Yankees vs. Red Sox for all the marbles. Don't expect any blowouts during the series. There might be a blowup or two—but no blowouts.

Bill Nowlin: The Yankees got their Boss, and the Red Sox have theirs: John W. Henry. He doesn't just own the Red Sox (and Fenway Park). He owns the *Boston Globe*, the Liverpool Football Club (in England), and Roush Fenway Racing, which competes in NASCAR events. He used to own the Marlins, and even a small share of the Yankees. His Fenway Sports Group represents a number of clients, including basketball superstar LeBron James.

Most importantly, though, is Henry's track record in baseball. In the 16 years that his group has owned the Red Sox, the team has won four World Series and lost zero. In that respect, they're the winningest team of the twenty-first century.

It's been a weird feast or famine stretch, though. Drama, for sure. First there was 2003, which I'd rather not think about. Then there was 2004, which I suspect the Yankees manager would prefer to pretend didn't happen. The Red Sox won again in 2007, 2013, and then in 2018. Forgive me, but it feels good to just reel off those years any excuse I get. But there was famine, too. I'm thinking of 2012, when the Sox finished last, and 2014, when they also finished last (bracketing the World Series win in 2013), and then again in 2015, when they finished last. Maybe that builds character. Or something. The Red Sox went on to win the AL East each of the last three years. And won it all again in 2018.

It's this 2018 ballclub that's taking the field tonight. Could you ask for better momentum? A first-year manager who seemed to earn the respect of all and built one of the most harmonious clubhouses Sox fans have ever seen. Everyone pitched in, even first-year pitching coach Dana LeVangie, who'd been an advance scout, bench coach, and put in five seasons as Boston's bullpen coach. Talk about promoting from within and showing faith in your staff—here he is debuting as a big-league pitching coach and seeing Red Sox pitchers record 108 wins, more than any team since 2001.

A number of pitchers needed to be rested. LeVangie spread the work around; no pitcher lost more than seven games. Nathan Eovaldi joined the team at the end of July. Come September and October, he really settled in and contributed.

They were a true team, winning both home (57–24) and away (51–30). Maybe the schedule provided favorable opponents, but heck, the 1998 Yankees beat the Athletics and Devil Rays by a combined 21–1 record. Not exactly the toughest competition.

It was the spirit of the team that prevailed. Mookie emerged to become the MVP, as solid on defense as he was on offense. The Sox had the best defensive outfield in all of baseball—witness two Gold Gloves in Betts and Jackie Bradley Jr., and Andrew Benintendi came in second for the Gold Glove in left. Who knows how many hits or runs they saved? The Sox pitchers, catchers, and first basemen all converted more than 99 percent of their chances without an error. The only true weak spot was third base, and Rafael Devers only turned 21 years of age midseason. He hit 21 homers and drove in 66 runs.

The club designated J. D. Martinez to hit—and he did! He led the majors in runs batted in, with 130. He hit 43 homers and recorded a major-league-leading 358 total bases. He even won TWO Silver Sluggers! He won one as DH and the other as an outfielder. No one in major-league history has ever done that. (He started 57 games as an outfielder.)

The X-Man, Xander Bogaerts, drove in 103 runs. His middle-infield partner, second baseman Dustin Pedroia, was physically unable to play in more than three games. A four-time All-Star and former MVP, in many ways the spark plug of the team for several years, he wasn't there—but the team came together and made it work. Eduardo Nunez and Brock Holt filled the gap, as did Ian Kinsler.

They'd been counting on Hanley Ramirez for offense, but cut him loose in late May and made it work. Benintendi had 15 game-winning hits.

Steve Pearce came over from the Blue Jays at the end of June and helped out a lot—he even became the MVP of the World Series!

That's the way it was all year, it seemed. Players stepping in and contributing when needed. A true team effort. Little drama off the field, plenty of drama on the field. There was never a day they weren't in first place, tied, or with a lead.

They'll be facing one of the best teams of all time. This is a special team. The Red Sox are ready.

EDITOR'S NOTE

The following simulation was supplied by Dave Koch and the good people at Action! PC Baseball.

In anticipation for this simulation, we supplied Action! PC Baseball with the following:

- The two teams chosen (the 1998 Yankees and 2018 Red Sox)
- Team with home-field advantage (Red Sox won via coin toss)
- Stadiums being used[1]

Once that information was supplied, Action! PC Baseball ran a simulation for a seven-game series, which included play-by-play, box scores, and stats for each game. The additional full series stats that appear at the end were compiled internally so that advanced statistics could be supplied.

Once we at Sports Publishing received these simulations, the authors were sent one game at a time to avoid any possible spoilers. Once we received their postgame notes from the first game, they would receive the simulation for the second game, and so on. Aside from selecting the team, location, and home-field advantage, everything to follow was left up to the simulation.

Additional Note

We informed Action! PC Baseball to use the rosters for these two teams. While the starting pitchers for Game One were chosen by who started the first game of each team's World Series appearance, the rest was left up to the simulation.

---

1 The authors agreed to use the current (2018) dimensions for both Yankee Stadium and Fenway Park.

1998 New York Yankees @ 2018 Boston Red Sox
Game One, Series Tied, 0–0
David Wells (18–4, 3.49 ERA) vs. Chris Sale (12–4, 2.11 ERA)
Time 3:30, 60°, Clear, Light Rain, Wind: 13 MPH Out to CF

```
Inn Out B-S  On  NYY-Bos  Result
                          1-New York
 1   0  0-1  -    0-0     Jeter flied to center, 1 out
 1   1  3-2  -    0-0     Raines grounded to first, 2 out
 1   2  1-2  -    0-0     Williams flied to deep left, 3 out
--------------------------------------------------------------
                          1-Boston
 1   0  2-1  -    0-0     Betts hit a solo homer to left center,
                             Boston 1 New York 0
 1   0  0-2  -    0-1     Benintendi struck out, 1 out
 1   1  3-2  -    0-1     Pearce struck out, 2 out
 1   2  0-1  -    0-1     Martinez hit a solo homer to left center,
                             Boston 2 New York 0
 1   2  1-0  -    0-2     Bogaerts grounded a single between
                             third and short
 1   2  2-0  1    0-2     Devers flied shallow down right field line,
                             3 out
--------------------------------------------------------------
                          2-New York
 2   0  1-1  -    0-2     Brosius grounded to first, 1 out
 2   1  2-2  -    0-2     Posada struck out, 2 out
 2   2  3-2  -    0-2     O'Neill struck out, 3 out
--------------------------------------------------------------
                          2-Boston
 2   0  0-2  -    0-2     Kinsler grounded to first, 1 out
 2   1  0-2  -    0-2     Leon struck out, 2 out
 2   2  1-0  -    0-2     Bradley Jr. grounded a single between
                             first and second
 2   2  1-1  1    0-2     Betts flied to deep left center, 3 out
--------------------------------------------------------------
                          3-New York
 3   0  1-2  -    0-2     Martinez struck out, 1 out
 3   1  0-2  -    0-2     Knoblauch struck out, 2 out
 3   2  3-1  -    0-2     Curtis walked
 3   2  0-2  1    0-2     Jeter flied to right, 3 out
--------------------------------------------------------------
                          3-Boston
 3   0  0-2  -    0-2     Benintendi struck out, 1 out
 3   1  0-2  -    0-2     Pearce flied to deep left center, 2 out
 3   2  0-1  -    0-2     Martinez doubled off the wall down the
                             left field line
 3   2  2-1  2    0-2     Bogaerts lined a single to left,
                             Martinez scored, Boston 3 New York 0
 3   2  0-2  1    0-3     Devers popped to the catcher, 3 out
--------------------------------------------------------------
                          4-New York
 4   0  3-2  -    0-3     Raines lined a single up the middle
 4   0  2-1  1    0-3     Williams hit a two run homer to left,
                             Boston 3 New York 2
 4   0  1-0  -    2-3     Brosius grounded to first, 1 out
 4   1  2-1  -    2-3     Posada grounded to third, 2 out
 4   2  3-2  -    2-3     O'Neill singled to left center
 4   2  1-2  1    2-3     Martinez popped to second, 3 out
--------------------------------------------------------------
```

```
Inn Out B-S  On  NYY-Bos  Result
                          4-Boston
 4   0  1-2  -   2-3      Kinsler popped to second, 1 out
 4   1  1-2  -   2-3      Leon singled on the infield
 4   1  0-1  1   2-3      Bradley Jr. hit by pitch, Leon to 2nd
 4   1  3-1  12  2-3      Betts walked, Leon to 3rd, Bradley Jr. to 2nd
 4   1  0-1  123 2-3      Benintendi flied very deep down the
                             left field line, sacrifice, Leon scored,
                             2 out, Boston 4 New York 2
 4   2  3-2  12  2-4      Pearce struck out, 3 out
-----------------------------------------------------------------------
                          5-New York
 5   0  3-2  -   2-4      Knoblauch grounded to short, 1 out
 5   1  1-0  -   2-4      Curtis lined to third, 2 out
 5   2  3-2  -   2-4      Jeter walked
 5   2  0-0  1   2-4      Jeter stole 2nd
 5   2  1-0  2   2-4      Raines struck out, 3 out
-----------------------------------------------------------------------
                          5-Boston
 5   0  1-1  -   2-4      Martinez flied deep down the left field line,
                             1 out
 5   1  0-2  -   2-4      Bogaerts grounded to third, 2 out
 5   2  0-0  -   2-4      Devers popped to second, 3 out
-----------------------------------------------------------------------
                          6-New York
                          >Barnes pitching
 6   0  2-2  -   2-4      Williams grounded to first, 1 out
 6   1  2-2  -   2-4      Brosius hit a solo homer to right,
                             Boston 4 New York 3
 6   1  0-1  -   3-4      Posada doubled off the wall in right center
 6   1  3-2  2   3-4      O'Neill struck out, 2 out
                          >Workman pitching
 6   2  1-2  2   3-4      Martinez struck out, 3 out
-----------------------------------------------------------------------
                          6-Boston
 6   0  1-2  -   3-4      Kinsler grounded to short, 1 out
 6   1  0-2  -   3-4      Leon grounded to third, 2 out
 6   2  0-2  -   3-4      Bradley Jr. grounded to first, 3 out
-----------------------------------------------------------------------
                          7-New York
 7   0  0-2  -   3-4      Knoblauch grounded to second, 1 out
 7   1  3-2  -   3-4      Strawberry walked
                          >Kelly pitching
 7   1  0-0  1   3-4      Strawberry stole 2nd
 7   1  0-1  2   3-4      Jeter grounded to third, 2 out
 7   2  1-2  2   3-4      Raines struck out, 3 out
-----------------------------------------------------------------------
                          7-Boston
 7   0  2-0  -   3-4      Betts singled to right center
 7   0  0-0  1   3-4      Benintendi flied to very deep left center,
                             outfield error, Betts to 3rd, 1 out
 7   1  0-0  3   3-4      Pearce grounded to the pitcher, 2 out
 7   2  3-2  3   3-4      Martinez intentionally walked
 7   2  2-2  13  3-4      Bogaerts struck out, 3 out
-----------------------------------------------------------------------
```

```
Inn Out B-S  On  NYY-Bos  Result
                          8-New York
 8   0  2-1   -     3-4   Williams grounded to the pitcher, 1 out
                          >Wright pitching
 8   1  0-2   -     3-4   Brosius flied to shallow center, 2 out
 8   2  1-0   -     3-4   Posada flied to shallow center, 3 out
-------------------------------------------------------------------
                          8-Boston
                          >Stanton pitching
 8   0  3-2   -     3-4   Devers hit a solo homer to right center,
                            Boston 5 New York 3
 8   0  2-2   -     3-5   Kinsler flied to right center, 1 out
 8   1  2-1   -     3-5   Leon flied to left, 2 out
 8   2  0-2   -     3-5   Bradley Jr. hit a solo homer down the
                            right field line, Boston 6 New York 3
 8   2  0-1   -     3-6   Betts lined to left, 3 out
-------------------------------------------------------------------
                          9-New York
 9   0  0-2   -     3-6   O'Neill struck out, 1 out
 9   1  0-2   -     3-6   Martinez flied to shallow left center, 2 out
 9   2  3-1   -     3-6   Knoblauch walked
 9   2  1-1   1     3-6   Strawberry lined to right, 3 out
```

Game One	1	2	3	4	5	6	7	8	9	R	H	E
1998 New York Yankees	0	0	0	2	0	1	0	0	0	3	5	1
2018 Boston Red Sox	2	0	1	1	0	0	0	2	-	6	10	0

New York	AB	R	H	RBI	BB	K	LOB	PO	A	E
Jeter, SS	3	0	0	0	1	0	1	0	1	0
Raines, DH	4	1	1	0	0	2	2	0	0	0
Williams, CF	4	1	1	2	0	0	0	3	0	1
Brosius, 3B	4	1	1	1	0	0	0	0	2	0
Posada, C	4	0	1	0	0	1	0	7	0	0
O'Neill, RF	4	0	1	0	0	3	0	2	0	0
Martinez, 1B	4	0	0	0	0	2	2	4	2	0
Knoblauch, 2B	3	0	0	0	1	1	0	2	0	0
Curtis, LF	1	0	0	0	1	0	0	2	0	0
Strawberry, PH-LF	1	0	0	0	1	0	1	2	0	0
	32	3	5	3	4	9	0	22	5	1

New York		IP	H	R	ER	HR	BB	K	Pit	S	B	ERA	BF
Wells	L(0-1)	7.0	8	4	4	2	2	6	119	87	32	5.14	32
Stanton		1.0	2	2	2	2	0	0	23	16	7	18.00	5
		8.0	10	6	6	4	2	6	142	103	39	6.75	37

Boston	AB	R	H	RBI	BB	K	LOB	PO	A	E
Betts, RF	4	1	2	1	1	0	1	2	0	0
Benintendi, LF	3	0	0	1	0	2	0	1	0	0
Pearce, 1B	4	0	0	0	0	2	2	8	1	0
Martinez, DH	3	2	2	1	1	0	0	0	0	0
Bogaerts, SS	4	0	2	1	0	1	2	0	1	0
Devers, 3B	4	1	1	1	0	0	1	1	2	0
Kinsler, 2B	4	0	0	0	0	0	0	1	1	0
Leon, C	4	1	1	0	0	1	0	9	0	0
Bradley Jr., CF	3	1	2	1	0	0	0	4	0	0
	33	6	10	6	2	6	0	27	6	0

Boston		IP	H	R	ER	HR	BB	K	Pit	S	B	ERA	BF
Sale	W(1-0)	5.0	3	2	2	1	2	5	96	63	33	3.60	20
Barnes		0.2	2	1	1	1	0	1	20	13	7	13.50	4
Workman		0.2	0	0	0	0	1	1	21	16	5	0.00	3
Kelly		1.0	0	0	0	0	0	1	10	7	3	0.00	3
Wright	S(1)	1.2	0	0	0	0	1	1	21	15	6	0.00	6
		9.0	5	3	3	2	4	9	168	114	54	3.00	36

GAME ONE POSTGAME COMMENTS

Red Sox Manager

Any time we play a game at home and needn't bat in the bottom of the ninth is a good game in my book. I told the team to be aggressive against Wells and our two big bats both struck in the first inning—Betts and J. D. Martinez hitting solo home runs.

And Chris Sale shut them down in the first two innings, though he doesn't normally walk as many as he did. That was indeed a surprise.

J. D. got a hold of another one for a double and Bogey brought him home.

Benintendi struck out twice, but then hit a sac fly for what proved to bring in the game-winner. He had 15 game-winning hits in the 2018 season, four of them on sacrifice flies. This fits with that, his best year yet at the plate.

Sale's pitch count was getting up there and was taken out after five—I assume to keep him fresh. The homer by Bernie Williams was a concern. Likewise the two walks. Brosius did a little damage, too.

It was kind of a game of home runs, wasn't it? I figured the light rain would dampen down the bats, but Devers—he's only 21—and JBJ each homered in the eighth. I was glad to see Steven Wright do so well in the eighth. The computer decided to let him work the ninth as well and give Kimbrel a needed extra day of rest.

Tomorrow's another day. I'm proud of our team. This is a great start.

Yankees Manager

Shocking. That's my reaction. A Yankees-Red Sox game played in three hours and 30 minutes? Why the rush? Oh, I see. The 1998 champions mustered just five hits off Boston pitching. That makes for a lot of quick half-innings. My boys did work the count, earning four free passes, but you can't expect to win ballgames in Fenway Park with only nine batters reaching base safely over an entire game. So kudos to Mr. Sale and his supporting cast for holding down the vaunted New York offense.

Two areas strike me as factors of immediate concern, and both involve left-handed batters facing left-handed pitchers. Paul O'Neill was completely handcuffed by Sale to the tune of three strikeouts. (Mr. Henry, the Yankees organization will, of course, reimburse the Red Sox franchise for all damage incurred to the dugout space heater, and replace the water fountain located in the tunnel leading to the clubhouse.) It's not a sin to strike out against Sale; he makes a living punching out opponents—especially those who face him while standing in the left-handed batters' box. But with David Price's turn in the rotation coming up, my team will need O'Neill to be in a positive mental state the next time he faces a lefty pitcher, and I'm confident Paulie will have a warrior mentality for that upcoming battle.

The other lefty-lefty match-up that causes concern is the fact that Mike Stanton surrendered two home runs—both to left-handed batters. Devers and Bradley Jr. took Stanton deep in the bottom half of the eighth, extending a one-run Boston lead to a three-run cushion that our team could not overcome.

Luckily for our team, one game does not make a series. If the Yankees can take Game Two and leave Boston with a split, I like our chances when the series moves to the Bronx.

1998 New York Yankees @ 2018 Boston Red Sox
Game Two, Boston Leads, 1–0
David Cone (20–7, 3.55 ERA) vs. David Price (16–7, 3.58 ERA)
Time 3:02, 62°, Wind: 11 MPH In from LCF

```
Inn Out B-S  On  NYY-Bos  Result
                          1-New York
 1   0  0-2  -    0-0     Jeter hit a solo homer to center,
                              New York 1 Boston 0
 1   0  0-1  -    1-0     Raines grounded to short, 1 out
 1   1  2-2  -    1-0     Williams singled to center
 1   1  0-0  1    1-0     Brosius bunted out to the catcher,
                              Williams to 2nd, sacrifice, 2 out
 1   2  1-2  2    1-0     Posada struck out, 3 out
-------------------------------------------------------------------
                          1-Boston
 1   0  1-1  -    1-0     Betts grounded to second, 1 out
 1   1  2-0  -    1-0     Benintendi grounded to second, 2 out
 1   2  1-1  -    1-0     Martinez grounded to third, 3 out
-------------------------------------------------------------------
                          2-New York
 2   0  2-2  -    1-0     O'Neill struck out, 1 out
 2   1  0-2  -    1-0     Martinez struck out, 2 out
 2   2  1-2  -    1-0     Knoblauch singled on the infield,
                              Knoblauch to 2nd
 2   2  0-1  2    1-0     Curtis grounded to second, 3 out
-------------------------------------------------------------------
                          2-Boston
 2   0  1-1  -    1-0     Bogaerts flied to deep right center, 1 out
 2   1  0-2  -    1-0     Moreland lined to right, 2 out
 2   2  0-2  -    1-0     Devers grounded to first, 3 out
-------------------------------------------------------------------
                          3-New York
 3   0  1-1  -    1-0     Jeter hit a solo homer to right center,
                              New York 2 Boston 0
 3   0  1-1  -    2-0     Raines grounded to third, 1 out
 3   1  2-1  -    2-0     Williams grounded to short, 2 out
 3   2  1-2  -    2-0     Brosius struck out, 3 out
-------------------------------------------------------------------
                          3-Boston
 3   0  0-0  -    2-0     Kinsler grounded to first, 1 out
 3   1  2-0  -    2-0     Leon doubled off the wall down the
                              right field line, out at 3rd, 2 out
 3   2  2-2  -    2-0     Bradley Jr. struck out, 3 out
-------------------------------------------------------------------
                          4-New York
 4   0  2-2  -    2-0     Posada struck out, 1 out
 4   1  1-2  -    2-0     O'Neill hit a solo homer to center,
                              New York 3 Boston 0
 4   1  0-0  -    3-0     Martinez flied to right, 2 out
 4   2  1-2  -    3-0     Knoblauch flied to right, 3 out
-------------------------------------------------------------------
                          4-Boston
 4   0  0-1  -    3-0     Betts popped to short, 1 out
 4   1  2-0  -    3-0     Benintendi popped to the catcher, 2 out
 4   2  2-0  -    3-0     Martinez flied deep down the left field line,
                              3 out
-------------------------------------------------------------------
```

```
Inn Out B-S   On   NYY-Bos  Result
                             5-New York
 5   0   0-1   -    3-0      Curtis grounded to third, 1 out
 5   1   1-2   -    3-0      Jeter flied to right center, 2 out
 5   2   1-2   -    3-0      Raines flied deep down the right field line,
                               3 out
-------------------------------------------------------------------------
                             5-Boston
 5   0   0-2   -    3-0      Bogaerts struck out, 1 out
 5   1   1-1   -    3-0      Moreland grounded to second, 2 out
 5   2   2-2   -    3-0      Devers struck out, 3 out
-------------------------------------------------------------------------
                             6-New York
 6   0   1-1   -    3-0      Williams grounded a single between
                               third and short
 6   0   3-1   1    3-0      Brosius hit a two run homer down the
                               left field line, New York 5 Boston 0
 6   0   1-1   -    5-0      Posada grounded a single between
                               first and second
 6   0   0-2   1    5-0      O'Neill flied to deep right center, 1 out
 6   1   0-1   1    5-0      Martinez flied to center, 2 out
 6   2   3-2   1    5-0      Knoblauch walked, Posada to 2nd
                             >Barnes pitching
 6   2   3-2   12   5-0      Curtis lined to short, 3 out
-------------------------------------------------------------------------
                             6-Boston
 6   0   1-1   -    5-0      Kinsler flied to deep right center, 1 out
 6   1   1-2   -    5-0      Leon singled on the infield
 6   1   2-1   1    5-0      Bradley Jr. singled to right center,
                               Leon to 2nd
 6   1   3-1   12   5-0      Betts walked, Leon to 3rd, Bradley Jr. to 2nd
 6   1   2-2   123  5-0      Benintendi struck out, 2 out
 6   2   1-1   123  5-0      Martinez grounded to third, 3 out
-------------------------------------------------------------------------
                             7-New York
 7   0   2-2   -    5-0      Jeter grounded to third, 1 out
 7   1   0-1   -    5-0      Raines grounded to short, 2 out
 7   2   1-2   -    5-0      Williams struck out, 3 out
-------------------------------------------------------------------------
                             7-Boston
 7   0   2-2   -    5-0      Bogaerts grounded a single between
                               third and short
 7   0   1-1   1    5-0      Moreland flied down the right field line,
                               1 out
 7   1   0-0   1    5-0      Devers grounded to third, forcing Bogaerts
                               at second, 2 out
 7   2   1-1   1    5-0      Kinsler grounded to second, 3 out
-------------------------------------------------------------------------
                             8-New York
 8   0   1-1   -    5-0      Brosius hit by pitch
                             >Thornburg pitching
 8   0   3-1   1    5-0      Posada grounded to short, second to first
                               double play, 2 out
 8   2   0-0   -    5-0      O'Neill lined a triple down the
                               left field line
 8   2   2-2   3    5-0      Martinez flied to right center, 3 out
-------------------------------------------------------------------------
```

```
Inn Out B-S  On  NYY-Bos  Result
                          8-Boston
8   0   0-1  -    5-0     Leon lined a single up the middle
8   0   3-0  1    5-0     Bradley Jr. flied shallow down right field
                              line, 1 out
8   1   1-0  1    5-0     Betts singled to right center, Leon to 2nd
8   1   0-1  12   5-0     Benintendi grounded to second, forcing Betts
                              at second, Leon to 3rd, 2 out
8   2   3-2  13   5-0     Martinez struck out, 3 out
------------------------------------------------------------------------
                          9-New York
9   0   2-2  -    5-0     Knoblauch hit a solo homer down the
                              left field line, New York 6 Boston 0
9   0   0-0  -    6-0     Curtis grounded to second, 1 out
9   1   3-1  -    6-0     Jeter grounded to third, 2 out
                          >Velazquez pitching
9   2   2-1  -    6-0     Raines grounded to third, 3 out
------------------------------------------------------------------------
                          9-Boston
9   0   3-2  -    6-0     Bogaerts singled to right center
9   0   1-2  1    6-0     Moreland grounded to short, Bogaerts to 2nd,
                              1 out
9   1   3-0  2    6-0     Devers walked
9   1   0-1  12   6-0     Lin grounded to second, forcing Devers
                              at second, Bogaerts to 3rd, 2 out
9   2   0-2  13   6-0     Leon struck out, 3 out
```

Game Two	1	2	3	4	5	6	7	8	9	R	H	E
1998 New York Yankees	1	0	1	1	0	2	0	0	1	6	10	0
2018 Boston Red Sox	0	0	0	0	0	0	0	0	0	0	7	1

New York	AB	R	H	RBI	BB	K	LOB	PO	A	E
Jeter, SS	5	2	2	2	0	0	0	3	1	0
Raines, DH	5	0	0	0	0	0	0	0	0	0
Williams, CF	4	1	2	0	0	1	0	2	0	0
Brosius, 3B	2	1	1	2	0	1	0	1	3	0
Posada, C	4	0	1	0	0	2	1	7	0	0
O'Neill, RF	4	1	2	1	0	1	0	3	1	0
Martinez, 1B	4	0	0	0	0	1	1	9	0	0
Knoblauch, 2B	3	1	2	1	1	0	0	1	7	0
Curtis, LF	4	0	0	0	0	0	2	1	0	0
	35	6	10	6	1	6	4	27	12	0

New York		IP	H	R	ER	HR	BB	K	Pit	S	B	ERA	BF
Cone	W(1-0)	9.0	7	0	0	0	2	6	125	79	46	0.00	35
		9.0	7	0	0	0	2	6	125	79	46	0.00	35

Boston	AB	R	H	RBI	BB	K	LOB	PO	A	E
Betts, RF	3	0	1	0	1	0	0	4	0	0
Benintendi, LF	4	0	0	0	0	1	0	0	0	0
Martinez, DH	4	0	0	0	0	1	5	0	0	0
Bogaerts, SS	4	0	2	0	0	1	0	1	5	1
Moreland, 1B	4	0	0	0	0	0	0	11	0	0
Devers, 3B	3	0	0	0	1	1	0	0	5	0
Kinsler, 2B	3	0	0	0	0	0	1	2	2	0
Lin, PH	1	0	0	0	0	0	0	0	0	0
Leon, C	4	0	3	0	0	1	2	6	1	0
Bradley Jr., CF	3	0	1	0	0	1	0	3	0	0
	33	0	7	0	2	6	8	27	13	1

Boston		IP	H	R	ER	HR	BB	K	Pit	S	B	ERA	BF
Price	L(0-1)	5.2	8	5	5	4	1	5	96	70	26	7.94	26
Barnes		1.1	0	0	0	0	0	1	23	15	8	4.50	5
Thornburg		1.2	2	1	1	1	0	0	22	12	10	5.40	6
Velazquez		0.1	0	0	0	0	0	0	4	2	2	0.00	1
		9.0	10	6	6	5	1	6	145	99	46	4.50	38

GAME TWO POSTGAME COMMENTS

Yankees Manager

The Bronx Bombers lived up to their name in Game Two, with five home runs accounting for all six runs scored to secure a much-needed victory and even the series at one game apiece.

Derek Jeter led the way with two homers, and although he's not known for his long-ball prowess, it comes as no surprise. Jeter has stellar career numbers against Price (20 hits in 65 at-bats with an OPS of .845), and hit a memorable home run off the lefty for career hit number 3,000. Scott Brosius hit another homer and now has gone deep in both games. The 1998 World Series MVP continues to raise his game in an important series, and the hunch to bat him in the clean-up position against the two left-handed pitchers (Sale and Price) is paying immediate dividends.

While the Yankees own David Price—and he knows it—the offense wasn't the real hero of Game Two. That mantle belongs to David Cone, who pitched masterfully by scattering seven hits to earn a complete-game shutout. He cruised through the first five innings while facing the minimum 15 batters (thanks to Sandy Leon being thrown out at third base trying to stretch a double) and needed to face just 35 batters over the entire game in order to record 27 outs. His only stressful inning was the sixth, when he wriggled out of a bases-loaded jam by striking out Benintendi and then inducing Martinez into a harmless ground out to snuff the lone Red Sox rally.

My team is under strict orders not to play "New York, New York" on the boom box. Yet the players know this is a significant victory worthy of celebration, as it now gives the Yankees home-field advantage as the series moves to the Bronx. The Bleacher Creatures will be in full throat.

Red Sox Manager

Tough game for Price. He probably was the co-MVP of the 2018 Series and we all thought his success would dispel any sort of a postseason jinx. He missed with his curve on that 0-2 count to Jeter and the ball ran right over the plate. Jeter took advantage. And he pounced again in the third inning. The computer had to get him out of there in the sixth.

All the home runs did the Red Sox in.

Sandy Leon—three hits. That was a bright light, but he got a little too aggressive in the third. I thought we had something going in the bottom of the sixth. Bases loaded, just one out.

Credit Cone. He pitched a heck of a game.

We'll take the day off and see you in New York.

1998 New York Yankees vs. 2018 Boston Red Sox
Game Three, Series Tied, 1–1
Andy Pettitte (16–11, 4.24 ERA) vs. Rick Porcello (17–7, 4.28 ERA)
Time 3:35, 63°, Wind: 13 MPH Left to Right

```
Inn Out B-S  On  Bos-NYY  Result
                           1-Boston
 1   0  0-0  -    0-0      Betts grounded a single between third
                               and short
 1   0  0-1  1    0-0      Benintendi hit by pitch, Betts to 2nd
 1   0  3-0  12   0-0      Pearce walked, Betts to 3rd, Benintendi
                               to 2nd
 1   0  0-2  123  0-0      Martinez struck out, 1 out
 1   1  1-1  123  0-0      Bogaerts flied to center, Betts scored,
                               Benintendi to 3rd, Pearce to 2nd, 2 out,
                               Boston 1 New York 0
 1   2  1-0  23   1-0      Devers lined a single to right center,
                               Benintendi scored, Pearce scored,
                               Boston 3 New York 0
 1   2  0-0  1    3-0      Devers caught stealing 2nd, 3 out
-----------------------------------------------------------------
                           1-New York
 1   0  2-2  -    3-0      Jeter grounded to the pitcher, safe on
                               an error
 1   0  3-1  1    3-0      Knoblauch flied to center, 1 out
 1   1  2-1  1    3-0      Williams lined a double to right center,
                               Jeter to 3rd
 1   1  3-2  23   3-0      O'Neill walked
 1   1  2-0  123  3-0      Strawberry grounded to first, second to first
                               double play, 3 out
-----------------------------------------------------------------
                           2-Boston
 2   0  0-1  -    3-0      Kinsler grounded to first, 1 out
 2   1  1-1  -    3-0      Leon grounded to second, safe on
                               throwing error
 2   1  2-2  1    3-0      Bradley Jr. flied to deep left center, 2 out
 2   2  1-2  1    3-0      Betts struck out, 3 out
-----------------------------------------------------------------
                           2-New York
 2   0  1-1  -    3-0      Martinez doubled off the wall in right center
 2   0  2-1  2    3-0      Brosius grounded to third, 1 out
 2   1  1-2  2    3-0      Posada flied to right, 2 out
 2   2  0-2  2    3-0      Curtis struck out, 3 out
-----------------------------------------------------------------
                           3-Boston
 3   0  1-2  -    3-0      Benintendi lined a single over second
 3   0  3-0  1    3-0      Pearce walked, Benintendi to 2nd
 3   0  1-2  12   3-0      Martinez grounded to short, second to first
                               double play, Benintendi to 3rd, 2 out
 3   2  3-2  3    3-0      Bogaerts walked
 3   2  3-2  13   3-0      Devers struck out, 3 out
-----------------------------------------------------------------
                           3-New York
 3   0  0-1  -    3-0      Jeter grounded to second, 1 out
 3   1  2-2  -    3-0      Knoblauch struck out, 2 out
 3   2  2-2  -    3-0      Williams struck out, 3 out
-----------------------------------------------------------------
```

```
Inn Out B-S  On  NYY-Bos  Result
                          4-Boston
 4   0  2-0   -    3-0    Kinsler grounded a double down the
                              first base line
 4   0  1-1   2    3-0    Leon popped to third, 1 out
 4   1  2-0   2    3-0    Bradley Jr. flied to right center, 2 out
 4   2  3-0   2    3-0    Betts walked
 4   2  2-0  12    3-0    Benintendi grounded to third, 3 out
------------------------------------------------------------------------
                          4-New York
 4   0  2-0   -    3-0    O'Neill grounded to third, 1 out
 4   1  1-1   -    3-0    Strawberry hit a solo homer to right center,
                              Boston 3 New York 1
 4   1  0-2   -    3-1    Martinez struck out, 2 out
 4   2  1-1   -    3-1    Brosius grounded to the pitcher, 3 out
------------------------------------------------------------------------
                          5-Boston
 5   0  0-1   -    3-1    Pearce popped to short, 1 out
 5   1  1-2   -    3-1    Martinez flied to very deep left center,
                              2 out
 5   2  0-2   -    3-1    Bogaerts struck out, 3 out
------------------------------------------------------------------------
                          5-New York
 5   0  1-0   -    3-1    Posada singled to left center, out at 2nd,
                              1 out
 5   1  2-1   -    3-1    Curtis grounded to the pitcher, 2 out
 5   2  2-0   -    3-1    Jeter flied to deep center, 3 out
------------------------------------------------------------------------
                          6-Boston
 6   0  1-2   -    3-1    Devers grounded to second, 1 out
 6   1  1-2   -    3-1    Kinsler struck out, 2 out
 6   2  2-0   -    3-1    Leon hit a solo homer to left,
                              Boston 4 New York 1
 6   2  1-1   -    4-1    Bradley Jr. grounded to first, 3 out
------------------------------------------------------------------------
                          6-New York
 6   0  1-2   -    4-1    Knoblauch flied to deep center, 1 out
 6   1  1-1   -    4-1    Williams grounded to third, 2 out
 6   2  1-0   -    4-1    O'Neill grounded to second, 3 out
------------------------------------------------------------------------
                          7-Boston
 7   0  3-2   -    4-1    Betts flied to deep left center, 1 out
 7   1  3-1   -    4-1    Benintendi walked
 7   1  1-1   1    4-1    Pearce hit a two run homer down the
                              left field line, Boston 6 New York 1
                         >Holmes pitching
 7   1  0-0   -    6-1    Martinez grounded to short, 2 out
 7   2  1-2   -    6-1    Bogaerts hit a solo homer to right center,
                              Boston 7 New York 1
 7   2  2-2   -    7-1    Devers grounded a single between first
                              and second
 7   2  1-2   1    7-1    Lin grounded to second, 3 out
------------------------------------------------------------------------
```

```
Inn Out B-S  On  NYY-Bos  Result
                          7-New York
                          >Lin playing 2B
 7   0  1-2  -    7-1     Strawberry struck out, 1 out
 7   1  0-0  -    7-1     Martinez hit by pitch
 7   1  1-2  1    7-1     Brosius flied to deep left center, 2 out
 7   2  2-2  1    7-1     Posada grounded to short, forcing Martinez
                              at second, 3 out
----------------------------------------------------------------
                          8-Boston
 8   0  1-2  -    7-1     Leon struck out, 1 out
 8   1  0-0  -    7-1     Bradley Jr. lined a single to right
 8   1  1-1  1    7-1     Betts flied to left, 2 out
 8   2  2-2  1    7-1     Benintendi flied to left, 3 out
----------------------------------------------------------------
                          8-New York
 8   0  3-2  -    7-1     Ledee grounded a single up the middle
                          >Barnes pitching
 8   0  2-2  1    7-1     Jeter struck out, 1 out
 8   1  0-1  1    7-1     Knoblauch grounded a single up the middle,
                              Ledee to 3rd
 8   1  3-1  13   7-1     Williams lined a double down the
                              right field line, Ledee scored,
                              Knoblauch to 3rd, Boston 7 New York 2
 8   1  3-2  23   7-2     O'Neill walked
 8   1  1-2  123  7-2     Strawberry struck out, 2 out
                          >Workman pitching
 8   2  3-1  123  7-2     Martinez walked, Knoblauch scored,
                              Williams to 3rd, O'Neill to 2nd,
                              Boston 7 New York 3
 8   2  0-2  123  7-3     Bush singled on the infield, Williams scored,
                              O'Neill to 3rd, Martinez to 2nd,
                              Boston 7 New York 4
                          >Wright pitching
 8   2  1-2  123  7-4     Posada flied to left center, 3 out
----------------------------------------------------------------
                          9-Boston
                          >Bush playing 3B
                          >Ledee playing LF
 9   0  1-1  -    7-4     Pearce grounded to short, 1 out
 9   1  1-0  -    7-4     Martinez grounded to short, 2 out
 9   2  3-1  -    7-4     Bogaerts walked
                          >Buddie pitching
 9   2  2-2  1    7-4     Devers hit a two run homer to right,
                              Boston 9 New York 4
 9   2  0-1  -    9-4     Lin grounded a single between first
                              and second
 9   2  0-2  1    9-4     Leon flied to right center, 3 out
----------------------------------------------------------------
                          9-New York
 9   0  2-0  -    9-4     Raines flied to center, 1 out
 9   1  3-2  -    9-4     Jeter grounded to short, 2 out
 9   2  3-1  -    9-4     Knoblauch grounded to short, 3 out
```

Game Three	1	2	3	4	5	6	7	8	9	R	H	E
2018 Boston Red Sox	3	0	0	0	0	1	3	0	2	9	11	1
1998 New York Yankees	0	0	0	1	0	0	0	3	0	4	8	1

Boston	AB	R	H	RBI	BB	K	LOB	PO	A	E
Betts, RF	4	1	1	0	1	1	1	1	0	0
Benintendi, LF	3	2	1	0	1	0	3	0	0	0
Pearce, 1B	3	2	1	2	2	0	0	9	2	0
Martinez, DH	5	0	0	0	0	1	0	0	0	0
Bogaerts, SS	2	2	1	2	2	1	0	1	3	0
Devers, 3B	5	1	3	4	0	1	2	0	3	0
Kinsler, 2B	3	0	1	0	0	1	0	1	2	0
Lin, PH-2B	2	0	1	0	0	0	1	1	0	0
Leon, C	5	1	1	1	0	1	1	7	0	0
Bradley Jr., CF	4	0	1	0	0	0	0	6	1	0
	36	9	11	9	6	6	8	27	13	1

Boston		IP	H	R	ER	HR	BB	K	Pit	S	B	ERA	BF
Porcello	W(1-0)	7.0	5	2	2	1	1	5	109	68	41	2.57	27
Barnes		0.2	2	2	2	0	1	2	23	13	10	10.13	5
Workman		0.0	1	0	0	0	1	0	9	5	4	0.00	2
Wright	S(2)	1.1	0	0	0	0	0	0	18	9	9	0.00	4
		9.0	8	4	4	1	3	7	159	95	64	4.33	38

New York	AB	R	H	RBI	BB	K	LOB	PO	A	E
Jeter, SS	5	0	0	0	0	1	0	1	5	0
Knoblauch, 2B	5	1	1	0	0	1	0	2	2	1
Williams, CF	4	1	2	1	0	1	0	5	0	0
O'Neill, RF	2	0	0	0	2	0	0	0	0	0
Strawberry, DH	4	1	1	1	0	2	3	0	0	0
Martinez, 1B	2	0	1	1	1	1	0	9	0	0
Brosius, 3B	3	0	0	0	0	0	0	1	1	0
Bush, PH-3B	1	0	1	1	0	0	0	0	0	0
Posada, C	4	0	1	0	0	0	4	6	1	0
Curtis, LF	2	0	0	0	0	1	1	3	0	0
Ledee, PH-LF	1	1	1	0	0	0	0	0	0	0
Raines, PH	1	0	0	0	0	0	0	0	0	0
	34	4	8	4	3	7	8	27	9	1

New York		IP	H	R	ER	HR	BB	K	Pit	S	B	ERA	BF
Pettitte	L(0-1)	6.1	6	6	6	2	5	5	114	64	50	8.53	30
Holmes		2.1	3	2	2	1	1	1	39	25	14	7.71	11
Buddie		0.1	2	1	1	1	0	0	12	10	2	27.00	3
		9.0	11	9	9	4	6	6	165	99	66	5.19	44

GAME THREE POSTGAME COMMENTS

Red Sox Manager

When you head into "opposition territory," it's always good to get a quick win if you can. The Yankees might have shut down that first inning with just the one run scored but then Devers slapped a clutch two-out single to right, giving the Red Sox three quick runs. How about the kid, Devers, going 3-for-5 with four runs batted in? He practically won the game by himself. I can't get over it; he just turned twenty-one at the end of July. My cleats are older than that!

Strawberry got a good pitch from Porcello and didn't miss. Yet another Yankee homer, but fortunately the only one for them. Our guys beefed up a bit with four of our own. Leon didn't let up. This time he put one out.

Porcello probably shouldn't have started the eighth, but I guess the computer had a good feeling about him against Ricky Ledee. It didn't work out. Barnes worked hard, but those '98 Yankees are one tough group. I'm glad Workman settled things down. I still don't understand why the computer seems fixated on Steven Wright. He wasn't even on the team's postseason roster. But it picked Wright over Kimbrel from the 53 players who appeared in games in 2018—and it paid off.

Looking for a strong outing from Eddie Rodriguez tomorrow.

Yankees Manager

All signs pointed to Andy Pettitte coming up big in Game Three. Instead, after 15 pitches the Yankees were trailing by three runs. They had a chance to make a statement in the bottom of the inning by loading the bases, but Darryl Strawberry rapped into a twin killing to extinguish a golden opportunity. This time the Straw did not stir the drink. He did slug a solo homer in the fourth, but we needed the long ball from him in the first. Oh well, that's baseball.

Chuck Knoblauch got the yips again, but thankfully his throwing error didn't cost us. The team needs Derek Jeter to get going. He's 2-for-13 in the series, with both hits coming in our Game Two victory. As our leadoff batter goes, we go.

My team is down two games to one—just like we were in the '98 ALCS against Cleveland. Then Orlando "El Duque" Hernandez won the fourth game, and that tipped the momentum back to our side. We're going to need another stellar performance from the Cuban wonder if we have any hope of catching Boston and making this a series.

1998 New York Yankees vs. 2018 Boston Red Sox
Game Four, Boston Leads, 2–1
Hideki Irabu (13–9, 4.06 ERA) vs. Eduardo Rodriguez (13–5, 3.82 ERA)
Time 4:21, 63°, Clear, Light Rain, Wind: 5 MPH Out to CF

```
Inn Out B-S  On  Bos-NYY  Result
                          1-Boston
 1   0  0-0   -    0-0    Betts grounded a single up the middle
 1   0  0-1   1    0-0    Benintendi grounded to second, Betts to 2nd,
                            1 out
 1   1  1-2   2    0-0    Martinez lined to left, 2 out
 1   2  3-2   2    0-0    Bogaerts grounded to third, 3 out
-------------------------------------------------------------------
                          1-New York
 1   0  0-0   -    0-0    Jeter singled between third and short
 1   0  0-0   1    0-0    Jeter stole 2nd
 1   0  0-1   2    0-0    Raines struck out, 1 out
 1   1  0-2   2    0-0    Jeter stole 3rd
 1   1  0-1   3    0-0    Williams struck out, 2 out
 1   2  0-2   3    0-0    Brosius grounded to first, 3 out
-------------------------------------------------------------------
                          2-Boston
 2   0  3-2   -    0-0    Moreland walked
 2   0  0-2   1    0-0    Devers struck out, 1 out
 2   1  2-0   1    0-0    Kinsler grounded to short, second to first
                            double play, 3 out
-------------------------------------------------------------------
                          2-New York
 2   0  3-1   -    0-0    Posada lined a single to left
 2   0  1-0   1    0-0    O'Neill lined a single up the middle,
                            Posada to 2nd
 2   0  1-1  12    0-0    Martinez lined a single between first
                            and second, Posada to 3rd, O'Neill to 2nd
 2   0  1-2  123   0-0    Knoblauch grounded to the pitcher,
                            Posada scored, O'Neill to 3rd,
                            Martinez to 2nd, New York 1 Boston 0
 2   0  3-0  123   0-1    Curtis walked, O'Neill scored,
                            Martinez to 3rd, Knoblauch to 2nd,
                            New York 2 Boston 0
 2   0  2-0  123   0-2    Jeter lined a single to right center,
                            Martinez scored, Knoblauch to 3rd,
                            Curtis to 2nd, New York 3 Boston 0
 2   0  1-0  123   0-3    Raines lined a single to left,
                            Knoblauch scored, Curtis scored,
                            Jeter to 3rd, New York 5 Boston 0
 2   0  3-2  13    0-5    Williams struck out, 1 out
 2   1  3-2  13    0-5    Brosius walked, Raines to 2nd
 2   1  0-2  123   0-5    Posada grounded to third, second to first
                            double play, 3 out
-------------------------------------------------------------------
                          3-Boston
 3   0  3-2   -    0-5    Leon grounded to the pitcher, 1 out
 3   1  2-1   -    0-5    Bradley Jr. lined to second, 2 out
 3   2  3-2   -    0-5    Betts walked
 3   2  2-0   1    0-5    Benintendi grounded to the pitcher, 3 out
-------------------------------------------------------------------
```

```
Inn Out B-S   On   Bos-NYY  Result
                             3-New York
 3   0  1-2    -     0-5     O'Neill struck out, 1 out
 3   1  3-2    -     0-5     Martinez struck out, 2 out
 3   2  0-0    -     0-5     Knoblauch lined a single to center
 3   2  3-2    1     0-5     Curtis walked, Knoblauch to 2nd
 3   2  2-1   12     0-5     Jeter lined to short, 3 out
-----------------------------------------------------------------
                             4-Boston
 4   0  1-2    -     0-5     Martinez singled to left center
 4   0  0-2    1     0-5     Bogaerts struck out, 1 out
 4   1  1-2    1     0-5     Moreland struck out, 2 out
 4   2  3-1    1     0-5     Devers doubled off the wall down the
                               left field line, Martinez to 3rd
 4   2  3-2   23     0-5     Kinsler walked
 4   2  1-1  123     0-5     Leon lined a single to right,
                               Martinez scored, Devers scored,
                               Kinsler to 3rd, New York 5 Boston 2
 4   2  1-2   13     2-5     Bradley Jr. grounded a single up the middle,
                               Kinsler scored, Leon to 3rd,
                               New York 5 Boston 3
 4   2  1-1   13     3-5     Betts popped to short, 3 out
-----------------------------------------------------------------
                             4-New York
 4   0  1-0    -     3-5     Raines grounded to second, 1 out
 4   1  1-2    -     3-5     Williams grounded a single between first
                               and second
                            >Velazquez pitching
 4   1  3-1    1     3-5     Brosius grounded to second, forcing
                               Williams at second, 2 out
 4   2  1-2    1     3-5     Posada struck out, 3 out
-----------------------------------------------------------------
                             5-Boston
 5   0  1-2    -     3-5     Benintendi struck out, 1 out
 5   1  1-2    -     3-5     Martinez flied to left, 2 out
 5   2  3-1    -     3-5     Bogaerts lined to third, 3 out
-----------------------------------------------------------------
                             5-New York
 5   0  1-1    -     3-5     O'Neill grounded to third, 1 out
 5   1  2-2    -     3-5     Martinez lined a double down the
                               first base line
 5   1  1-2    2     3-5     Knoblauch grounded to third, 2 out
 5   2  0-2    2     3-5     Curtis grounded to short, 3 out
-----------------------------------------------------------------
```

```
Inn Out B-S  On  Bos-NYY  Result
                           6-Boston
  6   0  1-0   -     3-5   Moreland hit a solo homer down the
                               right field line, New York 5 Boston 4
  6   0  3-2   -     4-5   Devers flied to deep right center, 1 out
                           >Buddie pitching
  6   1  0-1   -     4-5   Kinsler grounded to first, safe on an error,
                               Kinsler to 2nd
  6   1  2-2   2     4-5   Leon grounded to second, Kinsler to 3rd,
                               2 out
  6   2  1-2   3     4-5   Bradley Jr. singled to right, Kinsler scored,
                               Boston 5 New York 5
  6   2  2-0   1     5-5   Betts doubled off the wall down the
                               right field line, Bradley Jr. scored,
                               Boston 6 New York 5
  6   2  1-0   2     6-5   Benintendi flied to deep left, 3 out
---------------------------------------------------------------------
                           6-New York
                           >Workman pitching
  6   0  2-1   -     6-5   Jeter lined a single to left
  6   0  2-2   1     6-5   Raines struck out, 1 out
  6   1  1-1   1     6-5   Williams flied to deep right center, 2 out
  6   2  2-1   1     6-5   Brosius singled to left center, Jeter to 3rd
                           >Brasier pitching
  6   2  1-1  13     6-5   Posada grounded to third, 3 out
---------------------------------------------------------------------
                           7-Boston
  7   0  1-0   -     6-5   Martinez flied to shallow left center, 1 out
  7   1  0-1   -     6-5   Bogaerts lined a single between third
                               and short
  7   1  1-0   1     6-5   Moreland lined a single to right,
                               Bogaerts to 2nd
  7   1  0-0  12     6-5   Devers doubled off the wall down the
                               right field line, Bogaerts scored,
                               Moreland to 3rd, Boston 7 New York 5
  7   1  0-1  23     7-5   Kinsler intentionally walked
  7   1  2-0 123     7-5   Leon flied down the right field line,
                               sacrifice, Moreland scored, 2 out,
                               Boston 8 New York 5
  7   2  0-2  12     8-5   Bradley Jr. struck out, 3 out
---------------------------------------------------------------------
                           7-New York
  7   0  2-0   -     8-5   O'Neill singled on the infield
  7   0  2-1   1     8-5   Martinez popped to first, 1 out
  7   1  1-1   1     8-5   Wild pitch, O'Neill to 2nd
  7   1  2-1   2     8-5   Knoblauch grounded to first, O'Neill to 3rd,
                               2 out
                           >Kelly pitching
  7   2  0-2   3     8-5   Curtis struck out, 3 out
---------------------------------------------------------------------
```

```
Inn Out B-S  On  Bos-NYY  Result
                          8-Boston
 8   0  1-1  -    8-5     Betts grounded to second, safe on an error,
                              Betts to 2nd
 8   0  2-1  2    8-5     Benintendi lined to center, 1 out
 8   1  0-2  2    8-5     Martinez singled to left, Betts scored,
                              outfield error, Martinez to 3rd,
                              Boston 9 New York 5
 8   1  3-1  3'   9-5     Bogaerts flied to shallow left center,
                              Martinez scored, 2 out,
                              Boston 10 New York 5
 8   2  0-2  -   10-5     Moreland struck out, 3 out
------------------------------------------------------------------
                          8-New York
 8   0  2-2  -   10-5     Jeter struck out, 1 out
 8   1  3-1  -   10-5     Raines walked
 8   1  2-2  1   10-5     Williams struck out, 2 out
                          >Johnson pitching
 8   2  3-2  1   10-5     Brosius walked, Raines to 2nd
 8   2  2-1  12  10-5     Posada lined a single to left center,
                              Raines to 3rd, Brosius to 2nd
 8   2  0-2  123 10-5     O'Neill doubled off the wall in left,
                              Raines scored, Brosius scored,
                              Posada to 3rd, Boston 10 New York 7
                          >Walden pitching
 8   2  1-0  23  10-7     Martinez grounded to second, 3 out
------------------------------------------------------------------
                          9-Boston
 9   0  1-2  -   10-7     Devers flied deep down the right field line,
                              1 out
 9   1  1-0  -   10-7     Kinsler flied to deep right, 2 out
                          >Mendoza pitching
 9   2  2-2  -   10-7     Leon grounded to the pitcher, 3 out
------------------------------------------------------------------
                          9-New York
                          >Kimbrel pitching
 9   0  3-2  -   10-7     Knoblauch hit a solo homer down the
                              right field line, Boston 10 New York 8
 9   0  2-2  -   10-8     Curtis struck out, 1 out
 9   1  2-2  -   10-8     Jeter struck out, 2 out
 9   2  2-2  -   10-8     Raines singled on the infield
 9   2  0-2  1   10-8     Wild pitch, Raines to 2nd
 9   2  1-2  2   10-8     Williams doubled off the wall in left center,
                              Raines scored, Boston 10 New York 9
 9   2  2-0  2   10-9     Wild pitch, Williams to 3rd
 9   2  3-0  3   10-9     Brosius grounded to third, 3 out
```

Game Four	1	2	3	4	5	6	7	8	9	R	H	E
2018 Boston Red Sox	0	0	0	3	0	3	2	2	0	10	12	0
1998 New York Yankees	0	5	0	0	0	0	0	2	2	9	17	3

Boston	AB	R	H	RBI	BB	K	LOB	PO	A	E
Betts, RF	4	1	2	1	1	0	2	1	0	0
Benintendi, LF	5	0	0	0	0	1	2	0	0	0
Martinez, DH	5	2	2	1	0	0	0	0	0	0
Bogaerts, SS	4	1	1	1	0	1	1	2	1	0
Moreland, 1B	4	2	2	1	1	2	0	10	1	0
Devers, 3B	5	1	2	1	0	1	0	0	6	0
Kinsler, 2B	3	2	0	0	2	0	1	1	3	0
Leon, C	4	0	1	3	0	0	0	12	0	0
Bradley Jr., CF	4	1	2	2	0	1	2	0	0	0
	38	10	12	10	4	6	8	27	11	0

Boston		IP	H	R	ER	HR	BB	K	Pit	S	B	ERA	BF
Rodriguez		3.1	8	5	5	0	3	5	87	55	32	13.50	21
Velazquez	W(1-0)	1.2	1	0	0	0	0	1	27	19	8	0.00	6
Workman		0.2	2	0	0	0	0	1	17	10	7	0.00	4
Brasier		1.0	1	0	0	0	0	0	14	7	7	0.00	4
Kelly		1.0	0	1	1	0	1	3	21	13	8	4.50	4
Johnson		0.0	2	1	1	0	1	0	14	8	6	0.00	3
Walden		0.1	0	0	0	0	0	0	2	1	1	0.00	1
Kimbrel	S(1)	1.0	3	2	2	1	0	2	34	21	13	18.00	6
		9.0	17	9	9	1	5	12	216	134	82	5.50	49

New York	AB	R	H	RBI	BB	K	LOB	PO	A	E
Jeter, SS	6	0	3	1	0	2	2	1	2	0
Raines, DH	5	2	2	2	1	2	0	0	0	0
Williams, CF	6	0	2	1	0	3	0	1	0	0
Brosius, 3B	4	1	1	0	2	0	2	1	1	0
Posada, C	5	1	2	0	0	1	6	6	0	0
O'Neill, RF	5	1	3	2	0	1	0	4	0	0
Martinez, 1B	5	1	2	0	0	1	2	7	0	1
Knoblauch, 2B	5	2	2	2	0	0	0	2	2	1
Curtis, LF	3	1	0	1	2	2	2	5	0	1
	44	9	17	9	5	12	14	27	8	3

New York		IP	H	R	ER	HR	W	K	Pit	S	B	ERA	BF
Irabu		5.1	6	4	4	1	3	4	107	65	42	6.75	24
Buddie	L(0-1)	3.1	6	6	2	0	1	2	61	39	22	7.36	19
Mendoza		0.1	0	0	0	0	0	0	5	3	2	0.00	1
		9.0	12	10	6	1	4	6	173	107	66	5.40	44

GAME FOUR POSTGAME COMMENTS

Red Sox Manager

Talk about ups and downs in a ballgame! Back in the second inning when the Yankees broke out to a 5–0 lead before we even got anyone out, I was feeling pretty bad for Eddie. Then in the fourth my man Sandy came through yet again—a two-run single to pick up his pitcher. Then we added another run and were back in the ballgame. When Eddie reached 87 pitches, I agreed it was time to bring in Velasquez. He's been pretty good for us all season long, maybe a little under the radar. I'm sure glad we've got a full complement of staff in the bullpen—it's nice to have 23 pitchers to call on. We went through eight of them in this game alone.

And *seven* of our guys drove in runs. Everybody likes games when their guys score 10 runs. We needed every one of them. They got off to a big start, we picked up the next 10 runs, and then they put a scare on us by scoring twice in the eighth—maybe the computer put in Walden because it suspected the Yankees probably hadn't studied any film on him—and then, even with Kimbrel pitching the ninth, they got a couple more runs. So they scored early and late, but we got enough in between to pull through.

I'll tell you, it feels good being up three games to one, and I'm glad to have Sale pitching for us tomorrow.

Yankees Manager

Artificial intelligence can be dumbfounding. With the Yankees down two games to one, a well-rested Orlando Hernandez seemed the logical choice to start this crucial fourth game. Playing a hunch, the computer went with Japanese native Hideki Irabu.

Big mistake.

After being staked to a 5–0 lead, Irabu unraveled in the sixth. He came out, rookie Mike Buddie came in, and he couldn't hold it, either.

In Buddie's defense, he had none; three errors lead to four costly unearned runs, as the Yankees lose by one run. This is a stinging loss. The offense did its job, exploding for nine runs on 17 hits, yet it wasn't enough. Inexplicably, the computer simulation preferred Irabu and

Buddie pitching 8 2/3 innings over a ready and willing Hernandez in a critical game for the Yankees. Excuse me; I'm going to be sick.

A flawed algorithm might place too much emphasis on Irabu's regular-season workload (173 innings, 28 starts) to rank him as the fourth starter ahead of Hernandez (141 innings, 21 starts). I understand a fancy computer algorithm can't know Hernandez joined the team in June after defecting from Cuba and quickly gained a reputation as a "big game" pitcher, but a worthy algorithm should recognize El Duque's sparkling stats (12–4, 3.13 ERA) as being superior to Irabu's (13–9, 4.06 ERA). Starting Hernandez should have been a no-brainer.

The second-guessers can crow all they want, but rules are rules, so I'm told. The computer simulation was designed to utilize the team's entire 40-man regular-season roster. I could have insisted on utilizing only postseason rosters, making Irabu and Buddie disappear, but frankly, the notion to ask never occurred to me. Now my team is paying the price.

1998 New York Yankees vs. 2018 Boston Red Sox
Game Five, Boston Leads, 3–1
David Wells (18–4, 3.49 ERA) vs. Chris Sale (12–4, 2.11 ERA)
Time 2:34, 68°, Clear, Light Rain, Wind: 12 MPH Left to Right

```
Inn Out B-S  On  Bos-NYY  Result
                          1-Boston
 1   0  2-2   -   0-0     Betts struck out, 1 out
 1   1  1-1   -   0-0     Benintendi grounded to short, 2 out
 1   2  0-0   -   0-0     Pearce lined to third, 3 out
---------------------------------------------------------------
                          1-New York
 1   0  0-2   -   0-0     Jeter grounded a single between third
                            and short
 1   0  0-1   1   0-0     Jeter caught stealing 2nd, 1 out
 1   1  0-2   -   0-0     Raines grounded to the pitcher, 2 out
 1   2  0-2   -   0-0     Williams struck out, 3 out
---------------------------------------------------------------
                          2-Boston
 2   0  0-1   -   0-0     Martinez lined a single to left center
 2   0  0-1   1   0-0     Bogaerts grounded to third, Martinez to 2nd,
                            1 out
 2   1  0-0   2   0-0     Devers flied to right, 2 out
 2   2  0-0   2   0-0     Kinsler flied to right, 3 out
---------------------------------------------------------------
                          2-New York
 2   0  2-2   -   0-0     Brosius struck out, 1 out
 2   1  1-0   -   0-0     Posada doubled off the wall down the
                            third base line
 2   1  3-2   2   0-0     O'Neill grounded to second, Posada to 3rd,
                            2 out
 2   2  0-2   3   0-0     Martinez flied to deep right, 3 out
---------------------------------------------------------------
                          3-Boston
 3   0  1-2   -   0-0     Leon struck out, 1 out
 3   1  0-2   -   0-0     Bradley Jr. flied to left center, 2 out
 3   2  0-2   -   0-0     Betts grounded to short, 3 out
---------------------------------------------------------------
                          3-New York
 3   0  3-1   -   0-0     Knoblauch grounded to third, 1 out
 3   1  1-2   -   0-0     Curtis struck out, 2 out
 3   2  2-2   -   0-0     Jeter flied to left center, 3 out
---------------------------------------------------------------
                          4-Boston
 4   0  0-2   -   0-0     Benintendi struck out, 1 out
 4   1  1-2   -   0-0     Pearce struck out, 2 out
 4   2  0-2   -   0-0     Martinez struck out, 3 out
---------------------------------------------------------------
                          4-New York
 4   0  0-1   -   0-0     Raines grounded to short, 1 out
 4   1  1-2   -   0-0     Williams hit a solo homer to right center,
                            New York 1 Boston 0
 4   1  0-1   -   0-1     Brosius singled to center
 4   1  0-2   1   0-1     Posada flied to deep left, 2 out
 4   2  0-0   1   0-1     Brosius caught stealing 2nd, 3 out
---------------------------------------------------------------
                          5-Boston
 5   0  0-1   -   0-1     Bogaerts grounded to short, 1 out
 5   1  1-0   -   0-1     Devers grounded to the pitcher, 2 out
 5   2  1-1   -   0-1     Kinsler flied to right, 3 out
---------------------------------------------------------------
```

```
Inn Out B-S  On  Bos-NYY  Result
                          5-New York
 5   0  3-2  -    0-1     O'Neill flied to deep right center, 1 out
 5   1  2-1  -    0-1     Martinez grounded a single between first
                              and second
 5   1  2-1  1    0-1     Knoblauch grounded to short, second to first
                              double play, 3 out
-------------------------------------------------------------------
                          6-Boston
 6   0  0-0  -    0-1     Leon flied to right center, 1 out
 6   1  2-1  -    0-1     Bradley Jr. flied to deep right, 2 out
 6   2  0-2  -    0-1     Betts struck out, 3 out
-------------------------------------------------------------------
                          6-New York
 6   0  0-0  -    0-1     Curtis grounded to second, 1 out
 6   1  1-2  -    0-1     Jeter grounded to short, 2 out
 6   2  0-1  -    0-1     Raines grounded to third, safe on
                              throwing error
 6   2  0-1  1    0-1     Williams flied down the right field line,
                              3 out
-------------------------------------------------------------------
                          7-Boston
 7   0  1-2  -    0-1     Benintendi struck out, 1 out
 7   1  0-0  -    0-1     Pearce grounded to third, 2 out
 7   2  1-2  -    0-1     Martinez struck out, 3 out
-------------------------------------------------------------------
                          7-New York
 7   0  3-1  -    0-1     Brosius walked
 7   0  3-2  1    0-1     Posada flied deep down the left field line,
                              1 out
 7   1  2-1  1    0-1     O'Neill lined to second, 2 out
 7   2  2-0  1    0-1     Martinez flied to shallow center, 3 out
-------------------------------------------------------------------
                          8-Boston
 8   0  2-2  -    0-1     Bogaerts grounded to first, 1 out
 8   1  1-2  -    0-1     Devers flied to right, 2 out
 8   2  0-2  -    0-1     Nunez grounded to short, 3 out
-------------------------------------------------------------------
                          8-New York
                          >Kelly pitching
                          >Nunez, E playing 2B
 8   0  3-0  -    0-1     Knoblauch hit by pitch, Knoblauch injured
                          >Bush pinch runner at 1st
 8   0  2-2  1    0-1     Curtis grounded a single between first
                              and second, Bush to 2nd
 8   0  0-2  12   0-1     Jeter grounded to second, forcing Curtis
                              at second, Bush to 3rd, 1 out
 8   1  0-2  13   0-1     **Raines grounded to second, forcing Jeter
                              at second, Bush scored, 2 out,
                              New York 2 Boston 0**
                          >Hembree pitching
 8   2  0-0  1    0-2     Raines stole 2nd
 8   2  0-1  2    0-2     Williams intentionally walked
 8   2  2-2  12   0-2     Brosius lined a single to left,
                              Raines out at home, 3 out
-------------------------------------------------------------------
Inn Out B-S  On  Bos-NYY  Result
                          9-Boston
                          >Bush playing 2B
 9   0  1-0  -    0-2     Leon flied to deep right center, 1 out
 9   1  0-0  -    0-2     Ramirez grounded to second, 2 out
 9   2  2-1  -    0-2     Betts flied to very deep right center, 3 out
```

Game Five	1	2	3	4	5	6	7	8	9	R	H	E
2018 Boston Red Sox	0	0	0	0	0	0	0	0	0	0	1	1
1998 New York Yankees	0	0	0	1	0	0	0	1	-	2	7	0

Boston	AB	R	H	RBI	BB	K	LOB	PO	A	E
Betts, RF	4	0	0	0	0	2	0	2	0	0
Benintendi, LF	3	0	0	0	0	2	0	3	1	0
Pearce, 1B	3	0	0	0	0	1	0	7	0	0
Martinez, DH	3	0	1	0	0	2	0	0	0	0
Bogaerts, SS	3	0	0	0	0	0	0	3	4	0
Devers, 3B	3	0	0	0	0	0	0	0	1	1
Kinsler, 2B	2	0	0	0	0	0	1	3	2	0
Nunez, PH-2B	1	0	0	0	0	0	0	0	2	0
Leon, C	3	0	0	0	0	1	0	4	2	0
Bradley Jr., CF	2	0	0	0	0	0	0	2	0	0
Ramirez, PH	1	0	0	0	0	0	0	0	0	0
	28	0	1	0	0	8	1	24	13	1

Boston (A)		IP	H	R	ER	HR	BB	K	Pit	S	B	ERA	BF
Sale	L(1-1)	7.0	5	1	1	1	1	3	101	69	32	2.25	25
Kelly		0.2	1	1	1	0	0	0	19	13	6	6.75	4
Hembree		0.1	1	0	0	0	1	0	13	7	6	0.00	2
		8.0	7	2	2	1	2	3	133	89	44	4.91	31

New York	AB	R	H	RBI	BB	K	LOB	PO	A	E
Jeter, SS	4	0	1	0	0	0	0	0	4	0
Raines, DH	4	0	0	1	0	0	0	0	0	0
Williams, CF	3	1	1	1	1	1	1	4	0	0
Brosius, 3B	3	0	2	0	1	1	1	1	2	0
Posada, C	3	0	1	0	0	0	0	8	0	0
O'Neill, RF	3	0	0	0	0	0	0	5	0	0
Martinez, 1B	3	0	1	0	0	0	2	9	0	0
Knoblauch, 2B	2	0	0	0	0	0	1	0	0	0
Bush, PR-2B	0	1	0	0	0	0	0	0	1	0
Curtis, LF	3	0	1	0	0	1	0	0	0	0
	28	2	7	2	2	3	5	27	8	0

New York		IP	H	R	ER	HR	BB	K	Pit	S	B	ERA	BF
Wells	W(1-1)	9.0	1	0	0	0	0	8	95	78	17	2.25	28
		9.0	1	0	0	0	0	8	95	78	17	2.25	28

GAME FIVE POSTGAME COMMENTS

Yankees Manager

David Wells created a masterpiece by pitching a perfect game in 1998, and he nearly matched that magnificent performance with his effort in this game. He shut down the Red Sox to secure a much-needed victory to keep hope alive.

Boomer pitched the second greatest game of his "life," putting on a pitching clinic and was in complete command from beginning to end. Nine innings, one hit, no walks. You can't pitch much better than that! Boston placed one runner as far as second base—J. D. Martinez following his single in the second inning. And that was all she wrote for the Red Sox. Wells faced just one batter over the minimum.

In retiring 24 batters in a row, Boomer's control was so sharp he never went to a three-ball count on any batter. He also struck out eight and threw a total of only 95 pitches (78 for strikes) in the entire game, which lasted two hours, 34 minutes. To say he was on cruise control is an understatement.

While Wells pitched a gem, nothing can be taken away from the day Sale had. Bernie went boom in the fourth for a 1–0 lead, but neither team could solve the opposing pitcher. By the eighth, I was more concerned about winning the game. We scratched out a second run the old-fashioned way: get 'em on, move 'em over, and get 'em in. The RBI ground-out by Rock Raines was a thing of beauty. Down 0-2 in the count against Kelly, he refused to give in and got the job done. He then stole second base to get himself into scoring position, and though he was gunned down at the plate for the final out of the inning, I have no problem with the play. The third-base coach has to send the runner in that situation and force Benintendi to make a good throw, which he did.

Knoblauch got plunked and had to leave the game. I'm waiting for a report from the trainer, but hopeful he won't miss any games. It's all hands on deck. I told my guys: Don't worry about needing to win three in a row. Just win one game in a row three times and we'll take the series. One down. Now there are two to go.

Red Sox Manager

Sale did his job. Facing a team like the 1998 Yankees and holding them to one run over seven innings—you couldn't really ask for anything more. That's the second homer Bernie Williams hit off him, though—first in Game One and now in this one.

That said, the Yankees did get more. They got a near-perfect game from Wells. I don't know what kind of secret sauce he may have taken. He sure redeemed himself after Game One.

One hit by J. D. to lead off the second—a nice, clean, solid single. But then there was nothing else. I thought Mookie hit one in the top of the ninth, but O'Neill was playing him deep and pulled it in.

We put up some good defense. Yet again someone tried to take an extra base on Benny. They'll learn. He had 12 outfield assists in the 2018 season. Maybe they should have read their scouting reports a little better.

I don't have anything more for you tonight. We'll be back in Fenway after a day off. All we've got to do is take one of the two. Let's hope there aren't two, and we can wrap it up in six.

1998 New York Yankees @ 2018 Boston Red Sox
Game Six, Boston Leads, 3–2
David Cone (20–7, 3.55 ERA) vs. David Price (16–7, 3.58 ERA)
Time 3:44, 59°, Wind: 4 MPH Right to Left

```
Inn Out B-S  On  NYY-Bos  Result
                          1-New York
 1   0  2-1  -    0-0     Jeter grounded to third, 1 out
 1   1  3-2  -    0-0     Raines lined a single to right center
 1   1  0-2  1    0-0     Williams struck out, 2 out
 1   2  2-0  1    0-0     Brosius doubled down the right field line,
                              Raines to 3rd
 1   2  0-2  23   0-0     Posada struck out, 3 out
-----------------------------------------------------------------
                          1-Boston
 1   0  0-2  -    0-0     Betts struck out, out at 1st, 1 out
 1   1  1-0  -    0-0     Benintendi doubled to right center
 1   1  2-0  2    0-0     Martinez singled to center,
                              Benintendi scored,
                              Boston 1 New York 0
 1   1  1-0  1    0-1     Bogaerts hit a two run homer down the
                              left field line, Boston 3 New York 0
 1   1  3-0  -    0-3     Moreland walked
 1   1  1-2  1    0-3     Devers grounded to second, forcing
                              Moreland at second, 2 out
 1   2  1-1  1    0-3     Kinsler grounded to first, 3 out
-----------------------------------------------------------------
                          2-New York
 2   0  1-1  -    0-3     O'Neill grounded to second, 1 out
 2   1  3-2  -    0-3     Martinez hit by pitch, Martinez injured
                          >Sveum pinch runner at 1st
 2   1  1-1  1    0-3     Curtis hit a two run homer down the
                              left field line, Boston 3 New York 2
 2   1  3-1  -    2-3     Knoblauch flied to deep left, 2 out
 2   2  3-1  -    2-3     Jeter walked
 2   2  3-1  1    2-3     Raines lined a single to right center,
                              Jeter to 3rd
 2   2  0-1  13   2-3     Williams lined a single between third
                              and short, Jeter scored, Raines to 2nd,
                              New York 3 Boston 3
 2   2  1-2  12   3-3     Brosius struck out, 3 out
-----------------------------------------------------------------
                          2-Boston
                          >Sveum playing 1B
 2   0  2-0  -    3-3     Leon popped to short, 1 out
 2   1  3-0  -    3-3     Bradley Jr. walked
 2   1  0-0  1    3-3     Bradley Jr. stole 2nd
 2   1  0-1  2    3-3     Betts lined to short, 2 out
 2   2  0-2  2    3-3     Benintendi struck out, 3 out
-----------------------------------------------------------------
                          3-New York
 3   0  0-1  -    3-3     Posada flied to shallow right center, 1 out
 3   1  0-2  -    3-3     O'Neill flied to deep right center, 2 out
 3   2  1-2  -    3-3     Sveum struck out, 3 out
-----------------------------------------------------------------
                          3-Boston
 3   0  2-0  -    3-3     Martinez grounded to short, 1 out
 3   1  2-0  -    3-3     Bogaerts flied to deep left center, 2 out
 3   2  2-2  -    3-3     Moreland grounded to second, 3 out
-----------------------------------------------------------------
```

```
Inn Out B-S  On  Bos-NYY  Result
                           4-New York
 4   0  0-2  -    3-3      Curtis struck out, 1 out
 4   1  2-0  -    3-3      Knoblauch grounded to short, 2 out
 4   2  2-1  -    3-3      Jeter flied to right center, 3 out
-----------------------------------------------------------------
                           4-Boston
 4   0  1-1  -    3-3      Devers flied down the right field line, 1 out
 4   1  0-2  -    3-3      Kinsler struck out, 2 out
 4   2  1-2  -    3-3      Leon struck out, tagged out, 3 out
-----------------------------------------------------------------
                           5-New York
 5   0  1-1  -    3-3      Raines grounded a single between third
                                 and short
 5   0  3-1  1    3-3      Williams walked, Raines to 2nd
 5   0  0-2  12   3-3      Brosius struck out, 1 out
 5   1  0-2  12   3-3      Posada struck out, 2 out
 5   2  2-2  12   3-3      O'Neill struck out, 3 out
-----------------------------------------------------------------
                           5-Boston
 5   0  0-2  -    3-3      Bradley Jr. struck out, 1 out
 5   1  1-2  -    3-3      Betts struck out, 2 out
 5   2  0-2  -    3-3      Benintendi singled to left
 5   2  1-2  1    3-3      Wild pitch, Benintendi to 2nd
 5   2  2-2  2    3-3      Martinez grounded a single between first
                                 and second, Benintendi scored,
                                 Boston 4 New York 3
 5   2  2-1  1    3-4      Bogaerts doubled to left center,
                                 Martinez to 3rd
 5   2  1-2  23   3-4      Moreland singled to right, Martinez scored,
                                 Bogaerts scored, Boston 6 New York 3
 5   2  3-2  1    3-6      Devers walked, Moreland to 2nd
 5   2  1-2  12   3-6      Kinsler flied to shallow right center, 3 out
-----------------------------------------------------------------
                           6-New York
                           >Barnes pitching
 6   0  1-2  -    3-6      Ledee struck out, 1 out
 6   1  0-2  -    3-6      Strawberry singled to right center
 6   1  0-2  1    3-6      Knoblauch struck out, 2 out
 6   2  3-2  1    3-6      Jeter struck out, 3 out
-----------------------------------------------------------------
                           6-Boston
                           >Ledee playing LF
                           >Sojo playing 1B
 6   0  0-2  -    3-6      Leon struck out, 1 out
 6   1  0-1  -    3-6      Bradley Jr. lined to center, 2 out
 6   2  1-0  -    3-6      Betts grounded to third, 3 out
-----------------------------------------------------------------
                           7-New York
                           >Hembree pitching
 7   0  0-0  -    3-6      Raines grounded to short, 1 out
 7   1  3-2  -    3-6      Williams lined to second, 2 out
 7   2  0-2  -    3-6      Bush lined a single up the middle
 7   2  2-1  1    3-6      Posada doubled to right center, Bush to 3rd
                           >Brasier pitching
 7   2  1-2  23   3-6      O'Neill lined to short, 3 out
-----------------------------------------------------------------
```

```
Inn Out B-S  On  Bos-NYY  Result
                          7-Boston
                          >Holmes pitching
                          >Bush playing 3B
 7   0  2-1  -    3-6     Benintendi grounded to the pitcher, 1 out
 7   1  1-0  -    3-6     Martinez doubled to left center
 7   1  3-2  2    3-6     Bogaerts grounded a single between third
                            and short, Martinez to 3rd
 7   1  1-2  13   3-6     Moreland flied to deep right center,
                            sacrifice, Martinez scored, 2 out,
                            Boston 7 New York 3
 7   2  3-1  1    3-7     Devers walked, Bogaerts to 2nd
 7   2  1-2  12   3-7     Kinsler singled to left center,
                            Bogaerts scored, Devers to 3rd,
                            Boston 8 New York 3
 7   2  2-1  13   3-8     Leon grounded to first, 3 out
---------------------------------------------------------------
                          8-New York
 8   0  3-1  -    3-8     Ledee grounded to short, 1 out
 8   1  0-2  -    3-8     Sojo grounded to first, 2 out
 8   2  0-1  -    3-8     Knoblauch grounded to short, 3 out
---------------------------------------------------------------
                          8-Boston
 8   0  2-2  -    3-8     Bradley Jr. hit a solo homer down the
                            right field line, Boston 9 New York 3
                          >Mendoza pitching
 8   0  0-1  -    3-9     Betts doubled off the wall down the
                            right field line
 8   0  3-1  2    3-9     Benintendi walked
 8   0  2-0  12   3-9     Martinez doubled off the wall down the
                            left field line, Betts scored,
                            Benintendi scored, Boston 11 New York 3
 8   0  1-2  2    3-11    Bogaerts grounded to the pitcher,
                            Martinez to 3rd, 1 out
 8   1  0-2  3    3-11    Moreland struck out, 2 out
 8   2  1-2  3    3-11    Devers grounded to second, 3 out
---------------------------------------------------------------
                          9-New York
 9   0  1-0  -    3-11    Jeter grounded to third, 1 out
 9   1  1-1  -    3-11    Raines lined a single to right center
 9   1  1-2  1    3-11    Williams struck out, 2 out
                          >Thornburg pitching
 9   2  0-2  1    3-11    Bush hit a two run homer to left,
                            Boston 11 New York 5
 9   2  3-2  -    5-11    Posada struck out, 3 out
```

Game Six	1	2	3	4	5	6	7	8	9	R	H	E
1998 New York Yankees	0	3	0	0	0	0	0	0	2	5	11	0
2018 Boston Red Sox	3	0	0	0	3	0	2	3	-	11	13	0

New York	AB	R	H	BI	W	K	LOB	PO	A	E
Jeter, SS	4	1	0	0	1	1	1	3	1	0
Raines, DH	5	1	4	0	0	0	0	0	0	0
Williams, CF	4	0	1	1	1	2	0	2	0	0
Brosius, 3B	3	0	1	0	0	2	2	0	1	0
Bush, PH-3B	2	1	2	2	0	0	2	0	0	0
Posada, C	5	0	1	0	0	3	2	7	1	0
O'Neill, RF	4	0	0	0	0	1	4	3	0	0
Martinez, 1B	0	0	0	0	0	0	0	2	0	0
Sveum, PR-1B	1	1	0	0	0	1	0	2	0	0
Ledee, PH-LF	2	0	0	0	0	1	0	0	0	0
Curtis, LF	2	1	1	2	0	1	0	0	0	0
Strawberry, PH	1	0	1	0	0	0	0	0	0	0
Sojo, 1B	1	0	0	0	0	0	0	5	0	0
Knoblauch, 2B	4	0	0	0	0	1	0	0	3	0
	38	5	11	5	2	13	11	24	8	0

New York		IP	H	R	ER	HR	BB	K	Pit	S	B	ERA	BF
Cone	L(1-1)	6.0	7	6	6	1	3	7	102	66	36	3.60	28
Holmes		1.0	4	3	3	1	1	0	35	19	16	13.50	8
Mendoza		1.0	2	2	2	0	1	1	22	14	8	13.50	6
		8.0	13	11	11	2	5	8	159	99	60	5.54	42

Boston	AB	R	H	BI	W	K	LOB	PO	A	E
Betts, RF	5	1	1	0	0	2	0	1	0	0
Benintendi, LF	4	3	2	0	1	1	1	1	0	0
Martinez, DH	5	3	4	4	0	0	0	0	0	0
Bogaerts, SS	5	3	3	2	0	0	0	1	4	0
Moreland, 1B	3	0	1	3	1	1	0	7	1	0
Devers, 3B	3	0	0	0	2	0	1	0	2	0
Kinsler, 2B	4	0	1	1	0	1	3	1	1	0
Leon, C	4	0	0	0	0	2	2	13	0	0
Bradley Jr., CF	3	1	1	1	1	1	0	2	0	0
	36	11	13	11	5	8	7	27	8	0

Boston		IP	H	R	ER	HR	BB	K	Pit	S	B	ERA	BF
Price	W(1-1)	5.0	6	3	3	1	2	8	105	69	36	6.75	24
Barnes		1.0	1	0	0	0	0	3	22	18	4	7.36	4
Hembree		0.2	2	0	0	0	0	0	16	11	5	0.00	4
Brasier		2.0	1	1	1	0	0	1	25	18	7	3.00	7
Thornburg		0.1	1	1	1	1	0	1	11	8	3	9.00	2
		9.0	11	5	5	2	2	13	179	124	55	4.92	41

GAME SIX POSTGAME COMMENTS

Red Sox Manager

Very glad to win the series. I really thought it might go the full seven games. These are two truly superior teams. It only took this Red Sox team five games to win the 2018 World Series and the 1998 Yankees . . . well . . . they swept the Padres. When I really studied this Yankees team, I was apprehensive. I knew we had a great team, but what that team achieved kind of scared me. At the end of the day, I'm glad our guys came out on top.

We started David Price, of course. It was his turn in the rotation and we were sure he was due for a good outing. We got those three big runs in the bottom of the first. J. D. drove in Benny, and then Bogey homered. Then Curtis matched that—almost a carbon copy of the Bogaerts home run, both of them two-run shots by the Fisk Pole down the left-field line. Three runs for each team, then both starters settled down.

We got to Coney again in the bottom of the fifth with three more runs. He started out whiffing both Bradley and Betts, but then Benintendi singled and took second on the wild pitch. J. D. came through again, once more knocking in Benintendi. And Bogaerts got himself on again, too, this time with a double. With just a 2-1 count, J. D. wasn't running with the pitch and had to hold up at third. But Mitch Moreland—he's been platooning with Pearce and it paid off big here—came through with that sharp single to right, and it was 6–3.

We added a couple of insurance runs after the seventh-inning stretch. Again it was Martinez, Bogaerts, and Moreland. And in the eighth, Bradley hit that homer well past the Pesky Pole in right. Mookie had been struggling, but he doubled off that short wall in right, and J. D. came through (again) with his third and fourth RBIs of the game. It was all over. Homer Bush surprised us with that home run; he only hit one of them all year long. The Yankees had 11 hits; we had 13, but I guess ours were better timed.

It was great to see the guys celebrate on the field. To beat a team like the 1998 Yankees, that's about as special as it gets. The best team in more than 100 years of Yankees baseball and the Red Sox came out on top in six. That's big. I'm going to head into the clubhouse now. I have a feeling I'm going to get drenched in champagne.

Yankees Manager

Give the Red Sox credit. They proved their success in 2018 was no fluke. The team is well constructed and formidable in all facets of the game. The in-season trades strengthened the roster and made Boston a deeper team, capable of playing like one of the best of all-time.

Cone pitched masterfully in Game Two at Fenway, and there's no one we'd rather have on the mound for us in a big game. We were confident he'd take the ball and throw another gem. While warming up in the bullpen, Posada and pitching coach Mel Stottlemyre said Coney had all of his pitches working, and had pinpoint control throwing from all different arm angles. Unfortunately, he wasn't sharp once the game got underway. That happens sometimes.

Boston came out swinging, and we faced a three-run deficit right out of the chute. But then Curtis popped a two-run blast to make it a 3–2 game, so you thought, OK, we're going to get contributions from everyone, and you have a good feeling we're going to grab back the momentum. Then Coney settled down, retiring 12 of the next 13 batters. He cruised into the fifth, and I liked what I saw from him, especially after he struck out Bradley and Betts, and had Benintendi down 0-2 in the count. But the kid's a tough out. Benny singled, Coney uncorked a wild pitch, and then the floodgates opened: single, double, single, and we're down three runs again, 6–3, just like that.

They'll be more second-guessing from Yankees fans as to why Darren Holmes would be used in an elimination game trailing by just three when the bullpen was full of rested relievers with better track records. The pitching let us down, for sure, but it was missed opportunities from our offense that cost us the game. We banged out 11 hits, but it yielded just five runs. We left two runners on base in the first, second, fifth, and seventh innings. We had plenty of scoring chances, but we didn't cash in. Red Sox pitching, of course, had something to say about it. They struck out 13 of our batters, many at the most inopportune moments.

Woulda, coulda, shoulda. This loss will sting for a while. I genuinely liked my team's chances. We just didn't always put our best team on the field. So I'll say the 2018 Red Sox were the better team in *this* series. But I'm not prepared to say this simulation proves the 2018 Red Sox are superior to the 1998 Yankees.

MANAGERS' POST-SERIES PRESS CONFERENCE

Red Sox Manager

What a fantastic finish for a first-year manager! It was wonderful to see this Red Sox team set a franchise record for wins, and then go on to win the postseason—only dropping one game in each round. No disrespect to the Dodgers in the World Series, but going up against the squad my opponent selected as the best New York Yankees team of all time was probably our biggest challenge yet. I'm glad we came into it battle-tested and sufficiently rested.

And, of course, I'm pleased and proud that our guys prevailed.

But it wasn't easy.

Look at Wells and Cone. Wells practically no-hit us in Game Five. Toss in the game we got to him, back in Game One, and he still wound up with a 2.25 series ERA. And Cone topped that, with an ERA of only 1.80. But those ERAs come down when one of the two games you throw is a shutout. Coney shut us out in Game Two. It's a little hard to win a game in which your team doesn't score a run. Those were the only two games we lost—the two we got shut out. When we scored runs, we won.

We averaged nine runs a game in our four victories, but needed that 10th run in Game Four. They outhit us, 17–12, and almost caught us at the end, with two runs in the eighth and two more in the bottom of the ninth. They'd started off with a 5–0 lead, but we took advantage of three Yankees errors, which lead to four unearned runs in the sixth and eighth. Otherwise, that final push would have sunk us. We threw eight pitchers at them, and barely held on.

Chris Sale pitched great. I'm glad we rested him down the stretch. If he hadn't run up against Wells in Game Five, he might have had two wins. We would have had him ready to back up Porcello in Game Seven if it had come to that—Porcello did a great job in Game Three—but after this exceptionally long postseason everyone was glad to go home with bragging rights and get ready for the year to come.

Who was our MVP? We'll have to leave that to the designated sports-writers. With J. D., Xander, and Raffy each driving in six runs, you could almost think of sharing the honors. Devers had some big hits but didn't get on base quite as much, so the other guys scored twice as many runs. The simulation company voted J. D. as MVP in Game One and again in Game Six, but gave Devers the MVP in Games Three and Four. I think Bogey came out a little on the short end here. I think I'll stay out of this one. No point in getting caught up in something like this.

Have a good winter, everyone. I'll be enjoying this throughout the offseason myself. I expect I'll find myself musing, though, on how the 1912 Red Sox might have fared against the 1927 Yankees. But that's perhaps for another day.

Yankees Manager

If you score first in a baseball game, you have a much greater chance of winning that game. When a team scores the first run, you can usually bet that team is also in a better position to score *more* runs going forward. And if it's the home team that scores the first run, they also have more outs left in the game than their now-trailing opponent. So by scoring first, your team puts the pressure on the other team. It changes the way the opponent plays and gives your team more confidence. Score first and you usually win![1]

When the 2018 Red Sox scored first, they hardly ever lost. Really. They were 74–15 in the regular season when scoring first, and 10–0 in the postseason. So it's no surprise that the results of this series played out according to the script, as the team that scored first won five of the six games. Unfortunately, three of those victories belonged to the Red Sox, and only two to the Yankees. In the Boston wins, they scored two first-inning runs in Game One, three in Game Three, and three in Game Six. The only outlier was Game Four, when my team choked away an early five-run lead. That loss was a bitter pill to swallow.

Boston's victories in the two middle games proved decisive. In Game Three, with the series tied, we were counting on Pettitte to seize the

---

[1]   Per an article by Roger Weber of SportsLibrary.net, "The team that scores the first run of the game ends up winning the game close to 70%—actually 68.9%—of the time."

moment and throttle the potent Boston bats. His pedigree gave us the confidence to believe that victory was imminent. Instead, Andy surrendered three runs in the top of the first. Young Devers provided the dagger. With one run already in, he came through in the clutch by hitting a two-out single to knock in two more runs, putting us down, 3–0. It was a deficit from which we never did recover. And then coupled with the Game Four debacle? Well, I'm still wondering about one thing: Where was El Duque?

Still, you have to give the Boston pitchers credit. They held our guys in check most of the time and made quality pitches when the situation required. Kudos to the Red Sox bullpen. In the 20 innings the Red Sox bullpen pitched, they gave up 10 earned runs for a 4.50 ERA. The Yankees bullpen gave up 12 earned runs in only 9 1/3 innings pitched for an 11.58 ERA. Boston's relief pitchers were much stingier than New York's relievers. But if you'd told me Steven Wright would pitch the ninth inning and finish two games in the series, I'd have thought it would be in a mop-up role. In his six-year career, with 31 appearances coming out of the bullpen, Wright has only one registered save, which came in September of 2018. No disrespect intended, but the two saves credited to Wright's stat line is the most surprising result of this very surprising simulated series.

Wright could do no wrong, and neither could the Red Sox. Congratulations on your victory, Bill. Next time, we'll set it up so the Yankees put their best team on the field. Then a true champion can be crowned.

PARTING SHOTS

Bill Nowlin: This series played out nicely. I thought it might run seven and had no idea which team would come out on top. As we head into 2019, Red Sox fans are beginning to become a little more accustomed to winning, but here we were playing a great Yankees team—quite possibly the best Yankees team of all time (that was the idea, and I bow to Dave's judgment). It's not just that the Red Sox won, but the way we won (I'll say "we" because I identify with the team as most fans do) was gratifying, too. In this case, I had nothing to do with selecting the team. Dave

Dombrowski and the baseball operations people pretty much took care of that.

I have to say, though, I think it was a mistake for them to use the full-year rosters instead of each team's postseason roster, and there were some surprises there. When Marcus Walden turned up in Game Four, my immediate reaction (apologies to Mr. Walden) was "Who?" I had to look him up. Turns out he had appeared in eight games, threw 14 2/3 innings, and had a 3.68 ERA. Pretty good at the major-league level, but in the actual 2018 season, the last game in which he appeared was on May 3. Sent to Pawtucket, he was 0–4 with a 6.61 ERA in Triple A, and was sent down to Single A where he worked less than three innings. With the Sox battling the Yankees in a 10–9 game, why did the computer decide to put him in the game? It worked out well, though, as he retired the one batter he was asked to face. And Kimbrel came into a clean inning and did his thing. But that was one surprise. Thanks to the computer as well for asking Steven Wright to save a couple of games. In the latter weeks of 2018, Craig Kimbrel sometimes provoked some true anxiety. Maybe the computer thought it was safer to use Steven?

David Fischer: I had the exact same reaction ("Who?") when rookie reliever Mike Buddie came in to pitch for the Yankees in Game Four. I wholeheartedly agree that we should have used each team's postseason roster. That we weren't explicit with our wishes was our mistake. But it seems obvious that a postseason roster is the most indicative measure of a team's exceptionalism. I knew my team was in trouble when the starting pitcher for the crucial Game Four was Hideki Irabu instead of Orlando Hernandez. I was nauseous. Irabu and Buddie were left off the postseason roster for a reason—there were better options available. And even though El Duque wasn't asked to start a game, he certainly would have been a better long relief option than Buddie-boy. It proves that a computer cannot take into account which player has the hot hand and would perform better in an important series.

BN: I'd never heard of Mike Buddie and thought maybe it was a joke, but he really did have a respectable big-league career—though in 1998 he was 0–4 with a 5.62 ERA. Looking at his work in 1998, he had a few good games of more than an inning or two, but I don't think there was ever a time he seemed to have a hot hand. In Game Four of this series—with so much on the line—he did get badly burnt. He entered a game when the Yankees held a 5–4 edge and gave up two runs. But then he was brought out again in the seventh and gave up two more. And brought out in the eighth and gave up two *more*! The Red Sox only won by one run. There's no way to say anyone else *would* have been better, but there was hardly anyone on the team with a worse record in 1998, and Ramiro Mendoza (who was finally brought in at the very end) was 10–2 (3.25) that year and Graeme Lloyd was 3–0 (1.67). Where were they?

It really was feast or famine for the Red Sox, though. Either they scored zero runs at all—in the two games they lost—or nine-plus runs. In the 2018 regular season, the Red Sox did get shut out seven times. And they did get no-hit once, by the immortal Sean Manaea.

DF: Where was Mariano Rivera? Where was Jeff Nelson? The bullpen was one of the strongest units of the '98 squad and a big reason for the team's success. But Mariano was nowhere to be found. And when a reliever *was* called into the game, strange things happened. For instance, in Game One, with my team trailing by one run in the eighth, left-handed relief ace Mike Stanton came in to pitch with the hopes of holding the score right there. But, against all odds, Stanton surrendered two home runs in one inning—both to left-handed batters. That was an uncharacteristic result, and any hope of a comeback vanished.

While I'm ranting, how did Scott Brosius wind up as my team's cleanup batter in five of the six games? He had a career season in '98 (19 homers, 98 RBIs) and hit well enough in our simulation series, but manager Joe Torre's lineup card regularly listed Brosius in the ninth spot—not fourth. What gives?

I guess what they say is true: watch enough baseball games and you'll see something you never saw before.

BN: Yeah, like Sean Manaea no-hitting what was arguably the best Red Sox team of all time. Look at the bright side—algorithmic foibles aside, the Red Sox won.

Consider something else—the MVP designations the computer gave after each game. The two shutouts deservedly earned Cone and Wells MVP status for Games Two and Five. It was an old-time baseball strategy that worked: don't let the other team score any runs and you'll probably win. All four of the Red Sox wins saw a non-pitcher win. In fact, Rafael Devers won back-to-back MVPs for Games Three and Four. And J. D. Martinez bookended the series, named the MVP in Game One and the final Game Six. Sale had an excellent series, working two games with a combined 1.93 ERA, but the one run he gave up in the seven innings he worked in Game Five was enough that it cost him the game, given that Wells was hardly letting a Red Sox batter get on base, much less score a run.

DF: I'll stop griping about the algorithmic foibles and admit that the 2018 Red Sox won the old-fashioned way: they earned it. Every starting position player on your team scored at least one run in the series, and three players—Martinez, Bogaerts, and Devers—each drove in six runs. With the exception of Benintendi, Boston batters performed to the high standards set on the back of their baseball card. Some players even exceeded expectations, much to my dismay. I'm thinking about Sandy Leon driving in three runs and helping to power a Red Sox comeback victory in Game Four, and the surprising thumper, Jackie Bradley Jr., breaking out the whooping stick and posting a .667 slugging percentage. When the bottom-of-the-order batters do damage, it's a good sign your team will win.

Congratulations to the 2018 Red Sox. They're wicked good.

2018 Boston Red Sox Hitting

Pos	Name	G	PA	AB	R	H	1B	2B	3B	HR	RBI	BB	SO	SB	CS	BA	OBP	SLG	TB	HBP	SAC	ROE	GDP
RF	Betts	6	28	23	4	7	4	2	0	1	2	4	5	0	0	.304	.407	.522	12	0	0	1	0
LF	Benintendi	6	26	21	5	3	2	1	0	0	1	2	7	0	0	.143	.250	.190	4	1	0	0	0
DH	Martinez	6	26	25	7	9	5	3	0	1	6	1	4	0	0	.360	.385	.600	15	0	0	0	1
SS	Bogaerts	6	26	22	6	9	6	1	0	2	6	2	4	0	0	.409	.423	.727	16	0	2	0	0
3B	Devers	6	26	23	3	6	2	2	0	2	6	3	3	0	1	.261	.346	.609	14	0	0	0	0
2B	Kinsler	6	21	18	1	2	1	1	0	0	1	2	2	0	0	.111	.200	.167	3	0	0	1	1
C	Leon	6	25	23	1	6	4	1	0	1	4	0	6	0	0	.261	.250	.435	10	0	1	1	0
CF	Bradley Jr.	6	20	18	3	6	4	0	0	2	2	1	3	1	0	.333	.400	.667	12	1	0	0	0
1B	Pearce	3	12	10	2	1	0	0	0	1	2	2	3	0	0	.100	.231	.400	4	0	1	0	0
1B	Moreland	3	14	11	1	3	2	0	0	1	4	2	3	0	0	.273	.357	.545	6	0	1	0	0
PH-2B	Lin	2	3	3	0	1	1	0	0	0	0	0	0	0	0	.333	.333	.333	1	0	0	0	0
PH-2B	Nunez	1	1	1	0	0	0	0	0	0	0	0	0	0	0	.000	.000	.000	0	0	0	0	0
PH	Ramirez	1	1	1	0	0	0	0	0	0	0	0	0	0	0	.000	.000	.000	0	0	0	0	0

2018 Boston Red Sox Pitching

Pos	Name	W	L	ERA	G	GS	GF	CG	SHO	SV	R	ER	IP	H	HR	BB	SO	BF	H9	HR9	BB9	SO9	SO/W
SP	Sale	1	1	1.93	2	2	0	0	0	0	3	3	14.0	8	2	3	8	52	5.14	1.29	1.93	5.14	2.67
SP	Price	1	1	6.75	2	2	0	0	0	0	8	8	10.2	14	5	3	13	50	11.82	4.22	2.53	10.98	4.33
SP	Porcello	1	0	2.57	1	1	0	0	0	0	2	2	7.0	5	1	1	5	27	6.43	1.29	1.29	6.43	5.00
SP	Rodriguez	0	0	12.30	1	1	0	0	0	0	5	5	3.2	8	0	3	5	21	19.67	0.00	7.38	12.30	1.67
RP	Barnes	0	0	7.38	4	0	0	0	0	0	3	3	3.2	5	1	1	7	18	12.30	2.46	2.46	17.21	7.00
RP	Wright	0	0	0.00	2	0	2	0	0	2	0	0	3.0	0	0	1	1	10	0.00	0.00	3.00	3.00	1.00
RP	Brasier	0	0	3.00	2	0	0	0	0	0	1	1	3.0	2	0	0	1	11	6.00	0.00	0.00	3.00	0.00
RP	Kelly	0	0	6.77	3	0	0	0	0	0	2	2	2.2	1	0	1	4	13	3.38	0.00	3.38	13.53	4.00
RP	Thornburg	0	0	9.00	2	0	1	0	0	0	2	2	2.0	3	2	0	1	8	13.50	9.00	0.00	4.50	0.00
RP	Velazquez	1	0	0.00	2	0	1	0	0	0	0	0	2.0	1	0	0	1	7	4.50	0.00	0.00	4.50	0.00
RP	Workman	0	0	0.00	3	0	0	0	0	0	0	0	1.1	3	0	2	2	9	20.30	0.00	13.53	13.53	1.00
RP	Kimbrel	0	0	18.00	1	0	1	0	0	1	2	2	1.0	3	1	0	2	6	27.00	9.00	0.00	18.00	0.00
RP	Hembree	0	0	0.00	2	0	1	0	0	0	0	0	1.0	3	0	1	0	7	27.00	0.00	9.00	0.00	0.00
RP	Johnson	0	0	0.00	1	0	0	0	0	0	0	0	0.1	0	0	0	0	1	0.00	0.00	0.00	0.00	0.00

1998 New York Yankees Hitting

Pos	Name	G	PA	AB	R	H	1B	2B	3B	HR	RBI	BB	SO	SB	CS	BA	OBP	SLG	TB	HBP	SAC	ROE	GDP
SS	Jeter	6	29	26	3	6	4	0	0	2	3	2	6	3	1	.231	.286	.462	12	0	0	1	0
DH-PH	Raines	6	25	23	4	7	7	0	0	0	3	1	4	1	0	.304	.333	.304	7	0	0	1	0
CF	Williams	6	27	25	4	8	3	3	0	2	6	2	7	0	0	.320	.370	.680	17	0	0	0	0
3B	Brosius	6	24	19	3	5	2	1	0	2	3	3	4	0	1	.263	.375	.632	12	1	1	0	0
C	Posada	6	25	25	1	7	4	3	0	0	0	0	7	0	0	.280	.280	.400	10	0	0	0	2
RF	O'Neill	6	24	22	2	6	3	1	1	1	3	2	6	0	0	.273	.333	.545	12	0	0	0	0
1B	Martinez	6	21	18	1	4	2	2	0	0	1	1	5	0	0	.222	.333	.333	6	2	0	0	0
2B	Knoblauch	6	25	22	4	6	4	0	0	2	3	2	3	0	0	.273	.360	.545	12	1	0	0	1
LF	Curtis	6	18	15	1	2	1	0	0	1	3	3	5	0	0	.133	.278	.333	5	0	0	0	0
DH-LF-PH	Strawberry	3	7	6	1	2	1	0	0	1	1	1	2	1	0	.333	.429	.833	5	0	0	0	1
PH-3B-2B	Bush	3	3	3	2	3	2	0	0	1	3	0	0	0	0	1.000	1.000	2.000	6	0	0	0	0
PH-LF	Ledee	2	3	3	1	1	1	0	0	0	0	0	1	0	0	.333	.333	.333	1	0	0	0	0
PR-1B	Sveum	1	1	1	1	0	0	0	0	0	0	0	0	0	0	.000	.000	.000	0	0	0	0	0
1B	Sojo	1	1	1	0	0	0	0	0	0	0	0	0	0	0	.000	.000	.000	0	0	0	0	0

1998 New York Yankees Pitching

Pos	Name	W	L	ERA	G	GS	GF	CG	SHO	SV	R	ER	IP	H	HR	BB	SO	BF	H9	HR9	BB9	SO9	SO/W
SP	Wells	1	1	2.25	2	2	1	1	1	0	4	4	16.0	9	2	2	14	60	5.06	1.13	1.13	7.88	7.00
SP	Cone	1	1	1.80	2	2	1	1	1	0	3	3	15.0	11	1	5	13	63	6.60	0.60	3.00	7.80	2.60
SP	Pettitte	0	1	8.53	1	1	0	0	0	0	6	6	6.1	6	2	5	5	30	8.53	2.84	7.11	7.11	1.00
SP	Irabu	0	0	6.75	1	1	0	0	0	0	4	4	5.1	6	1	3	4	24	10.13	1.69	5.07	6.75	1.33
RP	Buddie	0	1	7.38	2	0	1	0	0	0	7	3	3.2	8	1	1	2	22	19.67	2.46	2.46	4.92	2.00
RP	Holmes	0	0	13.51	2	0	0	0	0	0	5	5	3.1	7	2	2	1	19	18.92	5.41	5.41	2.70	0.50
RP	Mendoza	0	0	13.53	2	0	2	0	0	0	2	2	1.1	2	0	1	1	8	13.53	0.00	6.77	6.77	1.00
RP	Stanton	0	0	18.00	1	0	1	0	0	0	2	2	1.0	2	2	0	0	5	18.00	18.00	0.00	0.00	0.00

EXTRA INNINGS

When the idea was broached of pairing me up with a dedicated Yankees fan on a book where we were expected to actually collaborate, there might have been a little trepidation on my end. Who is this guy? Is he one of those hyper-obnoxious Yankees fans I used to run into years ago? Can this really work? Will our editor, Jason Katzman, have to be as much of a referee as an editor? "Back to your corners, guys! And watch the low blows!"

It's not as though I'm a stranger to partisan prose. In the wake of the 2004 Red Sox triumph over the Yankees and Cardinals, Jim Prime and I wrote the 2007 book *Blood Feud: The Red Sox, the Yankees & the Struggle of Good versus Evil*. It was telling of the times that there was no need to explain—to anyone—who was considered good and who was considered evil.

That was mostly just good fun. But it was also true that most Red Sox fans harbored hostile attitudes toward the Yankees and their fans. A couple of words that come to mind as to the demeanor of the typical Sox fan of those times would be "resentful" and "surly."

Times have changed. Some of us have matured—myself included.

In fact, I already had several friends who were Yankees fans. Two of the other seven members on the current board of SABR are lifelong Yankees fans. We had a board meeting just outside New York back in 2007, in fairly early November. The Red Sox had just won the World Series, their second Series win in four years (after an 86-year drought, which was all I had ever experienced in life). I walked into the room and most of the board was already there. One of them, board president Vince Gennaro, greeted me by saying, "So, Bill, now you know what it's like to be a Yankees fan." Huh? I was taken aback for about 30 seconds, and then I realized what he meant, and its import. You could get used to winning.

Happily, I've continued to have more experience with my team winning. Four world championships in 15 years. It's not like what the

Yankees used to do—win 15 World Series in a row. (OK, that never happened. It just felt that way.) And by the time Vince had said that to me, I'd already written some notes to a couple of Red Sox–oriented message boards, along the lines of, "Hey, let's not get too full of ourselves. Let's not get arrogant. What goes up comes back down. Let's celebrate the Red Sox winning, but let's also be humble. Let's not be like Yankees fans." Not in so many words, but along those lines. There was a reason for my notes; I could see some Red Sox fans becoming a little too full of themselves— almost like *they* were the winners and not the players on the field.

Not all Yankees fans were self-centered boors. SABR's Publications Director Cecilia Tan is a Yankees fan and wrote the book *The 50 Greatest Yankees Games*. Great idea. I asked her about doing a Red Sox book, and we wrote it together: *The 50 Greatest Red Sox Games*. SABR treasurer F. X. Flinn is another lifelong Yankees fan. He was the other one in the room in 2007. All of us love baseball most of all. That transcends pure partisanship.

And, so, it was with Dave Fischer. We first met in the Sports Publishing office in New York. I was in town for a BLOHARDS luncheon (that's a venerable Red Sox fan club based in New York City) and the Red Sox-Yankees game that evening at Yankee Stadium (which the Red Sox won). Neither of us knew each other, but Jason knew us both and he picked wisely. He's a Mets fan, so he had no horse in the race (to toss in a mixed metaphor).

We had a common mission—to work on this book, to do our best working on it, to have it become a good book (which we hope it will be deemed), and to have fun working on it. We enjoyed the meeting, hit it off well enough, and for the past six-plus months have established a working relationship which has truly been fun—and rewarding. I learned an awful lot about the Yankees I hadn't known before. Reading the thoughtful and informed drafts that Dave put together, then discussing back and forth how to improve each other's drafts, I didn't actually become converted to Yankee fandom. But we developed a very smooth and mutually respectful working relationship.

I readily do admit this all might have been easier now that the Red Sox have significantly balanced the historical playing field.

When it came right down to it, the computer that ran the simulations was maybe the odd one in the room, as we both had to live with its quirky moves.

—Bill Nowlin

* * *

The message arrived unsolicited. Jason Katzman, editor at Sports Publishing, was reaching out to gauge my interest in a book idea. He said it was a book about the Yankees and Red Sox rivalry. *Yawn.* I've been there and done that. But wait. Jason's pitch had late life. He explained the book would be a unique way of looking at this 100-year-old rivalry—by pitting two partisan experts, one a lifelong Red Sox fan and one a lifelong Yankees fan—and asking us to choose the greatest single-season team for each franchise, as well as the top players at each position, with the idea of then running simulations for our all-time dream teams against each other. I found the idea to be fascinating, and accepted the assignment.

The first time I met Bill Nowlin during the summer of 2018 at the Sports Publishing office in New York, I tried not to seem intimidated. I'd done my homework on Bill and came away impressed, nay, jealous. He has authored more than 20 books on the Boston Red Sox and hundreds of articles for the Society of American Baseball Research's Baseball Biography Project, an invaluable source for baseball aficionados. But Bill's resume doesn't stop there. He's served as a director on the executive board of SABR for many years, and in 2011 accepted the Bob Davids Award, the Society's highest honor, which recognizes lifetime achievement to SABR and baseball. With Bill as co-author, there was no question I'd need to raise my game.

As far as being intimidated is concerned, I needn't have worried, for I quickly learned that Bill is as unassuming and without ego as anyone I've ever worked with. That's why a small part of me is sorry that he had to be paired with a typical Yankees fan: arrogant, cocky, entitled, and a crybaby when events don't go your team's way. Although my love of the Yankees developed during the early 1970s when the team was dreadful, it must be in every Yankees fans' DNA to feel a sense of bluster, to understand innately that the history of the Yankees is the history of major-league baseball.

The Yankees, with their unparalleled success and accompanying gallery of legends, have become a proud and distinct part of Americana. The popular stand-up comic Joe E. Lewis once commented on the coldly efficient, perpetually victorious Yankees: "Rooting for the Yankees is like rooting for US Steel." No team dominated for a longer period than did the Yankees from 1949 to 1964. During that era, the Bronx Bombers won an astonishing 14 American League pennants and nine World Series championships. Writing in the *New York Post*, Jimmy Cannon described the feeling of rooting for the Yankees. "I never have been on a yacht in my whole life. But I imagine rooting for the Yankees is like owning a yacht."

For Yankees fans, it sure has been smooth sailing for the past quarter-century. Since 1995, the Yankees have reached the postseason 20 times in that 24-year span and haven't experienced a losing season since 1992. Bill and his Boston brethren enjoy reminding us that the Red Sox have won four World Series titles in the last 15 years. I say, good for you! Keep up the current pace, and you'll catch up to the Yankees and their 27 championships by the year 2085.

By then, Bill and I will be somewhere in baseball heaven having a catch with Babe, Teddy, Mickey, and Yaz—and probably still having a good-natured argument over who's better, who's best. Hint: it's the Yanks.

—David Fischer

ABOUT THE AUTHORS

Bill Nowlin is a baseball author and historian. He was elected as SABR's Vice President in 2004 and re-elected for five more terms before stepping down in 2016, when he was elected as a Director. He has written dozens of books on the Red Sox and Red Sox players, including *Ted Williams At War*, *Mr. Red Sox* (on Johnny Pesky), *Love That Dirty Water*, and *So You Think You're a Boston Red Sox Fan?* and has co-edited a series of Red Sox "team books" written by numerous SABR authors that focus on different years when the Red Sox fielded exceptional teams. Bill is also co-founder of Rounder Records of Cambridge, Massachusetts. He's traveled to more than 100 countries, but says there's no place like Fenway Park.

David Fischer has written for the *New York Times*, *Sports Illustrated Kids*, and *Yankees Magazine*, and has worked at *Sports Illustrated*, the *National Sports Daily*, and NBC Sports. He is the author of several titles about the New York Yankees, including *Derek Jeter #2: Thanks for the Memories* and *Miracle Moments in New York Yankees History*. Fischer is also the editor of *Facing Mariano Rivera*. He resides in New Jersey but spends summer Sundays in the Bronx, where he's been lucky enough to witness two perfect games.